somebody's child

STORIES ABOUT ADOPTION

EDITED BY **BRUCE GILLESPIE** AND **LYNNE VAN LUVEN**

FOREWORD BY **MICHAELA PEREIRA**

TouchWood
Editions

TouchWood Editions
touchwoodeditions.com

LIBRARY AND ARCHIVES CANADA CATALOGUING IN PUBLICATION
Somebody's child : stories about adoption /
edited by Bruce Gillespie, Lynne Van Luven.

ISBN 978-1-926971-03-2

1. Adoption—Canada. 2. Adoptees—Canada—Biography. 3. Adoptive parents—
Canada—Biography. I. Gillespie, Bruce, 1975– II. Van Luven,Lynne

HV875.58.C3S66 2011   362.7340971   C2011-904178-2

Proofreader: Sarah Weber, Lightning Editorial
Cover image: Aleš Senožetnik, istockphoto.com. Drawing overlay, Pete Kohut

BRITISH COLUMBIA ARTS COUNCIL   Canada Council for the Arts   Conseil des Arts du Canada   Canadian Heritage   Patrimoine canadien

We gratefully acknowledge the financial support for our publishing activities
from the Government of Canada through the Canada Book Fund, Canada
Council for the Arts, and the province of British Columbia through the
British Columbia Arts Council and the Book Publishing Tax Credit.

MIX
Paper from
responsible sources
FSC® C016245

The interior pages of this book have been printed on 100% post-consumer
recycled paper, processed chlorine free, and printed with vegetable-based inks.

1 2 3 4 5 15 14 13 12 11

PRINTED IN CANADA

contents

foreword

MICHAELA PEREIRA

RECENTLY, I SPOKE AT a women's leadership conference. I had planned to tell the story of my life mostly from a professional perspective, but as often happens with me, I strayed from script and opened up to the crowd in a more personal way. I told the story of locating the family of my birth mother and what an impact the experience had had on me. Over a dozen years ago, I began my search and was heartbroken to discover that my birth mother had died following a lengthy illness. This was devastating news. I told the audience that I didn't understand why my birth mother had not told anyone about me before she died and how angry that had made me. After the conference had ended, several women came up to share their own adoption stories with me—and there were many. But one woman in particular will forever stand out in my memory. She was probably in her sixties, overcome with emotion. She grabbed me, holding me close in a firm embrace, and whispered in my ear: "Know that we were young and unprepared and afraid and not supported by family. And know that not a day has passed when you weren't thought of and prayed for. We did what we thought was best for you to have a chance of a better life." And she cried. We both did.

That moment changed it all for me. Up until that very second, I am not proud to admit, I always thought of adoption, of *my* adoption, from

1

the point of view of *me*, the adoptee. That special woman brought so vividly into view the fact that adoption affects so many people. Birth mothers faced with a terrible and lonely choice. Birth fathers, sometimes not in the picture but still connected. Grandparents, uncles, aunties, cousins. And the adoptive family, who choose to bring a child into their home, realizing that someday, they may have to share that child with another parent or sibling.

In our family, the word "adopted" was part of our vocabulary long before most kids even understood what it meant. Just as a young child can recite by rote his or her name, address, and age, by the time I was four years old, I was able to efficiently explain that I had been adopted when I was only three months old. And there was no mystery about it: my adoptive parents, Ainslie and Doug, are both Caucasian, whereas I am . . . well . . . brown, as are my four sisters, also adopted. Each of my sisters is First Nations, while I am a racial mix that includes Jamaican and Norwegian blood. We certainly were an unusual looking family growing up in rural Canada in the 1970s and '80s.

Now that I'm forty-one, I find it interesting to look back at how adoption shaped my life. For me, it was never a thing to be ashamed of; rather, I learned to be proud of being "chosen." I credit my parents with that. I remember Mom making a point of telling us that she had chosen us and didn't that make us special?

Our parents were trailblazers—renegades, really—on the adoption forefront. They adopted domestically, they adopted many, and they adopted outside their own race. As far as I can remember, they didn't turn to mentors or other adoptive parents for guidance. Dad worked for the federal government and his job moved us frequently. We lived in small towns on the Canadian prairies, towns like Creighton, Buffalo Narrows, even the now defunct Uranium City, Saskatchewan, at a time when we were absolutely the exception and never the rule.

Theirs was a tough job. And, now as an adult, I marvel at how they managed it at all; adopting five little girls . . . not just babies, but rather children who often arrived already loaded with baggage. Their job included convincing one child who had been bounced from foster home to foster home that she was with them to stay, that she didn't need to pack up her little suitcase every Sunday night to go off to a new home. It included carefully disciplining another child who probably had been the victim of abuse at the hand of a caretaker. And they achieved this while handling stares and questions from neighbours and co-workers: "Why on earth would someone adopt all of those children?" My parents always handled it with grace; my mother, especially, relied on humour. My favourite example: Once, soon after relocating in a new town following yet another transfer for my father, we attended service at a small local church. Understandably, many heads turned as the seven of us filed in, and nearly filled an entire row. After the service, a nosy-Nelly, busy-body type sidled up to my mother, pointed at us all, and whispered in a conspiratorial fashion, "Oh, my. Do tell. How does this all work?" To which my mother dryly replied, with excellent straight-faced delivery, "It's simple, really. All my children have different fathers." That hushed the woman up immediately and mortified my fifteen-year-old self. Today, I grin at my mother's temerity and cool.

My parents really did set the tone for me when it comes to how I feel about being adopted. In my experience, at home at least, it was never a stigma. As I get older, I am able to further grasp what it means to be adopted. Other people, besides Mom and Dad, have helped shape that definition for me through the years. I'm one of those people who tends to wear her heart on her sleeve; in fact I've learned to wear it there proudly. It feels authentic and true; yet at times, it leaves me incredibly vulnerable, something I've come to see as a strength and not always a weakness. In my effort to use this characteristic as a strength, I stay open about my adoption and the story of my family and will share it with anyone who displays even a remote interest. A friend once teased me about this years ago, and it almost made me self-conscious. But young people who have heard me speak publicly about my adoption stop me and shyly tell me that they too are adopted and that my story made them feel less alone and different. That shows me that sharing my story can have huge impact.

Early on, telling my story was like therapy: talking about my life made it real, less undefined. As time went on, I realized that my story was not unique, that the more I told it, the more it brought people and their stories out into the light. And in those stolen conversations in conference room hallways, in shared stories over cups of teas, there was and continues to be healing. The more we speak about what used to be unspeakable, the more we throw off the unnecessary weight of shame and secrecy.

By the same token, my heart swells from the beautiful gift I receive each time my "family" (and I've learned to define that word so much differently) expands. This past summer I met my beautiful, smart, and caring birth sister Marnie. And I cannot wait to introduce her to and share her with the rest of my ever-expanding family. I'd like to think the two dozen contributors to *Somebody's Child* are also part of that family — and will become part of yours.

Michaela Pereira is an award-winning television broadcaster and personality. She began her career in 1993 on CHEK-TV in Victoria, British Columbia, and has since worked in San Francisco and Los Angeles. Beyond her broadcasting achievements, Pereira is active in several community organizations throughout southern California that focus on at-risk and disadvantaged children and teens. She is a member of the National Association of Black Journalists and American Women in Radio and Television and is active with the National Association for the Advancement of Colored People. Pereira was born in Saskatoon, Saskatchewan, and is one of five adopted children. Her childhood was marked with diversity, as her parents and siblings do not share the same ethnic background. She enjoys travel and rare moments curled up with her e-book reader.

introduction

A THREAD CONNECTS US ALL

IN RECENT YEARS, AN old Chinese legend has become something of a touchstone for families involved with adoption. According to the story, an invisible, red thread connects people who are destined to be together; even if they are initially separated by ancestry or geography, the thread—sometimes called the red thread of fate—will eventually draw them together. It's a lovely, reassuring story with obvious appeal to adoptive families looking for ways to satisfy a child's endless appetite for "where did I come from" stories, as well as for adoptees seeking a connection to biological parents whom they may never meet.

As we set about collecting essays for *Somebody's Child*, I was particularly intrigued by the image of a red thread snaking its way across the world, extending from one family to another, creating new webs of relationships along the way. It seems a fitting metaphor for the vast networks built by adoption between people who might never otherwise know each other but are linked through love and children in unpredictable ways. Adoption is a big part of our world, even if we don't talk about it much. Which is odd: at a time when everything else seems to be acceptable in public discourse, adoption still smacks of stigma. Yet who among us has not been directly connected to an adoption or known someone who was involved in one?

The idea of connection and proximity guided the formation of this essay collection. While most books about adoption focus on one group—biological parents, adoptive parents, adopted children—we took another tack. We felt there was something to be gained from looking at adoption through a wider lens that included all of these perspectives side by side. That's why we've included viewpoints from siblings and grandparents of adoptees, people whose experiences might at first seem peripheral but upon closer inspection demonstrate how deeply adoption affects everyone connected to it. As the essays in this collection suggest, adoption is a subject we need to talk about more often, more openly. Indeed, as more and more governments across North America and around the world change their laws to open adoption processes and to give adoptees more power to learn about the circumstances of their birth, it has become essential to discuss all aspects of adoption with candour and sensitivity.

—Bruce Gillespie

❧ For a few years in my early childhood, I often entertained adoption fantasies. I usually indulged in such imaginings—even though I had not a whiff of hard evidence to suggest I was an adoptee—when I was at odds with one or both of my parents, especially when, in my estimation, they did not "understand me." How could I be expected to thrive in the middle of the prairies when I craved the streets of Dickensian London or the tea parties of Bloomsbury? How could I have a natural sibling whose values were so at odds with mine? In other words, I imagined I was adopted when I did not see my egocentric world view reflected by my family. I recall once, when I was about nine or ten, trying to trick my mother into admitting the truth.

"What made you decide to adopt me?" I asked her with feigned nonchalance, one night when we were doing the after-supper dishes.

"What?"

"Well, I'm adopted, right?"

My mother regarded me for a long, silent, scandalized moment.

(Perhaps she was recalling the considerable pain she suffered, at age nineteen, on the night of my birth.) "Whatever gave you *that* idea?"

"You mean I'm not?"

"You have far too much imagination for your own good," my mother replied, grimly swishing the dish cloth around the roasting pan.

Since then, I have learned that the Adoption Fantasy is as common as dirt among disaffected children who feel like misfits and believe life elsewhere would be better. Of course, all these decades later, I see my resemblance to my mother; I note that my two sisters and I sound alike on the telephone. And I can see extended family resemblances in my siblings' children. So, of course, my imaginings of adoption were ridiculous.

For the courageous contributors to *Somebody's Child*, the subject of adoption is a reality, one that sometimes has no humour attached to it. Ironically, because being adopted is so *real*, some actual adoptees for many years chose *not* to think about their roots at all. Some of them felt no need to probe and were happy not to question their own birth narratives. Still others obsessed about their beginnings constantly and only late in life came to peaceful acceptance of their early history.

In the process of assembling this powerful anthology, Bruce and I learned that "being adopted" is still not a neutral issue—nor is having "given a child up for adoption." The force, honesty, and beauty of the essays in *Somebody's Child* show us that the circumstances of our birth and the configuration of the families in which we spend our early years never lose their resonance. We are eleven years into the globalized virtual world of the twenty-first century, but the actual facts of each child's beginnings are perhaps more vital now than ever in human history. And *Somebody's Child* is here to prove it.

—Lynne Van Luven

edges

MICHELLE FRIED

I WAS PICKING THROUGH organic bananas when he walked in, his face exactly as I remembered: weathered, Salinas-sun dark, shadowed by the same broad-brimmed hat he wore the first time we met, twenty years before. He was sixty by now but looked much older, and if I hadn't known differently, if I hadn't known from first-hand, hard-acquired experience, I might have believed he was a wayward fisherman strayed mightily off course, haphazardly wandering the desert supermarkets of Utah. But I did know differently. I knew those pock marks, the red-streaked eyes, the too-thin frame; I knew they were reminders of boozing and hard drugs and late-night prostitutes. I hadn't seen him in years. I had hoped never to see him again.

It's a messy business when families are torn apart. Like paper, no matter how carefully the grown-ups fold and crease, it rips and shreds until you're left with two matching but imperfect halves. And even if, years later, another family comes along and tries to straighten it all out with cocker spaniels and peanut butter sandwiches, even if you grow up and have a Martha Stewart wedding and vote on the second Tuesday of every November, the edges never completely line up. Your friends, your kids, your husband, they may never notice, but you can feel it—something is smaller; you are smaller. So, you keep searching for those discarded pieces, and if you're very lucky—or, possibly, very unlucky—you might find a bit of what was lost: your first family, your blood family. You might find the man standing right in front of you, cigarettes in one hand and a bunch of celery in the other. And you may, like me, find yourself wishing you had never begun in the first place.

THE SEARCH

"Be careful, you're opening a can of worms," my adoptive mother, Rosanna, said when I told her I wanted to find my biological mother, Catherine. But over the years, I had learned to ignore the swarm of cautionary tales that hatched from her imagination—PTA plots, arsenic-filled Pixy Stix, serial killers living across the street. As insightful friends pointed out to me when I was growing up, my mother was "kinda weird."

Truth be told, she was unravelling. By Grade 6, our house had morphed into an odd storage facility, piled high with stacks of newspapers and zones of elaborately sorted trash. Soon after came her collections: stray cats, pedigree dogs, married men. While she spent her days in darkened rooms, I invented excuses to give her boss when she didn't show for work and secretly stuffed piles of trash into our neighbour's cans. And the more my adoptive mother fractured, the more I nursed my first-family fantasies. Is a rambunctious clan of brown-eyed little people waiting out there for me? Do they have tire swings and grandmas to spare and houses on the lake? Maybe Catherine is looking for me. Maybe she has regrets.

So, at seventeen, despite my mother's misgivings, I set off for Fresno, criss-crossed with thick tan lines and wearing a micro-mini skirt, filled with the kind of rock-hard, rock-headed certainty that only a teenager possesses. I was looking for cold, hard facts; I was attempting to lay down the what-ifs and whys I had been lugging around for most of my life.

But Rosanna's warnings were not paranoia. She'd seen the reports. She knew about the drugs, the evictions, the nights left alone in the crib. She knew about the man, too—his threats and his ultimatums. And she remembered my birth mother, barely nineteen, standing on our front porch with a stern man from social services, clutching a barely two-year-old me.

"Can you watch her for a couple of days?" Catherine had asked Rosanna. "Goddamned landlord locked us out. I just need to find us a place to stay, get some money together." She was dishevelled, in the same clothes she'd worn the night before, her voice shaking as she rambled on about allergies and sleep schedules.

"And one more thing," she added as she turned down the rocky driveway, the same driveway where I would learn to ride a bike and kiss my first puppy and call this stranger Mommy. "Please don't ever call her Shelly."

THE CALL

As I finished college, the call finally came.

"Michelle, this is Marty . . . Marty Lawson . . . Catherine's husband," the voice said.

I knew who he was. I was surprised they were still together. My heart was pounding, my chest tightened. I'd done it—I'd found my mother. "Can you put her on?" I asked.

"I'm so sorry, I can't. She's dead," he said, and in a moment, it was over. There would be no brick houses, no tree swings, no tearful reunions. "Just three months ago," he added, as if in consolation. "Uncle Charlie told me you were trying to find her."

So close—just aunts and great uncles and cousins away. Maybe if I had searched harder, called one more number, checked one more county record . . . Marty was still talking, but I wasn't listening, until the end when he added, "You have a sister, Sarah. I think she'd like to meet you."

THE MEETING

I drove from the Bay Area to Fresno the following Saturday to meet Sarah. When I pulled up, she ran across the yellowed grass to meet me trailing a puppy, a much older boyfriend, and a mass of bleached-blonde hair coiling down her back. When I stepped out of the car, she hugged me tightly, and we laughed, overcome with excitement and nervousness. I studied her carefully when I could catch a glimpse undetected, looking for some confirmation of our blood tie, some hint of Catherine revealed through her. Was it there, in her tiny hands, or there, in the strong curve of her hips?

Then, she stopped laughing. "Do you know what today is?" she asked. I shook my head. "February 18th," she said. "Our mom's birthday. She would have been forty-four today."

I stopped cold, feeling sick and strangely comforted at the same time. Was this what I'd been searching for, a divine message of sorts, guiding us together, guiding us closer?

That first day in Fresno, I crept around my shadow life, peering through windows, turning over stones. A box was placed in front of me, and I sifted through piles of faded pictures: Catherine opening presents in front of a spiny Christmas tree; Catherine roller skating in a white turtleneck and brown corduroy bell-bottoms; Catherine with her arms wrapped tightly around Sarah. I stared hard, trying to remember anything about her—her voice, her touch, her smell. Nothing. Only the same round eyes, the same high forehead, the same long neck and pronounced collarbones I see every morning in my own bathroom mirror. As I searched each box, I secretly hoped that somewhere, tucked carefully away, I'd find one of a little girl with wispy brown hair and enormous brown eyes. But there was no picture. There was no me.

After lunch, Sarah took me to Catherine's apartment across town, a small one-bedroom she'd shared with Marty. I picked up the Stephen

King book she was reading before she died, stroked her tiny dog, Trigger, drank water from her green ceramic mug. There were plants everywhere, green and vibrant. How did she keep them alive with so little sunshine? Here were the bowls I would have eaten from, the couch where we would have watched the daily soaps, the bed she slept on. I wanted to lie on that bed, put my head on her pillow; I wanted to take her brush, pull out the blonde hairs, touch something, anything, that was hers. All around, everything was carefully arranged; no hint of disorder, no whiff of chaos. I gulped it all in, engineering her, imagining the life I almost had.

But soon other stories poured in, stories Sarah needed to tell, stories I didn't want to hear. Catherine's childhood hopping between foster homes, her time on the streets, her dalliances in the occult, her cigarettes, her vodka bottles, her liver damaged beyond repair. "There . . . there is where she collapsed," Sarah said, pointing to a bright maroon rug on the bathroom floor. And there, in the living room, sitting before me, was Sarah's father, Marty, his sad eyes peering out beneath his broad-brimmed hat.

Marty stood to hug me, his breath a breeze of stale smoke and fresh beer. He was pale, like a man who'd just seen a ghost. I realized I was the ghost. He was sobbing, shaking his head. "Just like her," he whispered. "Just like her." Sitting next to him was Sherri, his new girlfriend, a late-night masseuse he'd run up a debt with. When Catherine died, Sherri moved in, crediting his three hundred and fifty dollars and splitting the rent.

Marty tried to collect himself, steadied himself on a stool, then spilled over like a flooded causeway, overwhelming us all with the sludge. "We were in Bakersfield one day . . . gassing up the car," he said quietly. "Catherine was really excited—she was ready to get you back. She wanted to pick you up from the foster home."

"And then . . . It was me . . . me. I told her no, I just couldn't do it." Marty hesitated. "I had a stepfather growing up—he wasn't the kindest person. I didn't think I could love a child that wasn't my own." He was quiet for a moment. We all took it in. "I don't think she ever got over losing you." Then, he was slurring. "I'm sorry, I'm sorry, I'm sorry."

THE WEIGHT

I suppose at that point I could have walked away, could have taken my answers and the Stephen King book and the picture of Catherine in the blue dress and just moved on. But I felt sad for Sarah, the way she disguised her opinions so carefully with questions, the way her smile never quite reached her eyes. And I felt a pull toward her, a comfort in her company, an intimacy that felt deeper than our time together warranted. I think together we felt less alone, less crazy to have one not-so-crazy relative. So, we realigned our lives and our loyalties; we developed a kind of dance to deal with our knotty past, delicately balancing, shifting and twisting, trying our best to act out the roles of sisters.

But lurking underneath, in a place so murky and grey we hardly recognized it, a fault line was slowly forming. She was jealous I got away; I was jealous she stayed. I reminded her of Catherine; she hated her mother. I resented Marty for having made Catherine choose; she knew he'd done me a favour. And as Sarah's life grew more chaotic, her relationships more tumultuous, her sadness more expansive, I began to resent the chaos leaking steadily into my life, into the new foundation I was trying so hard to build.

And always there was Marty, popping up unexpectedly, like a dead man stalking the living. One weekend, he showed up drunker than usual, reeking and blurry eyed. He waited for Sarah to leave the room, then came over and sat next to me on the couch.

"You're so beautiful, just like your mother." I froze. "You look just like her when she was your age." He reached over and tried to stroke my leg. I shifted, but his hand was running up my thigh. "You're so sexy," he whispered and leaned into me, his cracked, stale lips searching for mine. I raced for the door.

"Boundaries, I need boundaries," I decided on the long drive home.

THE PAST

But boundaries, like sand, shift and erode, and soon I would discover the past can't be tamed. History, my lost and found sister, her bleary-eyed father, would be there, lurking around in my life, in my head. Even when I married a great guy, had two giggling babies, bought a two-storey stucco home, even when I thought I'd contained the damage, contained Marty, the détente was short-lived. Life is strange like that: part destiny, part insanity. It steals round and round until twenty years later, you find yourself staring into a mirror wondering what the fuck just happened.

And so, when Sarah's second marriage headed into a tailspin, I wasn't surprised when she turned to me for comfort. The surprise came when I discovered her late at night finding comfort with my husband's brother instead. Soon enough, she'd moved in with him, seeping into every corner of my happy little life: every toddler birthday party, every bar mitzvah, every Las Vegas family get-away, with Marty trailing not far behind: Marty having steaks with my father-in-law; Marty playing cards with my brother-in-law. And with each excruciating encounter, with each attempt to keep her in my life but stay far away from him, I knew it was me who started it all, me who went poking around my past.

I have tried my damndest to sort this all out, to find peace, or forgiveness, or a priest who moonlights as an exorcist. I have found a therapist, a church, a doctor who's willing to prescribe me Ambien; none has quite done the trick. Some say I should embrace this new family, this bizarre twist of fate, our creepy Lifetime movie of the week. But it feels too much like a re-injury, a child picking at a scab, a remake of *Children of the Corn*. There are times I can laugh about it all, but not often enough, and that's what worries me most. Too often, I feel like I'm working way over my mental pay grade.

Sometimes I wish I'd listened to my mother's warnings. But the real question is, was that seventeen-year-old capable of listening? Could I have lived my life wondering if Catherine was out there, never knowing my story or how I came to be? Back then, I was certain my answers lay somewhere in the landscape of my past. But at forty, none of that certainty remains; there are no seamless connections, no absolutions, no guarantees. Only what's here, what's now, only me facing forward, trying hard to keep my attention firmly fixed on what lies in front of me—a tiny hand holding an inchworm, the dark brown eyes of my husband, the fat green tomato growing in my garden, the pink shadows crawling across the Wasatch Mountains.

People tell me I can't escape my past, and maybe they're right, because even now, in the foothills of the Rockies, even now, hundreds of miles from the fog and lettuce patches of Fresno, here is my past, poking produce, pushing his wobbly cart around my neighbourhood store, walking right toward me, toward the two little boys that could have been his, who would have been Catherine's, if he had just let me stay. He looks frailer, more stooped than I remember. For a moment, I consider introducing him to Eli and Seth. Then I think again, grab a banana, and head straight for the door.

Michelle Fried is a freelance writer and native Californian, transplanted to Utah where she lives with her husband and two sons. She was a community educator for a domestic violence agency and worked with foster teens in a group home. She is currently at work on her first novel.

the letter

J. JILL ROBINSON

THAT SONG LINE ABOUT the mother and child reunion being "only a motion away" runs through my brain as I concentrate, picking a card, the right card, the right paper, extra sheets of stationery and extra envelopes in case I fuck up; I'm sure to fuck up because it matters so much to get it right. The motion of writing, my hand out of practice writing longhand, but it has to be longhand, so I'm practising, forming the letters on a scrap sheet of foolscap. The stamp a pretty stamp, not a generic one of the queen or the maple leaf, no. And I kiss the front and back of the letter before dropping it in the mailbox, and then I stand there thinking. What will it be like when he opens the envelope, when that letter has completed its travel between Saskatoon and North Vancouver and falls through his mail slot? I stand waiting for revelation, and then I walk downtown along 9th Avenue, my heart and body alight.

I'd sworn I would never do it. Contact him. I'd always said that if he wanted to get in touch with me, I should and would be available to him through the birth registry in BC, but that I had no right to intrude on his life.

But I had changed my mind. In the months before I turned fifty, I thought a lot about mortality. How if I died, my son Emmett wouldn't know he had a brother, and that brother wouldn't know he had a brother. I wanted them both to know, and the feeling that contacting him was now the right thing to do became a drive that overrode my previous promise.

Even though the letter would be short, it took days to decide on the wording, and then to work on draft after draft to get it right. In the end the letter seemed simple and straightforward: I said that this was the only time I would contact him if that's what he wanted. That if I didn't hear back, I would make no more overtures, would withdraw completely, that it was to be his decision. I was writing now, I said, because I wanted him to know that he had a brother, Emmett, aged ten to his thirty-three. I included two pictures: one of Emmett, and one of me with my old boyfriend Gordy, taken the year after the baby was born. He was named David by his parents.

I told him that Gordy and I had loved each other very much. I told him that Gordy was my first boyfriend and that we had gone out for four years. I told him that we were fifteen and sixteen when we got pregnant, that we knew we were too young to be parents, and that we wanted people to raise him who were ready to raise him, people who would give him the best life possible. And I said that I hoped that had been the case, that he had been and was well loved, and happy in his life.

In the picture of Gordy and me, taken in early 1973, I'm wearing my dark grey boarding school duffel coat, and I'm hanging onto Gordy's arm as though he's a lifebuoy. He looks typically calm and obliging. His strawberry blond hair is combed in a long vee over his forehead. No jacket, and he's wearing the turquoise T-shirt I loved because it fit so snugly against his triangular chest, his strong smooth torso, his flat belly. It's tucked into the top of his tight jeans. Gordy and I lean lightly against his dark green 1969 Beaumont with the 396 engine.

I'm guessing that the photographs I'm enclosing are the first things David will look at when he opens the card, so I begin by saying, "Dear David, This is a picture of Gordy and me, your birth parents. I thought you might like to see what we looked like."

For over thirty years, whenever I told the story of my pregnancy it was a pat, bare-boned version that I thought summed up the experience and told the truth. I would say that I got pregnant when I was fifteen. That my mother had counselled abortion, but my boyfriend and I knew from the start that I'd have the baby and then we would give it up for adoption. That we were children ourselves. That he was born on February 2, 1972, and that Gordy and I signed the adoption papers on Valentine's Day and so that day always had a particular significance for me.

Sometimes I told a longer version, one that led up to the birth of my younger son, Emmett. I explained that I had thought for decades that I would never marry, let alone have children. How I had read that the first tree you see serves as the example for all the trees you see in the rest of your life, that if you say to a person, "Draw a tree," the result will differ depending on what tree was the person's example. An apple tree. A poplar. Mine is a cedar. And that you could extrapolate further: the first man, the first woman, the first mother. And so I believed I would be an angry mother like my mother and any children I might have would be doomed. I was approaching forty before I knew it didn't have to be that way.

I picked Emmett up at school and, instead of going home, I took him to the Dairy Queen, where for the first time we shared a banana split.

"This is weird," he said. "Not that I mind. Why are we doing this, Mum?"

"I have something important to tell you," I said.

"I'll guess," he said. "Okay?"

"You'll never guess," I said.

"I might."

"Okay."

"You met the Backstreet Boys."

"No," I said, laughing. "I didn't."

And then I reminded him of how, when he was three, he and I would sit on the lower stairs in the front hall and banter in nonsense language.

He would tell me about his eleven brothers and sisters who had names like Ngabooya, and Sticklamishtoonah-ah-ah and Pakumbala.

"That was pretty funny, wasn't it?" he asked happily, licking his plastic spoon.

"Well, Emmett, this is what I have to tell you. Besides those brothers and sisters, you also have a real one. A brother. Named David."

"I do?"

"He is a lot older than you, though. He is thirty-three."

"How did I get this brother?" asked Emmett, amazed.

I try to imagine my letter arriving at David's home. I try to imagine him picking up his mail—does he take it from a mailbox, or does he lean over or crouch to pick it up from the floor in the front hall? Does he sit down at the dining room table, or stand at the kitchen counter as he opens it? Does he tear it open, or slit the paper with his thumbnail, or a dinner knife, or a letter opener?

I don't know anything about him except his address, which I got from his name, which I got through a bureaucratic mistake. I don't know he if is a reader or writer; I don't know if he is a drug dealer; I don't know if he is tall or short, mellow or intense, or neither. Whether he has Gordy's fair skin and blond hair or my medium brown. For many of the years, I didn't know if he had grown up, if he were alive or dead, healthy, bright, or damaged by my teenage drinking (there was that party where I drank a whole mickey of vodka mixed with Tang and passed out cold).

Ten days later I take the bunch of mail out of the green mailbox beside my front door. When I see his letter my heart leaps. I carry it like a holy thing into the dining room and place it on the mahogany table that was my grandparents'. My great-grandfather scowls down from his portrait above the piano. I make a cup of Earl Grey tea and pour it into one of my mother's best china tea cups and stir it with a sterling silver spoon as if it somehow matters that I properly honour the letter's presence with the best I have to offer. I clear everything off the table except a coaster. The letter, addressed in his hand, lies gleaming on the wood. I turn off the radio and unplug all the telephones. I bring my father's letter opener from my office.

Inside the folds of his letter are six little elementary school portraits. I glance at them with great interest, but it's the letter itself that draws my closer attention. With an unfamiliar deep hunger I read his words. He tells me he is glad I have written. He tells me that he was indeed loved, and is loved, very much. He writes well.

He tells me that he runs the computers at a gold-mining company. And he writes that while he has never been one to believe in Fate, the arrival of my letter has given him pause. For one thing, it arrived on the third anniversary of his mother's death. For another, it was the day that he and his wife, Pamela, met a counsellor for the first time to discuss adopting a child. At the end, he asks tentatively if I think Gordy will be interested in meeting him.

I call Gordy at work. Dialling the still-familiar number, I remember how he had carried a picture of the baby in his wallet for years and years, so long that the baby was barely discernible. When he answers, I can hear the banging and crashing of tire moulds. I can picture him, hands and face blackened and sweaty, old jeans, blonde hair pushed off his face with his forearm. His voice so familiar in his "Hullo?" His voice breaking with emotion by the time I say goodbye.

Every day after work—his job was preparing and then putting truck tires into giant moulds to retread them by cooking on a new outer layer, cooling them, and then taking them out again, and then repeating the process—Gordy drove in to see me at the United Church Home in Burnaby, to pick me up, take me to Langley to eat supper made by his mum, and then to watch TV before he drove me back in time for curfew. Back and forth, back and forth, how many dozens of times across the Pattulo Bridge? Through Whalley, onto the Number Ten where it splits off from the King George, onto the bridge and over the Fraser River.

And I? I spent my days waiting for Gordy. I erected a monumental wall around me so that I couldn't see myself, didn't see my body and what it was doing inside and out. I smoked cigarettes and ate and ate and endured. I waited for it to be over, for things out of my control to reach their resolution.

Two months before the baby was born, my social worker, Alice, kind and young, told me she had found people who might be perfect parents for my baby. She couldn't tell me much about them, but she said they had adopted a child already, a son. That adoption was going so well that now they very much wanted another baby.

It's June before David and I meet at a park in North Vancouver. I pull my '76 VW van into the parking lot and kiss my rescue dog, Jersey, on her nose before I climb out. I see Gordy leaning up against his car about twenty yards away. He sees me and we smile and wave. I start walking toward him but out of the corner of my eye I see someone getting out of a car in a different row. A tall man. And I know it's him. I veer away from Gordy and move rapidly toward David. I feel a physical pull, a magnetic yank, my body drawing me to him.

"David!" I say in a voice squeezed tight with emotion.

"Hi," he says shyly, and we move into each other's arms.

I have never felt anything like it: my whole body warm and awash with life, every one of my cells aware of its reunion with him. My body knows him, remembers him completely, and yet the last time I held him he was a tiny baby just two days old, fresh out of my body.

I have tried, but I can't fully convey this reunion in words; if I close my eyes now, the best I can do is recall the emotion surging through me, and how, in astonishment and amazement, I could have stood there forever, my eyes closed, my body reunited with his six-foot-four body. His height, his brown hair and eyes, his nose are from my side of the family; the shape of his eyes, his broad shoulders, his hips and way of walking, his quiet, shy disposition are from Gordy's.

Trying to articulate what this experience is like for him, David says, "It's like you have lived in this house for a long time. This house you thought you knew pretty well. And then someone comes along and punches out one of the walls and suddenly you see this whole other part of the house you never knew was there before. It's amazing!"

A year later, Gordy and I are standing side by side on the deck of my family's cabin on Galiano Island, off the coast of BC, watching burgers on the grill. We like each other, can find pieces of the past we inhabited together to revisit with nostalgia, but it's still a little strange.

"Who would have thought, Gordy," I say, "that you and I would be standing here together all these years later?"

"Not me," says Gordy.

"I mean, who would have ever been able to predict such a thing — that we would be standing here looking over at the baby we made all those years ago, the baby now a fine grown man with a wife and baby?"

"Not me," says Gordy. "Not a chance."

Not my husband, Steven, either. (If it's all a little strange for me, it must be downright weird for him.) His preference is to dwell as firmly as he can in the present, though by now he knows enough of my history to get the picture. Steven is such an amiable man, I think, as I glance over at him. He's sitting at the picnic table drinking beer and talking to Gordy's mother, Norma, and Gordy's partner, Kathy. Gordy's granddaughter, Angel, is playing with bocce balls. Emmett is cooing at David and Pamela's baby, Maggie, who is standing up in her portable playpen waving a stuffed toy caterpillar. David and Pamela stand together slightly to one side, each with a beer, laughing. I feel so lucky. So fortunate. Talk about family reunion.

Later, I think how David and I, as well as our families, will need to travel quite a distance before we feel completely at ease with each other. I see it most clearly when Emmett is looking up to speak to David, his brother, whom he wants very much to love. David is like one of the trees Emmett has taken to climbing. He's trying to get a foothold.

When the two of them sit down to talk, the desire to connect is so clear in them both.

I take a walk by myself up the property and sit down on a mossy log to reflect, to attempt some perspective. It's such a paradox. Here David and I have this most intimate of physical bonds, but we do not know each other. We share the briefest of histories aside from the long, enduring histories of Gordy's and my families. Our lives have no connective tissue made of the dailyness of life but that which we are creating now. I feel lame, at a loss. When we talk, the desire to connect stilts our words, and both of us stumble. I am frustrated with myself: I want to know how to be, want to know what my role here is so that I can follow it. But there are no guidelines. When I get back to the cabin and David, I still find myself stumbling and trying too hard. Ah, we are better just walking slowly, down the grassy driveway, along the gravel road.

Five years later, on the May long weekend in 2010, Dave, Pam, and Maggie bring their tent trailer to Banff, our home now, to visit. Just the week before, Emmett, Steven, and I buried my father's ashes in the family plot in the Old Banff Cemetery. So one thing I want to do while Dave is here is to take him there. I lead the way, and we stand before the eight graves. The dozen yellow roses I laid, three along each side of my father's freshly installed rectangular stone, are drying out, and their petals are beginning to turn brown and curl.

The relatives in the Robinson family plot, I tell him, include three of my great-grandparents, two grandparents, and two children, one of them my father's little sister who died when she was five. David doesn't say a word, doesn't make a murmur. This unnerves me, and I babble on, giving details about the lives of the dead. Maggie runs from grave to grave in the peaceful, beautiful cemetery, identifying letters on the gravestones. Then she calls her father to her, and I stand in silence, remembering how Dave and Pam initially called us—his biological family—his "ghost family." Until right now I have liked this term; it has accurately described how, unseen and unknown, we lurked in the shadows behind David's "real" life with his parents, the people who raised him. But now here we are all present in his real life, while so many of his "real" family have passed away. They have become the ghosts, in a sense, I think, while his ghost family has become "real." Not in the same roles, not in the same light, but real nonetheless.

I don't think of myself as his mother, for I did no mothering. But he, that baby, this man, grew in my body, emerged from my body, was kissed and held by me, a dazed, exhausted, and ravaged sixteen-year-old girl traumatized by fear and pain, before I gave him up to his parents' care. So many years ago.

On the final day of the visit, the two brothers stand companionably side by side for a photo. Emmett, fourteen, with his curly and uncombed longish locks and Ironhead shirt, takes his favourite Austin Powers stance. David, thirty-eight, with his conservative clothes, short, short hair, and glasses, and with a small hint of a smile, stands straight, so straight, and tall. How different they are! Is this nurture or nature? David so carefully contained within himself, barely speaking except about Maggie or work. So gentle, intelligent, and hesitant with matters of the heart. While Emmett is a kook who careens from inside to outside himself, lively and expressive and open to the world. Emmett, who has not yet suffered.

I remain troubled by David's silence at the graveyard. How to read it? Lack of interest? Many people do not care about their roots. But I want to know. And so that final evening I ask him, and the next morning he tells me. That he was quiet because he was thinking of the generations of my family that are buried there. That he was thinking that there is no distinction among kinds of family for him anymore, that we are all simply "family." Yet how hard it was, standing in front of the graves, to feel emotionally connected to these people he didn't know.

"I don't even know what I want to know," he says. "I don't even know what I want to ask. But I'm interested." And so the silence. Which now I understand.

I hug him, hard, as we say goodbye, and he tells me, "I feel very close to you, even if I may not show it," and my heart leaps up. We are close, closer than we've ever been, and so, too, are the brothers.

J. Jill Robinson writes fiction and creative nonfiction. Her work has been shortlisted for National Magazine Awards and has twice won Western Magazine Awards. "The Letter" won *Event* magazine's creative nonfiction contest in 2009. Her most recent book is *Residual Desire* (Coteau, 2003). She lives in Banff, Alberta.

a familiar face

ANGELA LONG

IT ARRIVED DURING THE cold snap of 1994. A yellow envelope. A franked US stamp. If I'd recognized the return address, maybe I would have waited for a different moment to open it. A solitary moment in a quiet place. Instead, I opened it the way I usually opened letters back then, with a careless rip en route from the front door to the living room where my two roommates, the film students, sat watching movies all day.

I can't remember what they were watching, or whether they noticed the expression on my face. I remember going into my frigid bedroom and sitting on the futon, because suddenly I couldn't walk anymore. I put the letter down and looked out the window at the icy-white Montreal sky for a long, long time.

At some point I picked up the letter again. "Call me collect," she wrote. There was a phone number. A name signed with a flourish: Patricia Gallagher. My mother. The mother who gave me up for adoption when I was a baby. Gallagher. I tried the name on. I said it aloud. I stared out the window, watching the sky turn a pale rose, then sapphire.

When my boyfriend came home from work, I could barely speak I was so overwhelmed. "She wrote," was all I could say. But Sébastien knew whom I was talking about. I showed him the letter.

"Call her," he said.

I'd waited for this moment for so many years that, as I picked up the phone and stared at the numbers on the console, I couldn't bring myself to press them. Every number seemed to represent a different year of my life. Years when she hadn't been there.

I held the receiver away from me, thinking: How could a person who used such bright yellow stationery abandon her baby? Had she been living it up in Arizona all this time? I put the phone down. Slammed it a little.

Sébastien came back into the room. He gave me a long, hard look. "Call her, Angie," he said. "You don't know her story."

Maybe it was too late in Arizona to call, I reasoned. What was the time zone there anyway? Maybe it was best to wait until Sunday. Sunday afternoon when our roommates would be at the Cinéma du Parc. Sébastien kept looking at me. I took a deep breath and dialled.

℘ Even though my adoptive parents had done their best to make me feel like part of the family, I, a pale-skinned, blonde-headed wisp of a girl, might as well have been beamed down from Mars as picked up from a hospital ward in Ottawa. They and their two "naturally born" sons were a merry, olive-toned, large-boned bunch. Naturally, whenever the family appeared in public, strangers had wondered where I'd come from: "Where'd she get that blonde hair?" they'd asked. "Oh, her father was blonde when he was young," answered my mother, who had never lied otherwise.

This little white lie had never failed to make me wonder: what were they hiding? I began to feel like adoption was a dirty word. It was our little secret. My parents must have told me before I could talk; maybe they'd sung it to me in a lullaby. But they didn't tell me when I was old enough to know what it meant.

I'd learned what it meant in the schoolyard. It was something no one wanted to be. "You're adopted!" was a popular insult of the time. Being adopted was something I'd hidden on family tree day, drawing branches leading from one fictitious name to another. It had never occurred to me to learn of my adoptive family's ancestry. I must have figured it was better to lie than pretend to be someone I wasn't.

And who was I? I'd convinced myself the answer to this question lay in the discovery of my birth mother. I looked for her everywhere — the grocery store, the library. When I couldn't find her, I'd decided she must be famous. I'd narrowed it down to Farah Fawcett or Michelle Pfeiffer. Both were blonde. Both had probably run away to Hollywood after my birth, heartbroken.

Eventually I'd been forced to acknowledge I already had a mother, someone who taught me things like how to draw leaves and make grilled cheese sandwiches. Slowly I realized my childhood was a whimsical affair spent exploring meadows and putting on puppet plays. I had little reason to feel sorry for myself. But still, I was curious.

I was twenty-three before I did anything to satisfy this curiosity. My efforts were sparked by an encounter with a woman I met in French class during a brief stint at university. She too was adopted. She'd gone through the process of finding her birth mother and discovered she was the child of a rape. "But it didn't matter," she'd told me. She'd told me about instant bonds, about the pieces of her life falling into place.

I couldn't wait for the pieces of my life to fall into place. I'd called the Ontario Adoption Registry. They had told me forms would arrive soon. They'd asked: "Do you know if your name has been changed? Do you know your birth-registration number?"

I called my adoptive mother. "What?" she'd asked, surprised.

"Please don't take this personally," I'd said. Silence. "I just want to know my medical history and that kind of stuff," I'd lied.

I'd lied because I didn't want to hurt her feelings. How could I have told her I wanted to see someone who looked like me? How could I have told tell her I wanted an instant bond?

I prepared for the wait. I'd been advised the hiatus could last anywhere from months to years to infinity. I had to wait because a reunion could take place only if my birth mother also consented to be contacted. Someday, they'd told me, if all the pieces were found, a letter might arrive. Or a phone call.

🔊 The phone rang. Someone picked it up after the first ring, as though she'd been waiting. At first, I thought I was hearing my voice echo. "Hello?" I repeated. There was no sense asking the woman on the end of the line if she was Patricia Gallagher. "Hello?" she asked with the same soft voice I've been told I possess, a voice well-suited for phone sex or hypnotherapy.

"Angela?" she asked, just to make sure.

"Just call me Angie," I said.

"Just call me Pat," she said. We laughed.

When Sébastien left the room, I couldn't hold my emotions in any longer. Tears that had waited far too long to fall blurred my view of the Montreal sky. Suddenly it didn't make sense to try to make conversation.

But Pat sat there with me, three time zones away. She sat wherever she was sitting, staring out at whatever she stared out at. A cactus? A canyon? She wasn't going anywhere this time.

After a while, I began to sense the temperature had dropped outside. There was a stillness out there. The stillness of a cold where snow doesn't crunch beneath footsteps, where branches seize, where people barricade themselves indoors ferreting out warmth. I stopped crying.

"Maybe it's better if we meet in person," Pat said.

🔊 The airport in Albuquerque was a four-hour drive from Pat's home in Arizona's White Mountains. She had told me she'd meet me at the airport with her husband and son. There was a husband. A son. I slung on my backpack and began to walk in the direction of the arrivals lounge until my nerves got the better of me.

The entire journey had been a battle against nerves. Bouts of diarrhea and nausea. Sweaty palms and nonsensical conversation with fellow passengers and airline staff. At every checkpoint I'd debated turning back and calling it a day.

On the way to the arrivals lounge, I stopped in front of a Mexican restaurant. It was happy hour. I decided to delay reality a little longer. I ordered a margarita and ate tortilla chips with salsa. Spicy salsa with fresh cilantro. I convinced myself I was on a holiday. Just a simple holiday. I wasn't here to meet the woman who was my birth mother and her twelve-year-old son who, I realized with a start, was actually my half brother.

I knew they were waiting out there, but I couldn't move from the rattan seat. I admired the palm trees jutting toward the airport skylights and the southern accent of my waiter.

And then I saw her, rounding the bend near the magazine stand. She was with a skinny boy who looked even more nervous than I was. I knew it was her because she looked like a mid-forties version of me. Long, grey hair. Slightly frizzy. No makeup. Slight frame. She was wearing tight jeans and a sweatshirt printed with a wolf padding along the top of a mesa.

It was disconcerting to watch my older self scan the corridor leading to the baggage carousels with such a look of worry on her face. The boy looked in the direction of the restaurant with eyes I could tell were the same hazel as mine even from the distance of my table. Quickly, I settled the bill.

The moment I stepped out into the main corridor, my birth mother zoned in on me. She looked at me like you'd look at a glass of water after a long day in the desert. The look scared me so much that I looked toward the skylights again. The sky was darkening. Then I fiddled industriously with the straps on my backpack until she got so close I was forced to acknowledge her presence.

"Angie?" she asked, as if I could be anyone else but her daughter. She had a smaller version of my backpack slung over the same shoulder. I managed a nod. "I thought you'd decided not to come." she said.

It was time for the awkward moment then. The moment I'd spent years imagining.

I'd imagined many things: running into one another's arms; a frenzied embrace; copious tears. I'd imagined feeling like I'd finally landed on the right planet, like I was finally with my people.

I hadn't imagined a wide-eyed boy sizing me up or the smell of tequila on my breath. I hadn't imagined a woman as quirky as I was. A woman who goes into retreat mode when things become too emotional, like a turtle ducking under its shell waiting for the right moment to peek out.

The right moment wasn't here in the Albuquerque airport with Texans in cowboy hats looking on from the restaurant. The right time wasn't accompanied by announcements for departures to Salt Lake City.

We embraced. Quickly. I turned to her son, my brother, and we smiled at one another. "This is Lee," Pat said. He gazed at me like you'd only gaze at your long-lost big sister fresh from the North. "Hi," he said quickly and looked toward the magazine stand. Of course, he'd inherited the same habit of retreat. The husband, whose name I learned was Jimmy, hung back at a respectful distance. He had long grey hair too and waved at me. His beard and moustache were so overgrown I couldn't tell if he smiled.

The worst was over. That was the moment I describe every time someone finds out I've met my birth mother. "What was it like the first time you saw one another?" they inevitably ask. And I tell them. Sort of.

I tend to leave out the part about the restaurant and Pat's sweatshirt. I don't tell them about the black plastic comb wedged into the back pocket of her jeans. I don't tell them that when I first saw her it was obvious she wasn't Farah Fawcett or Michelle Pfeiffer. Pat was the kind of woman who rarely went to airports and hated driving in the city. She gripped her door handle as Jimmy drove to the Motel 76 alongside the interstate, where we waited out the darkness to drive into the mountains at first light.

I don't tell anyone how it all became pretty normal after that. We got ice from the ice dispenser and Dr. Pepper from the vending machine. Jimmy propped himself up against the pillows and flicked through television channels until he found a football game. Lee jumped up beside him.

Pat and I peeked out at one another from beneath our turtle shells, still waiting for the right moment. We sipped Dr. Pepper while sitting on top of the blankets of the other bed. I pretended I liked football. When the lights went out and Jimmy began to snore, Pat and I stared up at the ceiling. We both knew the other was awake. I was more nervous than I'd been on any first date. Much more.

"You know," Pat whispered, "I've thought about you every day for twenty-three years." She turned toward me. "Every single day," she said.

I turned toward her too. And we stayed like that, silent, waiting for our eyes to adjust to the darkness. Waiting to see a familiar face.

Angela Long's nonfiction, fiction, and poetry have appeared in numerous Canadian and international publications, including the *Globe and Mail*, *Utne Reader*, and *Poetry Ireland Review*. Her first collection of poems, *Observations from Off the Grid*, was published by Libros Libertad in 2010. She lives in a log cabin on Canada's northwest coast with her Sicilian husband, Giuseppe, and Penelope the tortoiseshell cat. She met her birth mother sixteen years ago and still keeps in touch.

these foreign places we call home

KELLY RUSSELL

FRANK SINATRA CROONS "New York, New York" from the lobby of the Pennsylvania hospital. I believe it is a sign. New York. *We are going home, baby.*

My lips meet the curve of my son's cheek. The translucence of skin is luminous against the just-born blue of his eyes. The contrast is startling, beautiful. I am memorizing this face that is only forty-eight hours familiar.

I am nervous waiting for David to pull the car around to the hospital doors. I know he is crouched down on the hot pavement of the parking lot, meticulously checking and rechecking the car seat we had installed three weeks ago. *Hurry up, David.*

I am conspicuous, holding a newborn baby in the hospital lobby without the soft bulge of midsection that accompanies most women heading home after giving birth. Without a trace of maternity skin, I feel exposed. I wish that I were at least sitting in a wheelchair instead of standing on my own.

I want to be the one to leave first, she says.

Her knees knock up against the metal of the wheelchair her mother pushes out of the room that we have slept in together over the past two days. I listen for her sobbing as she makes her way down the hall. The sound never comes. I marvel at her silence. I wipe my fingers, sticky from the Popsicles we shared in celebration of the final goodbye. I carry the taste of this parting on my tongue, now stained blue. I pick up my son and hold him cradled up against my chest. It is just the two of us for the very first time.

Before Jack was born, I had a dream I held a newborn baby in my arms. When I awoke, I could still feel the soft, silken hair of his scalp against my fingertips. I tell Angel about this image, and she gets quiet. The very first thing she asks her midwife when they pull Jack from her body is whether he has any hair. The nurses hold him up for all of us to admire. We discover he is bald. She smiles and rests her head back against her pillow. I am certain she is smug.

The call that Angel is in labour comes at 8:30 on an ordinary evening in June. David and I become this vaudeville act in motion, spilling the contents of our underwear drawer into plastic grocery bags and rushing to the car that has been packed with baby belongings for over a month. The three-hour drive between our arriving at Angel's bedside and our leaving the now topsy-turvy cottage, whose door we forget to lock, is a purgatory of wondering. What will we do in the delivery room? How are we going to feel? Will this baby really be ours? Hope is a turnpike that lengthens the distance between New York and Pennsylvania.

꧁ Everything pregnant is foreign to us and makes us feel envious. We travel the hospital corridors like interlopers looking for the maternity ward. The only experience we have with actual birth is what we have gathered from television programs, late-night medical dramas like *Grey's Anatomy* and *ER*. The sound of my flip-flops echoing against the tiled floor of the hospital corridor makes me feel conspicuous. I suddenly wish I had chosen to wear more sensible shoes.

The nurse who checks us in informs us that we will be issued only one hospital bracelet—the bracelet that is usually given to the father in those two-parent deliveries that are less awkward than our adoption triangle. *You take it*, David tells me. He nods his head in certainty. He chooses for me to have the privilege of wearing this signature of being Jack's parent. It is such a simple thing. I am overwhelmingly grateful.

Angel called me after taking the hospital tour in the weeks preceding Jack's birth.

Did you know that they have a chocolate fountain in the cafeteria? She bubbles over with unrestrained youth.

I have to remind myself, sometimes, that she is only eighteen and easily excitable. I shuffle my feet. I wipe the kitchen countertop for the seventh or eighth time since the beginning of our call. Despite the fact that the kitchen is immaculate, I find it necessary to keep my body in constant motion when we talk. I am anxious but unwilling to press her for delivery room details.

That's awesome! I try to temper my own impatience. *What else did they tell you during the tour?*

She hesitates before explaining the security system the medical bracelets provide.

I'm really happy the hospital has them. That means no one can up and steal a baby in the middle of the night. There is an edge of suspicion in her voice. I wonder who she is trying to reassure with this detail—me or herself.

In the delivery room, I stand, holding my breath, at her bedside. I watch her strain against the labour that I fear will break her tiny body in two. The nurse supports her legs. Spread open on the metal stirrups, she is more vulnerable than she has ever been. I should be embarrassed to be witness, but I cannot turn away. I lean in further to look for myself as I hear the doctor say, *Push. Keep pushing. He is almost here.*

When Jack's first cry, sonorous and staccato, fills the room, I can feel it in my bones. I know I will not let this child go. I have to bring this baby, my baby, home. I make a silent vow, with Jack no more than a minute old, that I will do whatever it takes to be his mother.

Jack is taken to the warmer on the other side of the room. No one but the midwife and her nurses have laid their hands on him. I try to maintain loyalty to Angel and the way that labour stole her breath. She lies exhausted and flat against the bed, looking nowhere but the ceiling. My body is starting to betray me: my fingers itch. My feet are turning outward to point in the direction of the baby. My eyes stray and stretch themselves across the room to where the nurses count ten perfect fingers, ten healthy toes. I long to go and learn the language of my son's body, press him tight against my skin. I do not move. I am riveted to the spot like a school-yard child in a game of Mother May I. I must wait for Angel to grant permission for me to see my son. He is no longer in her body, but he still does not belong to me. I wipe the sweaty tendrils of Angel's hair away from her forehead.

Go ahead, Momma. Go and get your boy. She is so generous then.

I do not wait for her to change her mind. I rush to where the nurses hold him out to me. I take him in my arms, swaddled tight and tender. I know that everyone is watching us. The room gets quiet. I tense. He does not know my smell, my voice, the feel of my palm, the crook of my arm; all of this is unfamiliar.

Angel once asked me if I wanted her to hold the phone up to her belly so I could talk to Jack. Her midwife had told her that by the fifth month it would be possible for a fetus to hear and react to voices outside of the watery womb that he was growing in. *I talk to him all the time when I lie in bed at night. He kicks up a storm.* I try to swallow my own jealousy when she tells me this.

When we were pregnant with the second of our three babies, each of which we would miscarry, I used to lie in bed at night with the ultrasound picture framed on the nightstand table. I would read to our never-to-be son poems by Pablo Neruda:

Now, I have all I have loved
Within my little universe
The starred order of waves,
The sudden disorder of stones

It seemed silly to read that when my uterus was empty. There was no longer a universe growing underneath my skin. All that I loved was outside of my body, and my hands were not long enough to touch. I wanted so badly to read to Jack growing inside another woman's body. I wanted to feel him undulate against me in the starred order of Neruda's waves. Instead, I pressed my lips against the phone and I told Jack, awkwardly and truly, that I was out there waiting for him. Then, I quickly hung up the phone and surrendered myself to crying.

I know you. I have always known you. This is what I whisper to my son as I stand holding him in a hospital room that does not belong to me. Angel pulls herself up on the bed into a sitting position. She watches with a face that is expressionless. I turn my body away as if to shield Jack. I do this on instinct. I am becoming his mother.

But I am not yet my son's mother in the eyes of the law. When the nurses take Angel to the bathroom to clean up, and David rushes into the hall to call our family, I am allowed to accompany Jack to the nursery. I stand on one side of a glass partition and watch as he is measured and weighed. Exhausted but exhilarated, I pull my face away from the nursery room window to rub at my watery eyes. My lips pressed up against the glass leave a subtle impression, the shape of a disappearing heart. I allow myself to think about the possibility of loss.

He isn't mine. I just feel like I am a surrogate for you and David. How many times in the months leading up to Jack's delivery did I take comfort in those exact words?

꧁ My parents arrive in the afternoon of the day Jack is born. Angel answers the door of the maternity room and they do not recognize her as anything but a stranger. After the awkwardness of introductions, my parents meet their first grandchild. Angel climbs into her bed and watches silently as I place Jack into my mother's arms. I stand with my hands wrapped around my mom's shoulders. I marvel at this moment of us mothering together. Angel's mother does not come to the hospital except to act as her ride home. It is only after Jack is safely home, and our relationship with Angel begins to unravel, that I wonder about all the things each of us did wrong.

Angel brought us photos of herself as a child the first time we met in person. We sat on our hotel bed and tried to picture an infant with her features. There was an indoor pool at the hotel. We invited her to swim. I cursed myself quietly in our bathroom as I changed into my suit. I had forgotten to shave my legs. How would she possibly think me responsible enough to mother her child if I could barely manage my own grooming? That night, we drove through the small town of York and stopped to look at Christmas lights. She showed us the church in which she hoped she would one day get married.

I already have my dress all picked out. I heard wistfulness in her voice that reminded me of myself every time I went to a baby shower or watched a mother push a newborn down the street in a baby carriage. I am constantly reminded that Angel and I are not such different women after all.

꧁ The first night after Jack is born, I wake up at 2:00 AM to the sound of someone crying. Jack is sleeping soundly in the bassinet that I have pulled to arm's length from the pullout couch on which I dozed off. Angel is not in her bed. I hear the muffled signs of distress coming from behind the closed bathroom door. I press myself against the frame and listen. Angel is arguing with someone about choices that need to be made. She is desperate, pleading. This one-sided conversation makes me queasy and afraid. Jack stirs. I go on silent feet to comfort him.

When Angel comes puffy-eyed from behind the bathroom door, I ask her if there is anything I can do to help, while Jack contentedly feeds in my arms, his tiny fingers wrapped around my left thumb. Angel climbs back into bed and asks me to join her. I climb up next to where she has pulled the covers to meet her chin. I place Jack in the hollow space that is between our bodies. As we lie side by side in silence, against the gentle rhythm of Jack's breathing, there are so many words left unspoken.

In the morning, the nurses come to tell us that Angel and Jack are being discharged later that day. We will have to spend at least the next week in hotel rooms, where we will create makeshift changing tables out of beds and learn to parent in foreign surroundings. We have to wait for the Interstate Compact to be signed by the proper authorities in New York and Pennsylvania. If we were to cross the state line to bring our son home before this paper was signed, it would be considered kidnapping.

David heads down to hospital administration to finalize the bill. I have brought a stack of books and sit happily in a rocking chair reading to Jack. The June sun shines in from between the venetian blinds. I feel a generosity swelling in my bones. We are leaving the hospital today. This knowledge gives me faith. I look over at Angel and she turns to me and smiles. We are all in this together.

You should have some time alone with Jack before we leave today. Even as I say this, I surprise myself. I go and sit in the lobby of the maternity floor. One of the nurses comes and makes conversation. She tells me that all the nurses are amazed at the relationship we have with Angel. People who adopt are often viewed as saints. I feel much more like a sinner when I return to Angel's room thirty minutes later, having been able to endure only a half hour of biting my nails and aching to fill my arms up again with Jack. Through the glass in the hospital door to Angel's room, I see them. She has Jack cradled, the palm of her right hand wrapped around the soft spot of his skull. With her other hand free, she reads to Jack from one of the books I have left on the table beside the bed. It is a well-worn copy of *The Giving Tree* by Shel Silverstein. This particular book has an inscription inside the front cover, written by David's mother. I remember packing this particular book in our suitcase before we left for Pennsylvania. I tucked it safely under hand-knit blankets and the *I love my Mommy* bibs, thinking that I would soon be able to pass along the tradition of mother reading to her son.

I stare into the glass window that separates me from Angel. She is holding my son. She is reading *The Giving Tree* to Jack. I want to come crashing through that door and rip the book and Jack from her arms. I want to stamp my feet and yell like a petulant child. *He is mine! He is mine! He is mine!* I want my son back. I am overcome with a mix of terror and hatred so pure I can feel my hands begin to shake as my fingers grip the door handle to turn the knob—until I stare more closely into the room. My rage begins to dissipate as I see the scene for what it is. Angel is reading Jack *The Giving Tree*. I see that *her* hands are shaking so violently she can barely hold the book between her fingers. There are tears streaming down her face, making exclamation points of her cheeks. I stand silent witness to her grief and realize I have no right to my own.

꧁ *We are going home, baby,* I whisper in Jack's ear as I stand nervously in the hospital lobby. David pulls our car up into the no-loading zone in front of the hospital. I cradle Jack's car seat/carrier close to my body, and I race toward the doors. I step out into the climbing heat of that June afternoon as the automatic doors close behind me with a *whoosh*. I do not look back as David pulls the car gently away from the curb and we drive off. I do not take my eyes off of Jack, fast asleep beside me. As we drive through the streets of York, heading for our hotel, I keep expecting someone to jump into the middle of the road to try to stop our car. I wait for the ringing of our cell phone, for a stern voice telling me to turn around and bring Jack back. I cannot believe that it is just the three of us, David, Jack, and me; finally, we are a family.

Why didn't you pick up the phone when I called yesterday? I had no idea what you were doing or where you were. You know, I still have twenty-five days left to change my mind. Every word Angel speaks in the weeks after we bring Jack home sounds like a threat.

After we are given permission to bring Jack home, Angel and I talk on the phone daily, despite the stress this causes. David is back at work, and I am home alone learning how to mother. Every time the phone rings, it jolts my nerves. New York state law gives the biological parents of any child that is being adopted forty-five days to change their mind. Angel is allowed to call the lawyers and demand we give Jack back to her at any time during that period. We would have to pack up the bibs, the bottles, and the bassinet he sleeps frog-legged in every night next to our bed and say goodbye. We would have no recourse. This threat looms large over my mothering. Angel uses it like a weapon. I find I am beginning to dread talking to her every time she calls.

I plead with Angel to understand. *Every time you call me and yell at me or cry about how hard this is for you, I don't know what I am supposed to say.* I beg her to give me the space required to mother. This is not what I had bargained for. This is not what any of us expected. *I feel so guilty that I am the one who is mothering Jack. I feel responsible for all of your pain.*

Angel is silent on the other end of the phone. It makes me wonder if this is exactly how she wants me to feel. Finally, she says, *You cannot understand any of this. You did not give birth to him. I did.*

I did not give birth to my son, Jack, but it does not change the way I love him. Inconsequential people have dared to say that I could not love my son who is adopted as much as I love my daughter. Molly was born from my body a year and thirteen days after the anniversary of Jack's birth. Those people will never understand how my children are two equal sides of my beating heart—seamless, without division.

Jack was three months old when I found out I was pregnant with Molly. Certain I would lose her like each of my three previous babies, I did not allow myself to wonder about who she would become until at least five months into the pregnancy, past the bouts of bleeding that would wreck me in the middle of the night, and the daily doses of medication to convince my body to do what it had refused to do before. Then, I would lie back against the bed pillow, with a belly that kissed the sky, reading from Pablo Neruda, Jack tucked safe and soft inside my arms.

A week before the very first Mother's Day that I would celebrate as Jack's mom, I come across the box that holds all the paperwork from his adoption. I sit on the floor of my bedroom, my belly swollen eight months full. I rub the space where Molly often kicks, under my ribcage on my left side. I read through all the cards and emails that passed between Angel and me all those months that she was pregnant. We thought it would be easier than it turned out to be. I come across a letter that I have folded tight and small. I pull it apart slowly and smooth out the wrinkles to see these words scrawled across the page: *I hate you. I hope that Jack grows up to hate you too.*

I wonder at why I have kept this note, tucked between the copies of Jack's inky baby footprints, medical bracelets, and hospital-issued knitted hat. Then, I remember. When I read those words for the first time, a torrent of relief coursed through me. That note is tangible proof—proof that Angel was too selfish a woman ever to have mothered my son. I think how easy it would be to pin this letter to my chest some day far off in the future, if and when Jack comes and tells me he wants to find his *real* mother. This letter might simply let me off the hook. It is means and maybe motive. I fold the note up again, over and over, until the tight corner creases cover the words. I fold that note down small enough to fit in the middle of my palm. I cover it up tight and trembling in my fist.

Momma!

Jack cries out from where he has been sleeping unaware and peaceful in the next-door nursery. We have painted his room Caribbean blue and decorated the walls with prints of ships, trains, and airplanes. I walk over to the wastebasket. I should throw this note away. My hand wavers over the white wicker next to the bedside table. This note should not exist. To throw it away would be evidence that I am not selfish. I want to do the right thing.

Momma!

Jack cries out in a voice that is little boy certain that his Mommy is coming to fetch him. The note is sweaty and stiff in my hand, a tight, shaky fist. I should throw this note away.

I should, but I don't.

I turn off the bedroom light and shut the door behind me. Carrying the past with me, pushed deep down in the right pocket of my maternity jeans, I walk quickly down the hall to where my son waits for me with arms outstretched in the dark.

Kelly Russell is a middle school reading teacher. She is writing, living, and parenting her two children in New York. You can find more of her writing at thehandinsideyou.blogspot.com.

my little sister

WILL JOHNSON

WHEN I FIRST TOLD my little sister Ashley that I was writing a story about her, she asked me what I was going to call it. She was sitting at the kitchen counter doing her homework, perched on a stool with her legs pulled up under her. She was surrounded on all sides by piles of dirty dishes, boxes of cereal, and the random assortment of belongings a large family leaves lying around. She was fifteen, her eyes a rich brown. Her hair hung softly down the sides of her face. In the past few months she had started to become a woman. She wore low-cut designer tops and expensive jeans. She was wearing cover-up to hide the slight sprinkle of pimples forming around her hairline, and her eyes were smudged with dark, thick mascara.

I had recently started taking classes at the University of Victoria but travelled to visit my family on the British Columbia mainland every few weeks. A quick ninety-minute ferry ride would bring me back to my childhood home in Tsawwassen, where my seven younger siblings still lived with my parents. Often they were busy with soccer practice or away at friends' houses, but on this particular visit Ashley was home trying to finish an assignment.

"I'm not sure what I'll call my story yet," I told her. "Maybe 'Pimple Face: The Adventures of a Really Ugly Girl.'"

Ashley lunged from the stool and punched me in the arm, making her best version of an angry face. She huffed at me theatrically, planted her hands on her hips, and asked again. "Seriously, William. What are you going to call it?"

I hadn't thought about it yet. I've always struggled with titles—but maybe I'd go for something simple. "My Little Sister?" Or maybe just "Ashley?"

It better be good, she told me. Better be.

Having spent over a decade living with Ashley, it's been weird to sort through my memories and try to organize her life into a narrative. It's been years since I've thought about her as anything more than a noisy teenaged nuisance. But then I think about the life she might have had if my parents hadn't decided to adopt. I wonder what might have happened to her, along with her three younger siblings. I picture our family portrait cut almost in half, four smiling faces missing.

On November 10, 1992, Ashley was born at the Royal Columbian Hospital in New Westminster. She was ten weeks premature and weighed four pounds. Suffering from neonatal abstinence syndrome, a withdrawal from her fetal cocaine addiction, Ashley spent the first month of her life in a hospital, hooked up to machines. There was a good chance she would die if the doctors sent her home too soon.

The first two years of Ashley's life are a shadowy mystery. She doesn't have the baby pictures or the memories that many people have. She can't remember her parents, her house, her life. All she has are bits and pieces of stories from her foster mom and the random information my parents have picked up along the way.

We do know that she spent twenty-two months with her birth parents before being taken away by the government. These were dark years of neglect, possibly of abuse. Her parents were troubled people, impoverished and addicted to drugs. They had moved after their first child was taken from them, to inhabit a slum on the Downtown Eastside of Vancouver. When the Ministry of Children and Families came to visit Ashley, they found her filthy and malnourished. She had a limited vocabulary, consisting mostly of swear words, and was terrified of grown-ups. She had gotten into the habit of cutting her food in half, giving the rest to her baby brother Cody. (Her parents often forgot to feed Cody and would leave him lying supine in his crib for hours. He was unable to move, so the pressure eventually flattened the back of his skull.)

In September 1994, Ashley was placed in a foster home in Ladner, along with Cody. Their younger sister, Amanda, had been taken from her mother at birth and had been living there since July. Finally, Tyler joined them after his birth in January 1996. Ellie, their foster mother, was an elderly energetic woman with an enormous collection of Disney movies. For most of their stay in Ellie's house, the kids were surrounded by two to five other children, most of them First Nations and many of them suffering from various disabilities.

This became Ashley's home for the next two years, until my family came along. Their social workers had been struggling to place the kids, as they hoped to keep the four siblings together. My parents, already with four birth children, had originally been considering adopting a sibling group of two. But upon meeting Ashley, Cody, Amanda, and Tyler, their plans instantly changed.

The adoption process was like a long courtship, with our family inviting the kids out on a number of dates. We drove them to the nearby park and fed the rabbits. We took them to Science World and the Vancouver Aquarium. My parents attended classes on the adoption process and went through a gruelling vetting process. We met with social workers and government officials.

Then, finally, in early December 1996, the four kids climbed into our hulking red twelve-passenger van, a new purchase. We strapped them into their brand new car seats and waved goodbye to Ellie. Then we brought them back to our house. At four years old, Ashley had finally found her home. We'd spent months preparing for the four siblings' arrival. The house was packed with garbage bags of donations from our local church, with everything from baby clothes to picture books and toys. Their bedroom, just down the hallway from my parents' room, was set up with brand new bunk beds. As my mom tucked Ashley in that night, Ashley asked her, "Is this where we're going to live forever now?"

Ashley has been diagnosed with Fetal Alcohol Syndrome (FAS), which is now known as Fetal Alcohol Spectrum Disorder (FASD). FASD hits every child in different ways. Depending on how severely their mothers abused alcohol, children that suffer from FASD struggle with everything from severe brain damage to crippling depression and memory loss. Some children born with FASD have serious health issues, including epilepsy, developmental delay, organ dysfunction, and birth defects. Many who suffer from FASD are unable to live ordinary lives and are forced to bear the burden of their mothers' mistakes.

Ashley doesn't wear any of the outside indications of her mother's addictions, and to the casual observer, she is an entirely normal teenage girl. She recently turned seventeen and got her driver's licence. She works in a jewellery store in the mall, lives with her boyfriend, and loves her new kitten. Growing up, she liked to plaster the walls of her room with glossy pictures of half-naked men with rippling abs, men who wore cowboy hats and tight jeans.

"She looks so normal, but has such struggles," says my mom. "It's almost harder, because people can't see her disabilities."

Not long after the adoption, my dad made pancakes when the kids woke up. It was Saturday, and he wanted to do something special — during the week, breakfast was often a mad dash through the kitchen to grab a quick bowl of cereal on the way. Ashley ate pancakes along with everyone else, but a couple of hours later she confronted my dad and accused him of not serving breakfast. "She's so set in her ways, so stuck on her routine, that she couldn't remember eating breakfast. To her, it had to be cereal. If it wasn't cereal, it wasn't breakfast," Mom explained.

Poor coordination, learning difficulties, lack of imagination, behavioural problems—Ashley disguises them well, but these problems bog her down regularly. She enrolled in a special program in high school and has been in the same grade as Cody since they began their education, though she is ten months older. Once, Mom overheard Ashley complaining that her birth mother had "messed up" her brain. Growing up, we were warned not to use words like "stupid" and "dumb" with Ashley, though these were common sibling insults. Ashley was particularly sensitive about her intelligence.

Although Ashley may not always understand her specific deficiencies, she sees them more as a nuisance in her social life—an obstacle to getting what she wants. One symptom of FASD is a lack of abstract reasoning, and Ashley understands only concrete facts. So, when her lack of mental faculties translates into something tangible (taunting at school, or limited opportunities), she gets upset.

"I'm smart, right?" Ashley asked me when she was fifteen, as we were sitting in the kitchen doing homework together. I told her about my own struggles with math and explained to her that different people are good at different things. I may not be good at math, but I'm good at writing. She may not be good at school, but she's great at making friends and getting what she wants.

"So, I'm street smart?" she asked.

"Yeah, you are."

Ashley is diligent about researching her history, about building her identity. She has a fierce need to understand and control the world around her. Watching Mom change Tyler's diaper when she was four, she asked, "Did you do this for me when I was Tyler?"

"No," Mom explained. "Your first mommy did that for you."

"My first mommy?"

First mommy, foster mommy, new mommy—these were important distinctions for Ashley to make. Of all the children, Ashley was the most preoccupied with titles. Maybe she thought if she could understand her history, then she could grasp her life and make it her own.

She likes to hear stories about herself, especially stories about her childhood.

Our first Christmas with her in 1996, she was confused by all the decorations and excitement. I doubt she ever had a proper stockings-over-the-fire, Christmas-tree, Rudolph-the-Red-Nosed-Reindeer celebration. As it turned out, she'd never even heard of Santa Claus. When she did, she was horrified. A strange, fat, bearded man was going to sneak into our house in the middle of the night? Who was this man? Why was he coming? How was he going to get in? Ashley threw an entirely justifiable tantrum when she learned of his clandestine chimney entrance, refusing to go to sleep until she was assured this man would not be allowed in the house.

"Oh, hi, Santa," Mom called from the front door, after answering a staged doorbell-ringing. "Well, thank you very much," she said overly loud, making sure Ashley could hear her. "Yes, see you next year!"

Once Santa had earned Ashley's trust with a ridiculous mountain of presents (most donated by the church and family friends), she grudgingly allowed Santa to use the chimney for access, and even insisted we leave out proper milk and cookies. My dad would eat half of them, then leave a trail of crumbs. One Christmas, Ashley was hurt that Santa hadn't drunk all of his milk.

"Don't worry, Santa was probably just full," said Mom.

🜲 Growing up with adopted siblings was a novelty. I enjoyed each time I'd tell someone new, bragging as if I'd done something heroic and selfless. "Your parents must be such amazing people," they would always say, and I'd look for some way to divert the attention back to me. Having adopted siblings felt like owning exotic pets, like alligators or parrots.

When we first adopted the children, I was halfway through Grade 7.

Although I wasn't the most confident kid in school, I knew how to throw my weight around at home and savoured my role as eldest child. When you're a twelve-year-old boy, you don't experience a troubled new sister as a victim or a charity case. She's only competition: a rival. I understood that Ashley had had a rough background, but once she came into our home, I didn't have pity for her; I only felt obliged to defend my status in the family. I was the oldest, and therefore, I was in charge.

When I first met her, she was standing in the messy living room of Ellie's house. My family had just walked in: six strange people were smiling warmly at her. She and her siblings were playing on the floor; Ashley stood up and strategically placed herself in front, shielding them. With her hands on her hips and her shoulders back, she radiated defiance. She was a protective wall, and if we wanted to see the kids, we would have to get through her first. She was three years old and she was ready to fight. I run this family, her face seemed to say. Who are you?

Once we had brought the group home, Ashley had the same attitude of control. She was constantly attempting to boss around her new siblings and refused to listen to anything we said. She had acknowledged my parents' authority over her, but had no respect for the older children. Why should she?

You're not my real brother!

You can't tell me what to do!

Shut up! You're stupid!

She was feisty, determined, and stubborn. I returned in kind. The following years were a constant battle for dominance. I had bonded with the other kids—particularly Cody—but Ashley was just someone to fight with. Being asked to tuck the kids into bed was a particular pleasure, as I got to dangle my later bedtime in front of Ashley like a trophy. I was a "big kid," she was a "little kid."

But once I moved out of the house, our relationship changed. "I think she feels closer to you because you're around less," said my mom once. "You're not an adversary anymore." Instead, Ashley quickly learned that I could be an ally, that she could use me. Once, I took her to get her nose pierced without parental permission. Mom was so livid she wouldn't even talk to me on the phone.

When Ashley was almost sixteen, I got a call in Victoria from my family. Ashley had run away from home with her friend Rachel. She'd left home in the middle of the night, and no one had heard anything from her. I spent the entire morning emailing all of her friends and calling the few I could find phone numbers for. Ashley had been having some trouble in high school. I had heard mutterings about drug dealers and catfights in the cafeteria, but I figured it was just normal teenage stuff.

Most of her friends replied quickly, letting me know that they didn't know what was going on. Her eighteen-year-old boyfriend sent me an infuriating email:

> Angels were meant to spread their wings. Sometimes all they need is the room to do so. She'll come around im sure. But for the time being she's learning about herself and this world. Unfortunatly i can't tell you where she is or where she's going cause i don't know. What i can tell you is if she runs into trouble ill be there in a heartbeat.

The police got involved and my parents spent the day driving from one friend's house to the next, ultimately figuring out where she was by a string of text messages. That night, nearly twenty-four hours after she went missing, she was picked up in Abbotsford. Apparently, she'd bused to downtown Vancouver, SkyTrained to Surrey, hitch-hiked to Langley, then finally ended up there. Where were they trying to go? Kelowna. Even though it was January, Rachel had heard it was warm. They had barely packed any clothes, didn't have any money, and had no real plan. The next day, I got an email from her:

Hey will, Im sorry for worrieing you and puting you through so much . . . I didnt mean to worrie you. well i got to go but i will talk to you later love you bye

Although things seemed to settle for a while, with Ashley doing well in school and working steadily at Dairy Queen, her relationship with her boyfriend started to become a problem. Often, my mom felt that she wasn't talking to my sister—she was talking to him. In time, Ashley was even helping him manage financially. As he struggled to find work and a place to live, she continued to devote herself to Dairy Queen. Hundreds of dollars were siphoned out of her account each month. When we expressed doubt that this was a smart idea, she always had a snappy response.

"That's what you do for people you love. You help," she'd say.

Tension grew between her and my parents. She was grounded often and got into screaming matches over the rules. She lied constantly and slipped stealthily out of the house in the middle of the night. She continually pointed out that our sister Kathryn, who is half a decade older, was allowed to do the things she wasn't. Then one weekend, while my parents were out of town, Ashley invited her boyfriend over. Despite warnings that her boyfriend was not allowed over while Mom and Dad were away, she tried to keep him hidden in her room. Kathryn was visiting from Vancouver and was watching over the house for the night. When she discovered that he was still in the house, the situation deteriorated quickly. Ashley accused Kathryn of being a "bitch." There was a struggle, Kathryn's boyfriend got involved, and Ashley called the police, who told Ashley's boyfriend that he was trespassing and that he needed to go home. Ashley was incensed and began packing her things.

When I think about Ashley, the first image that always comes to mind is that defiant little three-year-old with her hands on her hips, feet firmly planted on the ground. She was ready for whatever life had in store. In many ways, she hasn't changed at all.

During the summer of 2009, she spent a week at my apartment. While I went to work, she puttered around my house watching movies and texting on her cell phone. In the afternoons, we went to the beach or wandered around downtown. She convinced me to spend an exorbitant amount of money on her at the mall. She tried on several different dresses before deciding on the ones she liked. I wasn't old enough to legally supervise her, but I let her drive my car around Victoria. She squealed in excitement when I agreed to allow her to drive the car down the highway to the ferry terminal.

One day, we went to the beach and spent a lazy few hours suntanning on a pair of towels. I caught young boys doing double takes and whispering to their friends as they passed. Ashley was wearing a tiny bikini and had a sparkling diamond belly button ring dangling against her bronzed skin. She was effortlessly beautiful. I tried to go swimming but came panting out of the freezing water. She laughed and took pictures, then we walked along the water.

"You have to put these on Facebook," she demanded, as she scrolled through the pictures we'd taken over the past few days.

I asked her about life at home, how she felt to be going into Grade 11, how she was getting along with my parents. She talked a lot about her boyfriend. She repeatedly asked my opinion of her relationship; I tried to avoid the subject, but I eventually admitted that I have never really liked him. (However, I've never especially liked any guy who has dated any one of my sisters.) She was annoyed and went on at great length about how good he was to her and how happy she was.

"We're really going to make this work," she told me.

I asked her if she ever thought about her birth parents and if she thinks she'll ever try to find them. Ashley sifted through the sand with her feet, looking at the ground for a long moment before she answered. She said she wasn't sure if she wanted to meet them, though she was curious. She's mad at how they had failed her and not sure if she can forgive them. At the same time, she said she's learned from their mistakes.

"When I have kids, when I'm pregnant, I'm not even going to drink one drop of alcohol," she said. "Not even one drop."

Ashley is convinced she'll find her older brother one day. Last we heard, he was living somewhere in the US. She likes to imagine going on a road trip with Cody, Amanda, and Tyler. As we walked along, she looked out at the ocean. She said she wonders if he'll look like the other boys, and she wants to know if they'd all get along. I told that her if she ever tracks him down, I'll tag along for the ride. Then we walked back to the car and went for ice cream.

A couple of months later, Ashley moved to Chilliwack with her boyfriend. She passed her driving test, bought a cat, and got a job. My parents were devastated at her decision but allowed her to enrol at a new high school. A month later they gave her full access to her savings account. Whether they liked it or not, it was time to let her go.

I sometimes worry that the shadowy ghosts of her birth parents still linger in Ashley's mind. More and more, I'm learning to trust that she will be okay. She has big plans for her future. She wants to get married, have lots of children, and work as a hairstylist. She has her future carefully mapped out, and I really believe she can do it. In her photos on Facebook, her boyfriend stands behind Ashley with his arms wrapped around her. She clutches his forearms, her eyes squeezed tight as she smiles for the camera. There are pictures of her playing with dogs and young children. Pictures of her riding a ferry, going whale watching, or peeking out from behind the counter at Dairy Queen. Further along there are pictures of her jumping down sand cliffs or crashing through waves with her brothers and sisters. These are the souvenirs of a full life.

In one picture, Ashley laughs while I flex my bicep; in another I kiss her gently on the forehead. I'm nearly twice her size, a chubby, blond, curly-haired university student hulking over her slender frame. In the reflection of my aviator sunglasses, you can see my arm reaching out with the camera. Ashley smiles, slightly squinting in the sun, as the waves stretch out behind us. She leans her face toward mine, her hair resting on my shoulder.

We make an unlikely pair, and we couldn't be more different. But I love her without thinking about it, and I can't imagine my life without her. She is, for better or worse, my little sister.

Will Johnson recently graduated from the University of Victoria with a BFA in creative writing. An earlier version of "My Little Sister" was runner-up for Best Feature Article in Canadian University Press's 2009 John H. McDonald Awards. Will has worked for the *Whitehorse Star*, the *Trail Rossland News*, and *The Martlet*, the University of Victoria's student newspaper. His literary work has appeared in *The Fiddlehead*, *OCW Magazine*, *Pearls*, *This Side of West*, *Burner Mag* and *Strip Comics*. Please visit his website at goodwilljohnson.com.

abandoned
but loved

BETH GROSART

"OCTOBER 14, 1982, BABY girl abandoned by mother at hospital." The thin Korean man, sitting across the metal table from me, quoted from a faded manila folder. His manicured fingers flipped through the small stack of paper

I waited before reacting to his words, wanting to hear more, giving him the opportunity to realize his mistake. That wasn't me, I thought. My birth mother had other children, boys, and couldn't take care of me. She parted with me, knowing that she was giving me a better life, because she felt too old to be a good mother to a new baby. After giving it a lot of thought, she gave her only baby girl up for adoption. My parents had told me that story since I was young:

"Once upon a time you flew all the way across the world to come here to be our daughter. Your birth mother loved you so much that she wanted to let you have a better life than she could provide for you." Their bedtime stories enfolded what they were told by the adoption agency. But, now, here we sat, and the tale was different.

In 2008, at twenty-six years old, I returned to Seoul, Korea, with the mother and father who picked me up at JFK airport twenty-five years before. My younger brother, Alex, also adopted from Korea, two years after me, had moved back to Seoul after college to teach English, and we were there to visit. My mother and he came up with the idea to go to the adoption agency. It hadn't occurred to me. I was there to visit my brother and see some sights in the country where I was born. When they told me we'd be going to the orphanage, I was somewhat indifferent. "Sure," I said. "That could be neat." But, I didn't know the four of us would discover something so different from that sweet bedtime story I'd heard so many times before.

I leaned forward to listen closely as the man spoke. My mother, Susan, nervously twirled her blonde hair as he continued. *"The mother abandoned the baby, and the child was brought here to the adoption agency by a police officer who was notified by the hospital. Mother's name was Lee."* The man closed the folder and placed his clasped hands on top.

"I'm sorry, did you say 'Lee'?" I asked. Outside the Holt Adoption Agency, cars honked back and forth. One man yelled at another driver, displeased with the response of his fellow commuters. Multiple cars beeped in retort.

"Yes," he looked at the folder again. "Lee, her last name was Lee."

"We were told Beth's last name was Cho by the adoption agency." My mother looked at me as she spoke with the man. My brother shrugged.

The man sat back in his chair. "Often times, the orphanage gives the child a name of their own when they enter. So, most likely, you were given the name," he glanced down at his folder, "Cho Moon Hee."

I didn't say anything. The name he spoke, one I'd known and felt proud of for my whole life, felt, in that moment, odd and foreign. My mother looked at me and smiled. My dad had been silent most of the time we sat in that sterile room. I wrote down what the man said in a small notebook, processing the words as I wrote: My last name is actually Lee, not Cho. I wasn't given up for adoption lovingly; I was abandoned by some frightened woman. Abandoned. The moment she could get away from me, she did. As I scrawled out those last few words, I could feel the tears welling up, and I willed them to stop. I wasn't sure why I was crying. Not wanting my parents to think I was sad that I had been abandoned or left or given up for adoption, I looked down and focused on the pen in my hand, blinking the tears away.

"Can you tell us anything else?" Mom asked. "What was Beth's father's name? Anything else about medical history?"

The man pushed the folder away from him and placed others on top. "That is all to tell." His English faltered.

"Is there stuff you can't tell us?"

"That is it."

It wasn't exactly an answer to my question. He smiled kindly at me. I wondered how frequently he did this, told people things about their lives they never knew, things maybe they thought they wanted to know.

I wasn't ready to move from my chair yet. There was a lot to process. Something weighed on me that had not been there before this moment. For my whole life I had prided myself on being a drama-free adoptee. I didn't want to find my birth family; I felt issueless about my adoption itself. My parents had done a wonderful job letting my brother and me know we were adopted (I'm sure the fact they are both Caucasian, my mother a blonde, no less, would have given it away at some point). And for my whole life I have known I am their daughter, and, to them, I'm a gift. I didn't know that going to Korea to visit my brother on summer vacation would be such a life-changing experience. A perspective-altering experience.

"Thank you for meeting with us," my dad said, shaking the man's hand.

My mother took both his hands in hers. "Yes, thank you, so much. We are so thankful for all that you all have done for us." She touched my shoulder as I stood to leave. "You gave us our baby."

Mom cried as she moved to stand next to my dad. It was a positive experience for her, to be there and learn what she could about my beginnings. It didn't affect her in the way it did me. How could it? I felt like a piece of me had been unexpectedly taken away at that moment. On the one hand, nothing could suppress the gratitude and love I felt for my parents and the fact that they took me in as their own and gave me a happy childhood and a bright future. However, a piece of something else had been ripped from me when the little man had said, "Abandoned." The hole I felt sits with me still, and I'm not sure it will be filled. And, the hardest part is, I can't explain it.

As we stood in the room, I could tell my mother would have been happiest to go around hugging everyone in the agency. Instead, she had to be content holding the hand of the post-adoption agent, who looked no older than me and therefore had nothing to do with my specific adoption. Yet, still, she held onto him, thanking him for all he had done, not wanting to leave just yet. I, however, felt ready.

He smiled at my mother. "I will take you to the orphanage facility if you would like to see. It is the same place where your daughter was held before going to foster care, before coming to you. They do the same good work there today."

"Oh, yes, please," she said, and took my father's hand to leave.

We followed him next door to a larger building. My heart clenched in my chest as I saw the hallway. A police officer I'd never know brought me here for my first night of sleep. I saw the room where I was cleaned and examined by a doctor. There was a small playroom with playpens and old toys strewn about the floor. The place felt industrial to me, and yet a palpable warmth permeated each of the well-cared-for rooms.

As we came out of the final room, a nurse came into the hallway in front of us. Her back was to us, but a small hand rested lightly on her shoulder. As she turned, my breath caught in my chest, as she revealed a pink-clad baby girl. Her almond-shaped eyes were big as she took in the room. Her stare stopped on my mother's blonde locks.

"She has never seen blonde hair before. She came to us yesterday and is having her checkups. Ten months old."

My mother put her hand out and squeezed mine. Of course it touched her to see this baby girl here, waiting for her new life to start.

I knew a specific fond memory had entered my mother's mind. When I was little, I used to ask her, "Mom, was I a good baby?"

"Oh yes," she would reply.

"Did I sleep well, through the night?"

"Yes, you did. Except for the first few nights. We had you in bed with us, and you would stay up all night and twirl my hair in your little fingers. You couldn't keep your eyes off my blonde hair. You had only ever seen black. You were observant even then."

I had always loved that image of me taking in my new world so seemingly aware of what I did and did not know or recognize, even as a baby. Happy in my life. Unaware of anything but the love I was receiving from these two new people.

I turned away, not wanting my parents to see me crying. Tears flowed down my cheeks. I wanted to hold this baby, but I didn't know how to ask or if that was appropriate, so I simply stared. Like looking in a mirror that could transport you back in time, I saw myself as an infant, being held in that same hallway by a stranger. Did that stranger that held her, the kind nurse in a yellow dress, have more love for this baby than those people related to her by blood? Just as two strangers in the United States could have more love for a baby they knew only from a photo than that baby girl's own mother could have for her on the day she was born?

We left the orphanage that day and had lunch together quietly in a restaurant down the street. Koreans smiled at us, perhaps wondering at our relationship to each other. They are my parents, I thought to myself. I didn't speak much through lunch, afraid I would cry. The one thing I knew, even among the questions spinning around in my head, was that my life was a good one. Someone somewhere was looking out for me when they sent me to the US to grow up among the love of my parents.

I am thrilled to have been adopted and loved for my life. But I have discovered a confusion and sadness about being abandoned and unwanted by those who were supposed to love me most. In this trip to my birthplace, I discovered, there is a difference between being given, thoughtfully, to a better life and being left, tossed to fate. But, if fate smiles on you, and, like me, you end up in a place of love and care, then the loss cannot be yours. So, I thank my birth mother for leaving me in the hands of fate that brought me to Sue and Gary Grosart, a thoughtful, caring couple, patiently waiting in Marion, Massachusetts, for a child to become a part of their lives.

Beth Grosart lives in New Hampshire where she teaches high school English. She is currently working toward a second MFA in creative writing at Pine Manor College in Massachusetts with a focus on writing for young adults. She is at work on her first novel.

what it is: the unending incompleteness of life

FRANK KAFKA

WHEN MY SON DAVID first called one day more than a decade ago, my response was not, I think, what he expected. I wasn't shocked that a son whom I had let be given up for adoption had found me. I didn't fumble with a sense of what I would say to him or to others about him as, quite independently, I had begun my own efforts to discover his whereabouts, identity, and life path.

What turned out to be surprising to us both is that what we each wanted from the contact were quite different things. He wanted authenticity to his existence; he wanted to know who his parents were and the reasons he had been given up.

What I wanted was to try to resolve what I had come to see as the greatest failing of my life. The thing I had grieved over for much of my adult existence was what I did when my first love, my first sexual partner, my first intimacy outside of family, became pregnant. I—and it had been me, not Kathleen—had decided not to marry and so set in motion the chain of events that saw her leave school and enter a home for unwed mothers where she swelled, became morning sick, and bore David, only to give him up afterwards.

To understand my guilt fully, you have to understand the context surrounding David's coming into existence. Kathleen and I had been literal high school sweethearts. We had fumbled from first to second to third to sexual home plate without really knowing what we were doing. We fumbled in part because what we did in the context of the times seemed criminal. Nice teenagers—and we were nice teenagers—didn't have sex in the late '50s and early '60s. Bad people did. Loose people. Nice teenagers kissed and held hands and got married and then did something. We were, of course, going to get married because Hollywood told us love wasn't the gateway to societally approved lust, it was the portal to marriage. But the truth was that the nice high school sweethearts were going to school two thousand miles apart, and, in so doing, had been drifting apart in both love and lust over their freshman year; indeed, we had broken up once already that summer.

But our teenage relationship angst was also taking place within the context of a personal trauma worthy of the Greeks that had sundered Kathleen's family. Her professor of theology father, a man of goodness personified, had, after he had fathered four children, experienced a *coup de foudre* and fallen in crazy love with the ruby-haired wife of one of his colleagues.

The good man fell in love but fought it. He tried to go back to his wife, but desire and teenage-style, car-backseat groping eventually won out. And when it did, Kathleen's mother cracked and admitted herself to a mental hospital. And almost every night while she was there, Kathleen and I went to her now empty family home where I held her and we had sex as we tried to figure out how we children could advise her crazed in two senses parents on the correct paths of love and marriage and desire. Our method of birth control was the so-called rhythm method, because in the early 1960s, nice teenagers in love who slipped into sex didn't use condoms because that would suggest they were fully conscious of what they were doing. And if they were fully conscious of what they were doing, they would know it was wrong.

Trying to be the adult at nineteen amid the wreckage of Kathleen's family wore me out, and even as we wrapped ourselves around one another, I thought that when Kathleen went back to school, we would break up. But break up softly after giving in to the impossibility of a long-distance relationship. However, seeing her mother and father's marriage come apart in the thralls of illicit passion was more than a responsible eldest daughter could stand, and so, in October, Kathleen flew home with the idea she'd drop out of school, we would marry, and she would nurse her broken family back to wholeness if not true health. But her mother and I talked her out of that. We pointed out that she was roaringly smart and that smartness required not a jerry-rigged marriage but an education, and that an education would let her make her own way in a world where, no matter what she did, her parents would have to lead their own lives. Kathleen seemed to take solace in that, and the night before she was supposed to go back to school, we had sex for what I thought could have been the last time, sex in which I experienced for the first time the intensity of a woman's climax, a crying, heaving sexuality that dwarfed anything I had ever seen before and maybe since.

And that sex—that farewell sex, that therapeutic sex, that climactic sex—produced David and with him all of my guilt over Kathleen's abandonment. I felt I had betrayed not just her but romantic love itself. Some time later I realized I had come out of the experience fearing and despising the sexual intoxication the French call *amour fou*. I saw it not as some Hollywood movie romantic trill, but like the Greeks did—as madness.

But what about David, you might well ask? Did my guilt extend to him? Here was the great irony of his arrival in my life: I didn't feel guilty about him because, in many ways, my relationship to my son was supposed to have been deeply abstract. He was simply to have been: The Nameless Baby The Woman I Loved But Hadn't Married Gave Up. My principal role in the biology of his creation was not to tell anyone anything about what had happened because that would have, in the language of the times, ruined Kathleen's reputation. That meant I was not supposed to write to her or call her or think of her. My role was to become numb.

I particularly wasn't supposed to feel anything about the child, because that would have compounded my betrayal of Kathleen. The question would then become: if the fetus that became David truly mattered, why hadn't I married Kathleen? So, rather than think about him, I walked around my university campus with clenched fists, driving my nails into my palms. I pretended nothing had happened and that I didn't feel anything. Which wasn't true. I felt self-loathing. I felt scared. I felt as if I were living someone else's life. The only positive thing I was allowed to do was study harder than I had ever studied before and get straight As to show the world that the man who wouldn't marry the mother of his child could still do something right.

So, when David called and we spoke and I learned only a little about him, I did something I think he found both strange and awkward—I questioned him at great length about Kathleen. I wanted to know if she had survived my betrayal and callowness and youth. When he told me she had married and borne another son and gone on to get a PHD and lived what seemed a whole life, I wrote Kathleen a letter and asked David to forward it to her, as he had contacted her first. I didn't myself feel strange or awkward in this request, because the need to communicate with her felt like a dam burst of feeling that washed away all senses of propriety.

In the letter, I did several things. I tried to let her see who I had become in a kind of formal way: a husband, a father, a journalist. I was attempting to say that what had happened between us wasn't the expression of some personal pathology. I hadn't made a life of hurting and betraying women and children. And I apologized. I apologized for being afraid and young and knowing that I wouldn't be either a good husband or good father. I apologized for letting her, as biology demanded, bear our child without my having to carry it, something that always seemed unfair when I thought about it later. We both had lusted and been sexual criminals, but only her life had been dented by the act.

I apologized even though I continued to believe that marriage wouldn't have been some Hollywood romance but rather the prelude to a rotting relationship between two unripe child-adults who were fundamentally unready to become parents. Every time I looked back, I knew we wouldn't have remained together but rather would have eventually been ripped apart by the bitterness of a parenthood forced upon us. Our marriage would have become the embodiment of a failure to have become something other than parents.

But, most importantly, I suppose I reached out through that letter so that I might discuss that whole section of my early life that for more than thirty years remained numb and unspoken. Kathleen was the only person I could truly talk to about this past, because she was not just part of it, she was it. This was the reason I had been trying to find David. There was this rupture in my life, and I didn't understand what it meant. I didn't understand the relationship between what happened to teenagers in love and lust and everything that followed.

So, I sent the letter to Kathleen and waited like a penitent before the confessional. I wanted not so much to be forgiven as to be heard. But because life is not a Hollywood film, Kathleen didn't respond with an instinctive understanding of my wounds. When she wrote back, she didn't want to talk or forgive. She didn't want to hear from me again and was obviously still angry at me and what had happened. It was an anger that I have come to think reflects the difference between a male and a female in relationship to the child who has been given up to others. Kathleen felt, I think, that she had betrayed the child who grew inside her, who forced his way into the world through her and whom she saw before he was taken away.

What Kathleen wanted was not a healing with me but with the infant the society of the time and the scared boy-man forced her to give up to adoption. She *knew* him from birth; I didn't. Most men, I think, don't truly get to know a child until they can break free from mother love and mother nourishment and do that singularly human thing: talk. Kathleen didn't need anything from me, but she did need absolution from David.

I accepted that Kathleen's response meant no resolution to my numbness. I accepted I was still not supposed to communicate or feel or really even think about her. And I tried to help her reconcile with David by sending him the love letters she had sent me in university, which he later returned and I keep to this day. My idea was to let him know he was the fruit of love and desire and, in a profound way, innocence.

I see now, more than fifteen years later, that my response was almost hurtful in its obliqueness about David's sense of abandonment. If we had been so much in love, why couldn't Kathleen and I have summoned the power to make a loving place for him in our lives? I believed the answer was that our teenage love and lust wasn't about children; it was about body. But could David see that? Could he ever want to?

After we knew each other a bit, I visited with David the large house in the suburban New Jersey paradise where he had grown up. It was near the laboratory where he was doing postdoctoral research. It was the picket fence kind of place I would have placed him in, a place where he could be raised by richer, older, and, I thought, better people than me. When I saw where he had grown up, I felt another pang of guilt. I owed Kathleen much for bearing a child, and I owed David's adoptive parents even more for raising it. So I told him to tell his parents that I wanted to see them. And around 1995, on a visit to Colorado, I went into the mountain valley where they now lived and thanked a man and woman old enough to be my parents for raising my son. Thanked them tearfully, sobbing my gratitude for looking after my child when I knew I wouldn't have provided him with the balance that would let him get on with his life and education. I did it as well to say to his adoptive parents: I won't take him away from you. He is yours. I am just his rutted beginning; you were his road. I think it was good for them to meet me and see I wasn't some callous seducer, merely the grown-up version of a boy who slept with his first love, accidentally got her pregnant, and then withdrew.

But I don't know if the meeting was good for David, because, as I keep telling you, my story isn't a Hollywood romance. Dramatic reconciliation scenes don't change the traffic wrecks of human affairs. Part of the reason David was looking for Kathleen and me was because he had grown estranged from his parents, and particularly his adoptive mother, when he came out as a gay man. He and his mother had been very close, but the homosexuality had, in ways that only the human heart can understand, poisoned that. And they barely speak now.

I asked David some time later whether it was harder to accept being gay or being adopted, and he said being adopted. He had known from the age of eight or nine that he was gay, but he hadn't ever understood why he had been given up at birth. And meeting Kathleen and me didn't make that understanding any easier, because what he encountered were not frightened, lustful teenagers but adults, creatures who had ripened, prospered, and had families and who, in so doing, seemed more acceptable as parents than those stiffer, older, more conservative people who had raised him. Even more, he encountered people who were untroubled by his kind of sexuality.

I have not figured out how to make a bridge between the truth that I have no problem with his gayness now, but I did with his existence then. This discontinuity between who I am today and who I was then has continued, I think, to confuse and torment David, and to give us a very un-Hollywood, modern sort of relationship. Yes, I introduced him to my other children and met and spent time with him and his then-partner, and he came to my mother's funeral, but the truth is that I haven't made David part of my life. He remains, in ways I think he hates and in ways I can do nothing about, an otherness.

With Kathleen, I hope there is something better. He visits her brothers and sisters and her son, and she has, as far as I can tell, been better at mending the breach. In a way, David seems to me to have been at least partially re-adopted by Kathleen, and I hope that has helped her heal. I hope the more she loves him, the less she hates me. But I don't know if this is truth or fantasy, because the silence and numbness between Kathleen and me remains and David is angry when he speaks of her.

In place of any kind of re-adoption, David and I talk. We talk not really as father and son, but as congenial male adults. We talk about his career as a university science researcher and professor and the craziness of academic life. We talk about his broken relationship with his ex and his efforts to figure out what kind of sexual relationship to have with a subsequent partner who was HIV positive. We talk about my other children, how Frederick is getting married and how David will be invited to the wedding. But there is distance, because he is still less my physical son than the physical incarnation of my great numbness. When people ask me how many children I have, I don't know how to answer. I gave David life, but I didn't raise him, and thus I don't feel he is truly mine.

I don't know what David makes of this cathedral of incommensurateness. He is a deeply cautious person. He pauses and thinks before he speaks about anything, but there is sadness to him I feel, and there seems nothing I can do about that. He was born and lives and floats apart from the man who helped make him. And he doesn't really understand that, but that's where we now stand.

Each of us still apart. Nothing fundamentally resolved. No Hollywood ending. Just life. Just existence's unending incompleteness.

Frank Kafka is the pseudonym of a Toronto-based writer who is married and the father of two other children besides David.

sick sisters

KELLY R. LYNN

MY PARENTS WERE NOT secretive about my origins; I knew of my adoption before I could read. I remember Mom lifting me, three years old and dripping, out of the beige bathtub and wrapping me in a towel. With my swaddled figure perched on her hip, she danced over to the gilt-framed mirror and pointed to my reflection.

"You see that girl right there?"

I nodded and clung to her like an octopus, my legs wrapped around her waist, arms clutching her shoulders.

"That girl in the mirror there is special. Do you know why?"

I first shook my head no, then yes, up and down and around in that noncommittal way that kids do.

"Why is she special?"

Warm and damp in the humid bathroom air, I felt languid and cozy. "'Cause she's a dopted," I said, splicing the word into two parts: the article "a" and the made-up "dopted." That's what it sounded like to my young ears—I had no understanding of adjectives or nouns or participles. I don't know how old I was when I figured out that "adopted" was one full word, but there in the bathroom, I was still in the dark. Mom couldn't hear the difference between "adopted" and "a dopted," so she assumed I had said the word correctly, and that grammatical lesson was saved for some other time.

The adoption lesson, however, Mom repeated a lot for reinforcement. My parents did not want me to grow up not knowing I was "a dopted." And so, I knew. It became a part of the fabric of our existence in the same house together, all of us wrapped in the same cloth of adoption, like a towel that grew shabby with use, more forgettable with age.

"That's right," Mom said, dipping me with her hip and making me laugh. "She's adopted, that girl in the mirror there. Her Daddy and I wanted her very badly, but couldn't have her by ourselves. Her birth mommy and daddy couldn't take care of her, so those nice, good people let her be our daughter instead."

Watching our reflections bobbing up and down, I absorbed these mysterious doctrines. I knew that my parents wanted me but, even at age three, stoically accepted that they had got me because someone else didn't.

My parents' casual, though careful, treatment of my adoption and the nurturing environment in which they raised me cut down any budding bitterness. Besides, I was too busy begging my parents for a baby sister to fret about being adopted. I would have settled for a baby brother, but whenever I scribbled Christmas lists, "Little Sister" occupied the number one slot until it became apparent that the closest Santa would come to granting my request was a doll baby propped stiffly under the tree, its glass eyes gawking. I did not realize at the time how my innocent wish and my disappointment in its perpetual deferral must have pained my parents, my mother in particular, as she was literally unable to deliver. Sprouting fibroid tumours like weeds, her otherwise barren womb had been excised when I was four, terminating any possibility of children.

As I grew older, it occurred to me my biological parents had probably borne other offspring. However, I could never picture a scenario in which I would know them. I had been an only child my whole life;

how could I imagine anything different? For a long time, I had hoped that an infant would arrive on our doorstep, wrapped in a blanket and tucked in a basket. Sometimes I would hear a noise in the front yard, a soft mewling sound, and I would yank open the front door, preparing to welcome my baby sister into my home, ready to share my toys with her and let her sleep in my room. Of course, instead of a baby in a basket, it would be a stray cat, meowing for food. Eventually, by age ten, I gave up on getting a sister. I relegated the thought of a sibling, adoptive or biological, to the back of my mind and transferred my familial affection to my cousins, all of whom lived four hundred miles away in Kentucky.

This tactic merely reinforced my loneliness, my craving of a sororal companion. I was aware that I had biological parents, but I never gave them, abstract as they were, much thought. My parents gave me what little information they had: my bio-father was a redhead; bio-mother had been seventeen when I was born; one of them had allergies or asthma, which explained why I was likewise afflicted. Those meager details did little to stoke my imagination. Sometimes, I would pass a red-haired man on the street or encounter a woman with long, brown hair, like mine, in the mall, and I would fancy that it was "one of them." Mostly, though, I accepted that two unidentified people contributed their genes to my existence and let them, as well as any potential siblings, remain a mystery.

That is, until I got sick. When I was sixteen, I was diagnosed with ulcerative colitis, which the doctors could never control. Several years and surgeries later, we discovered that I had been misdiagnosed. I actually suffered acutely from Crohn's disease, an incurable condition that can range from mild to horrible discomfort. In my case, I had reached a state of constant pain and aggravation. I wanted answers. I wanted to know where it came from, if this wretched disease was genetic.

One evening in November 2004, I went to my parents' house. I had just been officially diagnosed with Crohn's disease after over a decade of believing I had something else. I needed to complain. After I complained to Mom in the kitchen, I went to the basement and complained to Dad. He was sitting on the tan and cream plaid couch that had been there since the 1970s; I slumped into a brown leather recliner that rocked back under my weight. Eyes downcast, I surveyed the basement floor, still covered in the brown and orange shag carpet I played on when I was little.

"Dad," I said. "I'm worried that I'll pass this along if I get pregnant."

He looked at me, his left hand folded under his chin, elbow propped on the arm of the couch. His forehead wrinkled. "The Crohn's, you mean?"

"Yeah. What if it's genetic? I don't know, because I have no clue if either of my biological parents have this, or anyone in the family. It's completely unfair that adoption records are sealed. I have a right to know my medical history, to know who these people are."

Dad sat while I ranted. He nodded as I spoke, mostly listening as he heard me rail about the injustice of keeping important medical information from adoptees. And then he said the words that would ultimately change my life.

"Well," he said softly. "I know her name."

"Wait, what?" I said, disbelieving my ears.

"I know her name," he said.

I stared at him. "Are you serious?"

"This is not the kind of thing you forget, though God knows I tried. I saw her name on the papers. At least I think it was her name. It wasn't supposed to be there. The lawyer messed up. They were supposed to black out her name, but I saw it."

I sat there and let his words sink in. "Are you really telling me that you know the name, the identity, of my biological mother?"

"Yeah," said Dad. "I saw it on those papers, next to 'birth mother.' The last name is 'Lit-gie' or something. I guess that's how you say it. 'Susan Littge.'"

As I sat in that chocolate brown recliner, my world suddenly shifted on its axis.

He continued. "I saw her name and then told myself, 'You weren't supposed to see that. Okay, forget that name, you never saw that name, put it out of your mind.'"

We both laughed, but as I laughed, I felt something uncork in my chest. It welled up in my throat, a hysterical bubble of some strange feeling I had never felt before, not about this. It was hope. For the first time, I felt hope. It wasn't a childish hope based on fantasies and dreams. This was real hope, based in fact. I could do something with "Susan Littge."

Due to someone's clerical error, my biological mother's name had been left on the adoption paperwork. Perhaps that person had just not had enough coffee that morning in October 1975. Whatever the case, the name was there on the adoption papers, and when Dad signed them, he saw it. He tried to forget, but in making a deliberate effort, perhaps this made the memory all the more potent. He secreted away the name "Susan Littge" for twenty-eight years, the name gnawing at the corners of his consciousness for decades until finally, one day, my sickness dislodged it. The name wriggled out into the open air at last.

"How is it spelled?" I asked.

"I'll write it down for you," Dad said. He rummaged around on the cocktail table for a piece of paper. With a black felt-tipped pen, he scrawled the name, Susan Littge, on the corner in his half-block-print, half-cursive handwriting. He tore off the corner and passed the name across the table to me. I gazed at the name on this scrap of paper, the name of my birth mother. Suddenly, this name was fraught with meaning. I had never heard the name before, of course, but if I had, it would have been meaningless. It was only in this context that the syllables "Susan Littge" held a kind of magical power. I felt as if I had been on a lifelong quest, and my prize was this tiny, frayed corner with a name printed in black ink. To anyone else, if I were to have dropped the paper on the street, this would have been a piece of trash to ignore, for the wind to pick up and flick into a puddle, for a bird to wedge into the construct of its nest. For me, though, the black name on white paper was a key to unlock the mystery of my existence, the crystal ball through which I hoped to peer and catch a glimpse of what the future may hold.

I took that name and tucked it deep into my wallet, checking several times to make certain it was safe. With this information, I made a post on an adoption reunion website. I filled in the details I knew, such as the name my adoptive parents gave me, my birth date, and the attending OB/GYN. The form asked for the attorney or agency through which the adoption took place. There had been no attorney or agency, so I wrote "Private (Dr. Kowalczyk?)." Mom's OB/GYN, who, as I had learned from Mom a few years previous, was also my birth mother's OB/GYN; he had arranged the whole adoption without the two ever meeting. Dr. Kowalczyk had been the source from which came the mysterious details about my biological parents that haunted me as a child and into adulthood.

The online form included a section for the adoptee to fill out whatever information she knew, if any, about the biological parents. Under the birth mother section, I keyed in what I had: first name, Susan; last name, Littge; age at birth, seventeen. That was all. I knew nothing about my birth father except the fact that he had red hair, but there was no section for "hair colour," an omission I found frustrating. How would they be able to find me if they weren't able to see that I knew my biological father had red hair? I wanted to fill out forms with everything I knew, every detail accounted for, no matter how seemingly irrelevant. Even though my information was limited, I was sure I had more in my tool belt than the majority of adoptees. Most adoptees in that era were handed over to an agency that acted as an intermediary, ensuring that no details could slip through the cracks. In my case, there was only one degree of separation between us; perhaps it was inevitable that a trickle of information would seep into the foundation of our lives, soaking in until, eventually, the whole thing broke wide open.

On May 11, 2006, I came home from work. I had just returned from a trip to Scotland, and each workday dragged on and on, wearing me out more than it would ordinarily. The red light on my answering machine blinked twice. I pressed the button and half-listened to the first message. I dropped my purse on the couch and stared out the window to the street. The machine beeped and the second message began. An unfamiliar female voice asked, "Kelly? Are you sitting down?"

I turned. "This is your bio-mom, Karen."

I should have sat. Her message nearly brought me to my knees, which buckled with the surprise. I caught the ledge where the answering machine rested so that I would not fall. "Oh my God, it's her," I said again and again. I wished I weren't alone—I wanted a witness to this moment, someone to share in my joy and incredulity. For the first time, I was hearing the voice of the woman who gave me life. Her voice went on to fulfill what had been my deepest, most secret desire for three decades: after thirty years of only childhood, I had a half-sister named Kacie. My resignation to a sisterless existence evaporated. I listened to the news again and again. "I have a sister," I murmured along with the tape.

I spoke with my biological mother and half-sister for the first time that night, marvelling at the surreality of the experience. When I spoke with Karen, I explained how my dad had remembered her name as Susan, not Karen. We agreed that even though he had gotten it only half-right, he remembered the right half. Had he not remembered the name "Littge," Karen's sister Nancy, the genealogist of the family, would have never found my posting on the adoption reunion website. Nancy had been looking on the Internet for information about her family's ancestors and found me instead.

After I spoke for a while with Karen, she asked if I wanted to talk to my sister. Of course, I said yes. Yes, please, let me talk with my sister. How strange, to hear myself saying these words, I thought. Kacie got on the phone and immediately began to babble. She seemed even more excited than I did. She had known about me. She had, perhaps, been primed from a young age for the possibility of our meeting, whereas I had always been braced for the probability that no such meeting would ever, could ever, occur. She knew that her older half-sister was out there, somewhere. I knew nothing of her except for a nebulous potential. Yet, here we were, talking. I was on the phone for the first time with my sister, Kacie Diane. How different we sounded, my sister and I: her chirpy soprano chattering counterpoint to my huskier alto. How young she was, only fourteen, with gushing speech patterns I associated with much younger children. She bubbled over with charm, naïveté and whimsy. I could not help comparing her to myself at her age, the complete opposite: sullen, dark, sarcastic.

Like me, Kacie had been raised an only child. Unlike me, Kacie grew up with the concrete fact that she had a half-sister, somewhere. Karen informed Kacie of my existence, ephemeral though it may have seemed. Karen knew that I had been adopted by a couple in the St. Louis area, but not much else. She knew that I had been born with a mass of dark brown curls. She knew that, for a brief while, I had carried the name she had given me: Kellie Rae.

My parents had also named me Kelly, though they had chosen the more conventional spelling. When Karen revealed that she had named me Kellie, "with an -ie," I knew that although I sometimes craved a more exotic name, my name was anything but common. It carried with it a kernel of fate, a crumb of mystery. How many people are named the same thing twice by two different people? On the phone that night with Karen, I divulged my own surprise: bored with the -y spelling in junior high, I had experimented with a variety of alternatives, finally settling on Kellie. I kept it that way through the end of high school, changing it back to Kelly only when I went away to college. Even my parents spelled it with an -ie; it took them a while to get used to writing my name with the spelling they themselves had selected. I asked my parents if they had seen my original name on the adoption papers, and if that was where the inspiration came from for naming me Kelly. They said they had never seen that name on any papers. My mother revealed that Dr. Kowalczyk told her, years later, that my birth mother had also named me Kelly. Regardless, my parents came up with my name independently, forsaking their other top picks (Ronnie and Shannon). I was born to be a Kelly, no matter what the spelling.

I admired the symmetry of the names Karen had given her daughters: Kellie and Kacie. Karen could have spelled her second daughter's name differently—Casey, or Kayce, or numerous other variants. Instead, she kept the first and last letters of the name she had given her firstborn daughter, the one she had given up, filling the bookends of the K- and the -ie with new phonemes. Perhaps this was her attempt, conscious or not, of keeping a part of me. I understood that, in her way, she had really wanted me. Our reunion was her long-awaited wish, as having a sister was mine.

֍ I discovered in that first conversation in 2006 that, according to Karen, Crohn's ran neither in her family nor in that of my biological father. As far as she knew, nobody in either family had Crohn's. Lung cancer, on the other hand, ran rampant through our branch of the family tree. I had been given something altogether new to worry about.

With information from Karen, I then contacted my biological father, Drew. He confirmed that none of his other three children and no one else in his family suffered from Crohn's either. I was glad that no one else had the disease that afflicted me and hoped that I was just an anomaly. But then, in March 2008, I got a text message from Kacie: she had just been diagnosed with Crohn's disease. She was sixteen years old—exactly the same age I had been when I developed the disease, although I had not been officially diagnosed until many years later.

I told my parents the news, and they were almost as upset about it as I was. I had told them immediately after getting in contact with my biological relatives, and their first question was whether any of my biological family members had Crohn's. Back then, the answer was no. We sat in my parents' living room that evening. For once, the television was off.

"I don't know anymore, guys," I said. "I thought I was in the clear to have children. Now, I'm not so sure."

Mom shook her head. "Kel, you never know what you'll get. You can't go into it thinking that your baby will have Crohn's. You just can't think like that."

I half-heartedly agreed. "It's just that I don't want anyone else to have to go through what I've gone through."

Dad spoke up. "At least you can help Kacie. You know what it's like."

"That's right," said Mom. "You've been through it already. If anyone can understand, it's you. You're her sister."

Researching the genetic odds of Crohn's has proven ambiguous. According to the National Institutes of Health's Genetics Home Reference website, "the inheritance pattern . . . is unclear because many genetic and environmental factors are likely to be involved. This condition tends to cluster in families, however, and having an affected family member is a significant risk factor." For me, learning that no one in my gene pool had Crohn's was a triumph; it put my fears to rest about potentially passing it on to my children. Unfortunately, the triumph was temporary, squashed by my sister's diagnosis.

Now that my biological mother's only other child has developed Crohn's disease, it appears to be obviously genetic. I had hoped that having a different father would stave off the disease for Kacie. From an unscientific perspective, both of us having Crohn's cannot be a coincidence; the disease must have been somehow inherited from our biological mother. Environmental factors do not seem to be the most prevalent link, as I have lived most of my life in Saint Louis, whereas Kacie has spent thirteen of her eighteen years in southeast Missouri, one hundred miles south of me.

My doctors don't know what caused it. My mother, in spite of more than forty years working in the medical field, has no answers. None of the doctors with whom she has spoken have any theories. Karen, a nurse, is nearly as stymied. However, she has provided one hypothesis. Karen's mother, when she was pregnant with her, contracted rubella in the second trimester. Rubella has been known to cause birth defects or other issues known as congenital rubella syndrome. When she was born, Karen did not manifest any known symptoms resulting from the rubella virus. Nevertheless, Karen now wonders if perhaps her mother's virus caused some mutation in her ovaries while she was in utero—a mutation that has subsequently affected me and Kacie.

With only anecdotal speculation and few statistics to work with, we can only wonder. I am still hesitant to have children, fearing that they will inherit the disease. Kacie, still a senior in high school, is I hope far from making these decisions. We have not had that conversation. Kacie and I talk about boys, friends, school, music, and clothes. We talk about dealing with Crohn's—about various medications, surgeries, social problems, other issues. We focus on building our relationship as sisters, in spite of the sixteen-year age gap. As sisters with sickness in common, we can help each other cope with the reality of life with a chronic illness. Perhaps together we can make sense of our situation. More importantly, Kacie and I can enjoy being part of each other's lives. Despite the pall of a shared disease, we are more than sick sisters.

Kelly Lynn is a writer, flutist, figure skater, voice actor, belly dancer, animal lover, and adoptee living in Saint Louis, Missouri. In 2011, she will graduate from Spalding University in Louisville, Kentucky, with an MFA in writing.

enduring the
goodness-of-fit

ELAINE HAYES

I GREW UP IN a foster home and was raised by foster parents. But I was not adopted. I was also not a surrendered child.

Who—what—was I?

If you were unable to identify me as a biological child of foster parents, you are not alone. Social workers and organizations dedicated to the fostering and adoption processes also overlook the fact that foster parents are, commonly, parents first, and the biological children—and their contributions and sacrifices—rarely receive acknowledgment. These host children truly are, to borrow from the title of a paper by Dr. Robert Twigg, a renowned researcher in this field, the "unknown soldiers" in the campaign of care for surrendered children.

In March of 1964, I was a disappointed eight-year-old when I discovered that our first foster child was a male infant. We were one of the original families to move into Chateauguay, a new suburban development across from the island of Montreal, and I yearned for someone other than my seven-year-old brother Gary to play with, for someone with a Barbie convertible or an Etch-a-Sketch with an intact screen.

Patrick was six days old when he came to live with us. His umbilical cord and St. Mary's Hospital bracelet—with a smudged "Boy Lambert" on it—were still intact. In a lined notebook, my mother recorded Patrick's arrival weight and height. As the months passed, she added the milestones of sleeping through the night, rolling over, and the shift from formula to whole milk. She traced a diagram of an open jaw and entered the date of each tooth's eruption. Patrick's hair grew long and blonde and curly. We began calling him Paddy.

Then, on September 8, 1965, eighteen months after Paddy's arrival, the Ville Marie Social Services delivered one-week-old Darlene Marie Perks. When Gary and I arrived home from school, my mother snapped a photo of me cradling Darlene. As I stroked her large, bald head, my mind flipped through a catalogue of dolls' bonnets and ruffled dresses that I had recently relegated to the bottom of my closet; I was weeks short of my tenth birthday and believed I was getting too old to play with dolls.

Much of the research about the biological children of foster parents attempts to categorize the nature of relationships within foster homes, and the consensus is that the age and gender of the children, both biological and foster, play a significant, determining role in the acceptance or rejection of relationships. For example, in "The Relationship Between Foster Children and the Foster Parents' Own Children: A Unique Entity," Cathy Bruce and Phillip Bruce identify four distinct relationship types displayed by biological children toward foster children: "mildly resentful," which is largely based on degrees of avoidance; "indifference," which is a neutral association with no sense of connection; "parentified," which positions a biological child in a caregiver's role; and "friendship," which is self-explanatory. In my experience with fostering, I initially viewed our foster children as potential friends and playmates, and in Darlene's case, as a potential ally against the boys. However, I slid, as many older siblings do, into the role of assistant caregiver: I sat on the toilet to supervise bath time; I was dispatched to bring my mother a clean burp cloth; I cleaned dropped soothers with my own saliva.

In "All in the Family Home: The Biological Children of Parents

Who Foster," Judith Heidbuurt identifies the organization of the entire family unit into three structural categories: the "open boundary" concept, in which individual family members choose to fully or partially integrate the foster children; the "solid nucleus," which draws a distinct boundary around the biological family unit; and the "contingency model," which applies selective integration of some foster children and not others. However, although my parents reminded me that my foster siblings were not my biological siblings, and the calls and visits from social workers punctuated those reminders, the boundaries—both physical and emotional—around our family quickly dissolved.

My brother shared his bedroom with Paddy. After a few months in my parents' bedroom, Darlene joined me in mine. Initially, I resented the intrusion, the loss of my privacy and two dresser drawers, the smell of sour milk and talcum powder that lingered even with the window open. And I complained when naptimes and feedings dictated our schedules, when the television volume had to be turned down, when mealtimes were delayed because boiling pots of nipples and bottles occupied the stovetop. But the foster children did not pose a threat to my dolls or clothes or friends, and the bleak images of television orphanages tempered my resentment of Darlene's entry into my space.

We all soon settled into a routine that involved treating Paddy and Darlene as our brother and sister, as my parents' son and daughter. We kids crowded together on Santa's lap for the Christmas photograph. In the summer, we all received kitchen haircuts in order to stay cool. And, when Paddy, and then Darlene, began walking, Mom took us to a Montreal store we'd been to dozens of times because it guaranteed precise fitting. We jostled each other and positioned our feet in the slots at the bottom of a large walnut box called the Fluoroscope. We peered into the viewing ports as it hummed and revealed the bones in our feet, as well as the outline of our shoes, all glowing green. Both foster children received leather walking boots, as my brother and I once had, to ensure the proper development of their growing feet.

And, when Paddy, and then Darlene, began speaking, they addressed my parents as Mama and Dada. No one corrected them.

 I taught Darlene to clap Patty-Cake, and I taught Paddy to say "Jesus Murphy," just like Dad said whenever he climbed on the roof to adjust the television antenna. And, from the foster children, I learned that a newborn's umbilical cord would scab over and fall off and maybe bleed a little (all of which led me to believe, for years, that the navel was the site of menstruation). I also learned the enthusiastic tradition of younger siblings joining forces to torment an older sibling. When Mom banished us to our rooms for "bickering," Gary taught Paddy how to ricochet a ball off the linen cupboard door so it would bounce into my bedroom. And, when I refused to agree with my brother's comment that our bedtime snacks were "like a little party before bed," Paddy, with teasing eyes and a smile, asked me over and over, every evening: "Is it time yet for our party?" My brother also showed Paddy how to use a wood-burning kit to etch his initials onto a toy, showed him how to shove it under the dresser when Mom summoned them for dinner, and how, when the bedroom filled with smoke, to redirect blame to the sister who'd refused, once again, to read the instructions aloud.

Both my brother and I also learned that there were rules, a growing list of what you could not—and should not—do with foster kids. Even if we could afford someday to develop the basement, Paddy could not sleep down there because a foster child's bedroom had to be "above grade." Paddy could wear a harness so he wouldn't wander off when we went shopping, but he could not be tied to the back door with a length of clothesline, even if he could bark like a dog. And, due to what my scowling teacher called "their unfortunate birth circumstances," and what my mother called "their situations," neither foster child could ever, ever, "God help us," be volunteered for the role of baby Jesus in my classroom's nativity pageant.

And, in November 1966, when Darlene was fourteen months old

and we received notice she was leaving, my parents informed Gary and me that she would leave while we were at school, as would Paddy, someday; the departures would be easier and less complicated that way, my mother said, promising that my bedroom would be "back to normal" when I got home. I'd be able, once again, to hang my Tiger Beat posters on all four walls of the room, she said. But what my mother didn't realize was that I would sleep through the night, too, after Darlene left, because I wouldn't wake with every murmur from her, wouldn't take her into my bed to comfort her. When I pressed my mother for details and explanations for the lack of warning that Darlene was leaving, Gary and I learned that we'd never had the option to adopt her. We could never adopt Paddy, either, because, as my parents explained, foster parents could not adopt their charges. Foster parents signed "important legal papers" agreeing to not even try to adopt the children they cared for, my parents said. The word "legal" conjured up images of TV lawyer Perry Mason and courtrooms and defendants who were always guilty of some heinous crime, so I did not challenge my parents' statements. We knew better because our parents held sway: our tantrums were ignored, and our confiscated toys remained on top of the fridge for a week. The threat of the wooden spoon garnered our immediate attention. A mere warning that our bedtime snacks—our "party"—would be withheld guaranteed our compliance. We lived in a vacuum, in that we did not know any other foster families, and we were unaware of statistics on children adopted from foster care by their former foster parents.

Paddy left one year later, in December 1967; he had been with us for almost four years. On the evening before his departure, the last night we would share our home with a foster child, the boys rough-housed in their room and ignored my mother's weary warnings that "someone would get hurt." I sat on the floor, with my back pressed against the knobs of the dresser damaged in the wood-burning incident. I pretended not to watch, pretended not to memorize every curl on Paddy's head, every crease on the soles of his feet. And I did not tattle on the boys. My silence, though, was not good-natured tolerance; I let them play on in the hope that a late-night run to the emergency department would delay the inevitable.

Paddy lay on the top bunk, which was my brother's, and they giggled as my brother rammed a baseball bat between the upper bed's springs, bouncing Paddy closer and closer to the edge. Then they wrestled on the floor and shadow-boxed. As though they were trying to cram years of pent-up activity into one night, they frantically yelled out Batman-like ka-pows and ka-bamms. Suddenly, my brother yelped and clutched his back. "He bit me! Mom, Paddy bit me!"

My mother appeared at the bedroom door and demanded to see the bite mark, but my brother protested. "He bit my bum," he said.

Paddy sat on the lower bunk, eyes lowered, lashes damp. He'd never bitten anyone before, although, when we'd played house, he'd often volunteered to be our dog because we put Darlene in the role of baby. Paddy would bark as he pretended to pee against the swing set poles. I decided my brother was exaggerating to get attention.

(In preparing this essay, I called my brother, who now lives in Toronto, and I asked him if Paddy's bite—with twenty teeth, according to my mother's notes from the departure day—left a scar. My brother cupped the receiver and called out to his wife: "Hon, do I have teeth marks on my butt?" His teenaged daughters moaned in disgust.)

꧁ The evening before Paddy's departure, I volunteered to hem his new pants. I measured each leg twice, as I'd been taught in Home Economics, and, with my mother's pinking shears, I cut once. I hemmed those pants with the hope that Paddy's new parents would return him to us because they worried he'd had polio, because they envisioned him in an iron lung or in shoes with one thick rubber sole, that they'd return him to us because in those pants it seemed one of his legs was much shorter than the other. I was not familiar with the term back then, but my objective was abrogation, which is the right of adoptive parents to legally return a child to the foster system. And, at Mass that week, I lit a candle and bartered with God and prayed that the adoptive parents would send Paddy and his polio-pants back to us.

When Darlene had left, my parents had immediately disassembled her crib and rearranged the remaining furniture in my room, which somewhat disguised the crib's absence; however, when Paddy left, there was no way to hide the removal of a bunk in my brother's room. The walls appeared taller, and the room rang hollow.

As days passed, time became marked by rituals and routines that would not allow me to forget he was gone: the plastic bottle of shampoo promising no tangles and no tears that disappeared from the space next to my mother's glass bottle of Breck; the four chairs that now had space to sit equidistant around the kitchen table; the empty hangers swinging in the front closet. In those moments, I believed Paddy lived in a parallel world, bathing when we bathed, eating when we ate, running around outside when we ran around outside. And after school, I pictured him with his head pressed against a screen door, his impatience and puzzlement growing as he waited for me to arrive and critique that day's artwork or sympathize with him about a skinned knee. How long would it take, I wondered, for him to realize that I'd never arrive, there, at his new house? How long would it take for him to forget us completely?

We should be glad that Paddy was going to a good home, my parents often said, and we should embrace the spirit of fostering and see the potential and the possibilities of our former charges' lives in new homes. We should not dwell on their departures, not search for Darlene's bald head or Paddy's blonde curls in the backseats of passing cars or in strollers at the bank. But I was unable to meet my parents' expectations of enthusiasm for the adoptions. I felt as though we had betrayed those two children, that we had failed them, abandoned them, Paddy, in particular. He had stayed with us for almost four years—I was eight when he arrived, twelve when he left—and he had become my brother.

On the December day that Paddy left, that last week of school before Christmas, I did not share the news of his adoption with my school friends. I could not yet speak of him without replaying the minute details of his departure, as I envisioned it. In my mind, he did not go quietly. He clung to my mother's arm, clutching at the tea towel that seemed to forever ride her shoulder, and through his peanut-butter breath, he asked, over and over: "Do I have to?" And I did not—could not—confide in friends over the following days, either. I waited until January, after Christmas break, when I could deliver the news of his adoption in a tone flat enough to deflect sympathy and animated enough to convey the joy I was supposed to feel.

~ My questions about my departed siblings evoked silence from my mother, or long, measured pauses and short, clipped answers. I learned to avoid mentioning their names. Layoffs at Canadair once again forced my father to exercise his seniority and bump other unionized workers from their jobs; consequently, he now worked swing shifts in the plant instead of a desk job. He began arriving home at odd hours and sometimes without warning, in a uniform that reeked of cigarette smoke and alcohol. Amber, quart-sized beer bottles occupied refrigerator space vacated by the gallons of milk our milkman no longer delivered.

In the following weeks and months, the stillness in our house grew, interrupted only by distant noise from construction in adjacent neighbourhoods. I escaped to those under-construction homes—most of which offered mirror images or slight variations on our basic bungalow—and entered them through unlocked doors or windows propped open to allow varnishes and glues to dry. But my grief and shame accompanied me. The bathrooms all had builders' grade, black-and-white tiled floors, as we did, but the luxury of choice that some homeowners enjoyed—a knotty-pine rumpus room, a lazy-Susan in a kitchen cupboard, wall-to-wall carpeting in a hallway or bedroom—increased my resentment toward my parents. I stared out from the blank windows of those new houses, and, with eyes overflowing the way our little pool overflowed when someone stepped on its inflatable wall, I realized that my own home felt more vacant than the houses in which I stood.

꒰ When my mother died in 1997, I found her little notebook with the details of Darlene's and Paddy's stays with us. I also found Paddy's hospital bracelet, the still-soft, tangible link to his birth mother. I do not remember if Darlene arrived with hers. I found it curious, too, that in my mother's belongings there was no trace of my hospital bracelet, nor that of my brother. Perhaps she believed that Paddy's adoptive parents would not want his; back then, adoptions were seldom discussed openly. (I experienced this secrecy first-hand; only when my father died in 1970 had my mother confided to me that he had been adopted.)

So it is quite possible that Paddy, who would be forty-six years old now, has no idea that he was fostered at birth or adopted in 1967.

There were no records of the funds my parents received for fostering, but, at the back of the notebook, my mother recorded cheques received from a provincial mortgage subsidy program for low-income families. Did my parents lie and say they had signed those often-cited "we-agree-never-to-adopt-our-foster-children" papers to screen us from the truth that they could not afford to adopt? Would they even have qualified, financially, in the eyes of the Ville Marie Social Services? I'll probably never have the answer to that question, and I'm not sure I want it.

For years, I viewed the other families' adoptions of Darlene and Paddy as a hard Christmas candy, and said: "That's what broke my tooth," "That's what broke my family." But, in hindsight, I suspect that ongoing financial strains and my father's increased drinking had worked for years to weaken our bonds. Mere months after Paddy's adoption, the bank seized our Chateauguay home, and, by May of 1968, we were relying on the benevolence of relatives for our own temporary shelter.

꒰ I have not actively searched for Darlene and Paddy, perhaps because I need to hold the nostalgia—the belief that we provided a positive, healthy foundation for them to thrive—intact. I have Googled their names, and I've tentatively searched ancestry websites, but I have no legal status to search beyond what is available publicly. Government agencies and adoption registries have mandates to serve only adoptees, birth parents, birth siblings, and birth grandparents. It appears that, within the foster and adoption systems, host children do not exist.

Today, individuals as well as couples are recruited to both foster and adopt; surrendered children are as likely to be returned to their birth homes as they are to be adopted. But it appears little has changed for the biological children of foster parents. In her article "Sons and Daughters of Foster Carers and the Impact of Fostering on Their Everyday Life," Dr. Ingrid Höjer argues that biological children continue to be viewed as mere extensions of their parents, and they are, therefore, simply deemed equally "competent and resilient." As well, according to researchers Redding, Fried, and Britner in "Predictors of Placement Outcomes in Treatment Foster Care: Implications for Foster Parent Selection and Service Delivery," the agencies responsible for evaluating placements focus on the "goodness-of-fit" between prospective caregivers and their charges. And that is as it should be; the urgent need for suitable foster care cannot be denied. Nonetheless, why do the relevant agencies and associations ignore the research and choose not to broaden that focus slightly? Why not afford the biological children the same degree of attention granted to their parents? Unfortunately, however, from my correspondence with Dr. Twigg and Dr. Tracy Swan, a professor in the School of Social Work at Memorial University in Newfoundland, those involved in placement decisions today largely overlook these issues. Just as shoe stores unthinkingly promoted the Fluoroscope, which emitted copious amounts of radiation, little attention today is directed on the lasting consequences of an apparent "good fit" in foster care." Due to the regional nature of adoption and fostering agencies, it is difficult to accurately determine the number of children currently in Canadian foster care, let alone the number of biological children in fostering homes. In 2003, the Child Welfare League of Canada estimated there were more than seventy-six thousand fostered children; Dr. Twigg estimates that this number now probably exceeds one hundred thousand. And fostering has become exceedingly complex, with a large percentage of homes caring for children with special needs. Yet, given the current lack of information and support available, it is likely that foster parents still do not adequately gauge the impact the experience will have on their own children. Their biological children, the foot soldiers, still charge, untrained and unaided, through the increasingly complex minefields of fostering.

These host children's lives dovetail with their foster siblings'; they share space, just as my brother and I shared space — at the dinner table, on the sofa, in bedrooms and blanket-forts and bathwater. Host children share, too, their parents' attention. In my situation, adoption was the ultimate goal, yet those adoptions served to deny all that was shared, all that was given and taken, taught and learned. This denial, this void, demanded a reaction; when Darlene and Paddy left, I struggled to reconcile my conflicting emotions. Sharing a home — a place of refuge — created an intimacy that I could not ignore, could not readily dismiss. I was unable to celebrate Darlene's and Paddy's adoptions. I could not celebrate my loss. But I was also old enough to recognize that fostering was a noble and selfless task. I understood that fostering provided surrendered children an opportunity to thrive in the stability of a family, rather than be sent into an institutional environment, and that it facilitated a transition to an adopting family. And, eventually, as the months and years passed, I grew to believe that my family had succeeded in that regard. According to Dr. Höjer, more than seventy-five percent of the biological children in her study claim that fostering was a positive experience.

✤ Today, I sort through the loose photos — twelve of Darlene, fourteen of Paddy — that my mother kept with her notebook. One captures our first camping trip together, a trip when Darlene slept in the tent with my parents, and my brother and Paddy and I slept in the station wagon in a tangle of blankets and limbs and deflating air mattresses. Others are typical childhood snapshots, snapshots that fill the cookie tins and desk drawers of many parents: a swaddled infant, two boys playing on a pile of dirt, a toddler's face hiding behind a plastic cereal bowl.

But two photos—one of Darlene, one of Paddy—stand out. My mother had cropped the sides of these photos to fit her wallet.

Distance and time now allow me to more objectively consider the foster child's well-being and point of view. But the selfish twelve-year-old inside me, I realize, is still alive. As I reread my mother's notebook and finger Paddy's hospital bracelet and the scissor-cut edges of those cropped photos, the loss—the legacy of my fostering experience—is still palpable. As well, I am reminded of this loss, and of Paddy, in particular, every Christmas. The memories, though, are not stirred by shortbread cookies or the toys I wrap for my two-year-old grandson. Instead, notices from Calgary's Humane Society recall that day in 1967, two weeks before Christmas, when Paddy left our home; the Humane Society discourages pet adoptions in December, not due to a lack of abandoned pets, but because newly adopted animals do not react well to the commotion of the holiday season and the subsequent disruption of their routines.

And, in once again considering the foster child's point of view, I can't help but wonder, as Paddy was tucked into bed on those first few nights in his new home, amid the flurry of Christmas visitors and activities, did he ask his adoptive parents: "Isn't it time for my party?"

Elaine Hayes recently graduated from the University of Calgary with a Bachelor of Arts in English and a concentration in creative writing; her fiction has appeared and is forthcoming in several Canadian literary magazines. She lives in Calgary, Alberta, with her husband, Gary, and her terrier, Oliver Twist.

adoptionland

OLA ZURI

FOR THE PAST TWENTY-EIGHT years, I've been trying to find my way through my own adoption narrative, a place we might call Adoptionland. My name is Ola Zuri, but it was not always so. When I was born, I was named Darlene until I was adopted. Then my name was changed to Alison, the name I would be known by in my new family. As I was growing up, I never felt like an Alison, nor, in fact, did I ever feel like a Darlene. Those names didn't reflect who I was: inside, something was still missing. In 1999, when I was pregnant with my oldest daughter, I realized what it was: I needed a name that meant something to me, for me, and was about me. I made a choice to give my children names that would reflect what I saw in them as infants, but I realized that my name was not as exotic or meaningful. I researched names and tried them on to find one that I would feel comfortable with. Then I changed my name legally—and now I feel this name reflects who I have always been.

I am forty-three. I live in the Okanagan Valley of British Columbia, where I raise four children of my own, yet I still question whether adoption is the blessing almost everyone says it is. I was born in 1966, in an era when having a child out of wedlock was still considered taboo, especially for a black woman who had been rejected by both her peers and her family. My birth mother was unable to keep me: she lacked the ability and the means to raise a newborn. In such circumstances, no one would have called me blessed.

෴ My adoption was bittersweet, melding happiness and sadness — and surprise. My twin sister was born prematurely, one hour and fifteen minutes before me. She was whisked away into the neonatal care unit. Then, I was born. I surprised not only the doctors, who were not expecting a second baby to pop out, but also the new mother who would soon turn me away forever. When I was a few days old, I was separated from my twin and placed into Quebec's foster care system. A few weeks later, my sister was placed in the system with me.

When I was two years old, my twin sister, Neva, and I were adopted by a white couple in what was one of the first transracial adoptions in both the province of Quebec and in Canada. Growing up in Montreal might have been a good thing: it would have provided richness in diversity, culture, and heritage. However, after the birth of their biological daughter, my adoptive parents decided to relocate to the white, redneck city of Calgary, Alberta. In those days, Calgarians were resistant to change and definitely looked askance at black children in a white family. When we were out together, people would stop and stare, point fingers at me, and laugh. Other children would say I was dirty; they would not come near me, they said, because they didn't want to look like me. And of course, like any child, I could never understand why I was treated so differently.

This feeling of separation, of difference, continued as I grew up. I never knew why, but my parents sent Neva and me to different schools. There were no other black children at my school or at my sister's school. So, even though we had each other when we were at home, we each had separate issues to deal with at school, on our own. Such separation was not beneficial: it left me feeling alone, marooned in my own world. Being alone in a white world had been challenging enough, but now I was at a predominantly white school with children who picked on me, called me names, teased me, and even hurt me, simply because I was not the same as them. I couldn't change the colour of my skin and, as much as I tried, I couldn't wash it off. These searing experiences were the beginning of my sadness.

"Dirty. Blackie. Mud. Ugly. Monkey Girl. Poop. Stinkpot." The boy in my Grade 2 class would not stop calling me names. I ignored him for a long time but finally burst into frustrated tears and hit him with my fist, hard, right in the face. His nose started to bleed. I hit him again in the stomach and again on the arm. The teacher grabbed me, took me to the office, and told me I had no right to pick on other children. The principal, she said, would give me the strap. Even when I told her what had happened, she did not believe me. So I got the strap—and detention.

My dad was angry when I got home, even though I tried to explain. I remember feeling really bad for getting in trouble at school and then even worse for causing trouble at home. After that incident, I never again told my parents about problems at school, nor did I speak with any teachers or confide in my sister.

When another brown girl came to my school in Grade 6, I felt a gravitational pull toward her. Her name was Audrey; she was taller than me, athletic, confident, and very sure of herself.

"Hey, Nigger. Blackie. You can't hang around with us." The same kids who consistently teased and harassed me tried name-calling with Audrey.

She turned on them in a flash. "I may be black, but I know how to treat people a lot nicer than any of you." With that she turned and grabbed my arm, and we walked away. That actually shut them up.

"My parents tell me there are lots of people who don't like black-skinned people like us," Audrey told me. "That doesn't give them the right to put us down or make us feel bad. My parents always tell me to stand up for myself."

Audrey was amazing to me, for me. We became good friends, and I was invited to spend time with her family. Audrey taught me about some of the foods she ate and traditions that she and her family celebrated. Consequently, Grade 6 was my favourite school year: I became a little more confident and, in the process, made a couple of good friends. By Grade 7, a new school, new friendships, sports, and different lifestyles began to strain my friendship with Audrey; we lost touch during junior high school.

At the time, I knew there was something about Audrey that I had longed for. It was exciting for me to see that there were other people — besides the ones I saw in the movies or on TV — who looked like me. I didn't recognize that my sister was as much of a resource for me as Audrey had been, because Neva and I were unable to discuss our experiences at school. My sister never wanted to talk about anything personal, nor does she share very much now as an adult.

As most teens did, I wanted to conform. I decided that I would do what the other girls did, so I took up modelling. After all, wasn't modelling for everyone, black or white?

"What makes you think you could ever be a model?" Tanya said at my first fashion show. She threw a *Vogue* magazine my way.

"Models are not black! You won't make it in this business," another girl chimed in.

With no black female role model to emulate and shattered by what those shallow girls thought of me, I withdrew, never to resurface as a model again. The issues I was trying to deal with were difficult, so I buried my conflicts deep within.

"Hi, Nanny! I'm here to visit." I strain to hear a voice saying a small hello. My father's mother resented the fact that her son had adopted children who were black. Indirectly, she conveyed her rejection despite my many attempts to please her. I cleaned her home, I was quiet when she wanted me to be quiet, I watched horror movies with her, and I even took up cross-stitch because she loved it. But when my sister or cousins, the biological children, were on the scene, she didn't notice me at all.

As I got older, I felt increasingly dejected by my never-adequate attempts to do the right thing for my family. I resented the fact that family didn't/couldn't/wouldn't do enough to help me through the racial insecurities I felt. They didn't/couldn't/wouldn't provide the guidance I needed. I've made a lot of mistakes in my life; would those times have been less painful if I'd had a supportive black family member?

By young adulthood, I'd become nervous, quiet, shy, and even ashamed of having been adopted. I felt pulled in two directions: I was growing up as an outwardly black youth who felt white inside. Even as an adult, I still find myself trying to fit in—into both white and black communities. Often, I sense this "not quite right" feeling in the air. Black communities tend to be fairly insular and ask to whom you are related, where you come from. For them, I'm not "black enough." For others, I'm just "too black."

In my job in the financial industry, I meet a variety of people daily. On this particular day, the bank is full and the line is backed up. All of us tellers are doing our best. My next client comes up to my station, a buddy in tow. Both are young white men, probably in their late teens.

"Hello, how may I help you?" I ask.

The customer rolls his eyes at his friend. "If you know how, I want some money from my account."

Of course, I courteously serve him, but his rudeness intensifies: he shoves papers at me impatiently. Throughout our transaction, he and his buddy laugh together.

"Yo, girlie, hurry it up already," says the customer's friend.

As they leave, they toss a piece of paper my way and take off out the door.

"Yo, Nigga!" says the note, "Ya'll don't belong here! Go back to your own country!" Even though I had heard it all before, tears pricked my eyelids.

"What else is new?" I muttered.

I'd experienced racist attitudes before, but my co-workers were surprised. When I talk about the many racist people I've encountered, I often see looks of genuine dismay on my colleagues' faces: what I'm saying cannot possibly be true, not here, not in Canada. Even my family members are surprised when I report racist comments. When I was younger, I didn't understand why my family discounted my experiences. Now I get it: my family and I encounter a vastly different society.

For instance, in advance of the recent presidential election in the United States, my aunt, who is white, and I were discussing what each candidate had to offer. When I mentioned Barack Obama's race, I was shocked by my aunt's reaction.

"What does race have to do with it?" she asked

"What do you mean, what does race have to do with it?" I asked, startled. "Really?" Race had everything to do with it. The newspaper headlines read, "Is America ready for a Black President?"

Many members of my family think we all should see things the same way because we share a family history, but some of them don't get what is different—my race. They don't see me as a member of both my race and my family and often can't comprehend why I get distressed or agitated about it. It has to be either/or.

Have I ever wondered why my birth parents gave me up? Yes, I've wondered. Have I watched people go by and wondered if any of them were somehow related to me biologically? Again, yes. Have I ever dreamed of belonging to a famous family? Definitely. Why wasn't I special enough to keep? What did I do wrong? My answer . . . I was born.

Looking back now, I realize that around age ten I started supporting everyone but myself. I never stopped to listen to my own feelings. But if I was being helpful to someone else, then it seemed like I almost mattered. I didn't see, until almost twenty years later, when I really examined my life, that if there was no one else to listen, then *I* had to start listening to myself.

There are more resources available now for children than when I was growing up. Often, children's books provide a way for parents to broach a variety of subjects with their children, including adoption, bullying, and racism. And that's why I wrote *Why Can't You Look Like Me?*, the first in a series. Following that, I created a program titled *Believe in Me* to provide positive literature to empower young readers.

And I've finally decided that adoption has been a blessing: it's enabled me to become a part of the healing process for generations to come.

Ola Zuri (olazuri.com) lives in Kelowna, British Columbia, with her family. She facilitates transracial parenting workshops, runs mentoring groups for children, and creates inspiring literature for children and families.

the right not
to know

STEPHANIE FARRINGTON

TWENTY-FIVE YEARS AGO, I was a pregnant young woman. I can hardly think of those months leading up to the birth. I was in free-fall. Physically, I had already been through several hospitalizations for menstrual hemorrhage. The first time it happened, I lost as much blood as it is possible to lose and survive. I had no idea it was so bad; I had no basis for comparison.

By the time I got pregnant, the doctors had told me my chances of being able to conceive would be pretty low. I was too young to worry about it, and it was possible that I might outgrow it, but when the time came to consider children, I was told, I would be wise to consult with a fertility expert. For that reason, apart from managing the bleeding, I was not terribly concerned with birth control.

For the first five months, I did not know I was pregnant. I didn't put on weight, and apart from some nausea, there were no real symptoms. At around twenty weeks, thinking I had a kidney infection, I finally saw the doctor about feeling sick, tired, and nauseated. When the doctor told me my urine sample showed a mild infection but, more importantly, that I was pregnant, I started to cry. I was not ready for a child and had no intention of keeping him. From the first moment I knew I was pregnant, there was no doubt in my mind that I would give the child to an adoptive family. If I had found out sooner, I might have chosen abortion. My life was no place for a child.

Two weeks later, the baby shifted into a painful position over my right kidney. The doctors said there were serious problems. They discussed the possibility of kidney stones, tested me again for infections, and eventually decided I would have to stay in the hospital for observation until they could address the pain, and I could put some weight on. I couldn't keep any food down because the baby was pinching off something vital, and that seemingly simple situation was endangering both our lives.

I shared my hospital room with a succession of women who had dramatic and frightening stories to tell. One had felt her placenta rupture and the water gush out only five months into her pregnancy; another had lost a baby nearly that age when she went to the bathroom. Everyone was terrified. Eventually, the common sense of a Jamaican-born nurse who had seen this sort of thing under worse circumstances told me I had to start moving the baby myself. In order to do this, she helped me to my hands and knees on the bed and then had me rest on my forearms, arms crossed in front of my head, with my upper body tilted at a much lower angle than my hips. If I leaned forward onto my shoulders, I could reach back and pull my belly forward a little. I could feel the baby start to budge as I did so; I could feel him start to pull away from my kidneys. It was uncomfortable, but it seemed to work. The nurse also insisted I get out of bed and walk, and that helped a lot. At the same time, a friend of a friend who worked as a paramedic looked at the drugs I was being given me and suggested I refuse the medication and see what happened. I decided to try both approaches. Within twenty-four hours, I was out of the hospital and was fine for the rest of the pregnancy.

On the advice of another nurse, I was able to put on some weight by drinking milkshakes, and by the time I was ready to deliver, the baby and I were both healthy. I stayed with friends and family, and I waited.

I waited for my life to come to some sort of conclusion and point me in a direction. I waited to perform a single action: deliver a baby and ensure his future was nothing like my past.

I saw a social worker about the adoption. Because I was neither a drinker nor a drug user, my file attracted a lot of applicants. One, an optometrist, said he wanted a child from a clean pregnancy and a pure birth because he wanted to be sure the child would be physically perfect. He offered a great deal of financial security in return. I rejected him. Another couple talked about how their lives would be devoid of meaning without children. They also went into the rejection pile. I could not stand the thought of my son carrying the emotional weight for a family, and as for the optometrist, money just wasn't that important. I wanted a family who would love the child and include him in their lives the way any child should be included. I did not want adoption to be the central theme of his existence.

Eventually, I chose a couple who said if they could not adopt, they would continue to be a family, but they would be a family of two, and they would like to adopt in order to become a family of three. They seemed balanced, genuine, and right for my son. They were teachers, they owned their home, and their mortgage was paid off. They were Unitarian and liked many of the same things I liked. I decided they would provide his home.

At the end of November, after a short, relatively painless labour, I gave birth to my son. It was a natural childbirth—no drugs, no interventions of any kind. He was perfect, and I was determined his life would be perfect, too. I stood, with my baby in my arms, looking out the window of my hospital room at the oak meadow. The wet green fields were dotted with bunnies. It was all very bucolic, like the text of a psalm. My son had been born and his parents were chosen. I had no idea how I could possibly go through with leaving him, but even if I had to find someone to force me, I was determined to do it. I had no doubt that I was doing the right thing for him.

My family was a wreck. My parents' marriage had never been stable; in fact, it was rarely congenial. They fought constantly, and my most vivid memory of them in my childhood was one of trying not to hear them yelling at each other in the middle of the night as I lay in bed with a knot in my stomach. Their experience as parents had been shaped by the death of my infant brother. I was a healthy, strong, and lively child. People took to me. When my sister arrived a year after my brother's death, she was a weaker baby with the same colouring as my late brother and a tendency to be sickly. Out of concern for her well-being, my parents left me more or less to my own devices. The neglect was palpable and caused me to ask questions about it from a very early age. They gave a number of reasons for this, foremost among them was the fact that I was doing well enough that I did not require their attention, whereas my sister did. I think this was genuine on my mother's part, but I suspect my father was just an indifferent parent. They were careful to raise me as a well-mannered little girl, but apart from stressing that it was not nice to show off, they paid little attention to me. I received most of my positive attention from teachers, strangers, and, when we were in the same city, other relatives. I grew up knowing I was on my own and feeling that my strength made me unlovable and my talents made me a show-off.

By the time I was thirteen, my parents separated. I don't remember being upset about the loss of my father, who had always been verbally, mentally, and emotionally abusive, but I was unprepared for what was to come. My mother became attached to a man who eventually fled the country to escape charges of child sexual abuse. By the time he had blackened my eye, I knew I would have to find somewhere else to live. So, only thirteen, I went to my father's, but he was clear that he didn't want me, so I tried my mother's again, only to have the violence escalate.

My childhood continued that way until I was sixteen, at which point I decided to house-sit for friends and look for work. Eventually, I got a job in retail and let life spin and flow around me. I was a passive observer of my own life, aware of my good looks and not much else. The few times my father complimented me during my adolescence it was to say things like, "If I looked like you, I'd never have to work a day in my life." He made it clear that he believed my only strength was my sexual appeal. There were a few good influences, but for the most part, I accepted that I was too stupid to go to university and too poor for much of anything else. I settled for looking good and going dancing, but in my spare time I somehow discovered Beethoven, Camus, Dante, and the CBC.

Somehow, I knew these things were important for me, but I knew equally well that given half a chance, my father would take them away. Consequently, I browsed old bookstores for back issues of *The New Yorker* and copies of books by John Hershey, Aristotle, Eugene O'Neill, Pearl S. Buck, anyone whose name I had ever heard whispered in conversations about smart people. When I took a bath, I would take one of the magazines or books with me. To be sure I understood them, I often wrote notes and questions in the margins to be researched later. I wanted new ideas in my life more than anything else, but I kept them hidden. They seemed risky. I knew I would be ridiculed for having them.

With the birth of my son, I knew, on one level, that something had to change for everybody. It suddenly seemed to me that the things I had taken pains to hide might be something I could have in my life, in plain sight. I thought they might be important and that I might be something more than what I had been raised to think I was. These were small and frightening thoughts at the time. I knew that acting on any of them would cause trouble, and I believed there would be a good chance that even if I did pursue these things, specifically pursue an education, because I was not bright, there was a good chance I would fail.

More importantly, I also knew my family was intent on bringing my son into their world partly because my they saw their son in my son and could not bear to think of losing him again. But I knew, if he entered their world, the things that mattered to me would not exist for him. I wanted him to grow up knowing he could be bookish or musical or anything he wanted to be, so I needed to keep the peace and stay hidden long enough to get him out of my life to become safe and sound, and that is exactly what I did. I was compliant, affable and took pains not to mention anything I was considering about my own life.

I made sure my baby roomed with me. I wanted him to know he was cherished from the moment he was born and, selfishly, I wanted time to be his mother. Most of the time, I held him. When he slept, he slept at the foot of my bed. I rarely allowed him to be taken to the nursery, but when I did, I made it clear which medical procedures were acceptable and which ones were off my list. I refused the pills to dry up my milk supply, just in case. I am still not sure if it was a good thing or not, but I gave us time to be in love with each other the way only a mother and newborn can be. I wanted that for both of us.

My son's father was in the room when he was born. His name is on the birth certificate. Both families were free to visit and both did. People held him and said their hellos and goodbyes. Some, like my mother, refused to do either. I didn't make a fuss about it. His father could have been anyone. I convinced myself I loved him for everyone else's sake, but honestly, I was indifferent. He loved me and he held out some promise of stability. I thought that was enough for me. I'm glad I knew it was not enough for my son.

I never expected to love a person the way I loved my son. The future of the universe seemed to depend on him. He was the most beautiful creature I had ever seen. This made it difficult to leave him, but it also strengthened my resolve. What would you hesitate to do to benefit someone you loved that much? Nothing—you do whatever it took to ensure his safety, to give him a shot at real happiness. To do less would be unthinkable. After he was born, people would sometimes say to me, "I could never do what you did. I could never be that brave." My answer then was the same as it is now: "If you love your child, you will do whatever it takes to secure his future."

Before he lost contact with me, I made sure he had a letter to carry with him. It was long and not entirely honest. In it, I said I loved his father, but I knew that was not true. I said I wanted a secure emotional future for him, and that was true, but inside, I knew I would have been a good mother. I quoted *The Little Prince* and told him about Beethoven. I told him I wanted more for both of us. I assured him that sending him to his new family was a gift of love and not a rejection of him in any way. I told him not to talk about me as his "real" mother—his real mother was the woman who would raise him and who would be there for every happy and sad moment. I told him he was lucky. Most people have only two parents who love them more than anything in the world—he had four.

Looking back, I knew giving him up was a gamble for his future but also for my own. Although I refused to admit it, I think I knew I would leave his father as soon as I could. I knew I would start trying to fix the thousand and one things wrong with my life, and I knew my chances of succeeding, completely alone, as I was, were slim, but I had to make the effort because suddenly I wasn't just a bit player in my parents' story anymore. I had produced a child—that meant I had a place in the world and had to make something of it. The fact that my son might never know it didn't matter, but the fact that he might—that did. Once he was born, drifting didn't seem so okay anymore. I knew that even if I failed, I had to make the effort not to be the same person as the half-conscious girl who had conceived him.

꙳ After the birth and his adoption, my social worker asked me to speak to a group of parents and take part in a support group for birth mothers. The group was intended to help us get through the emotional trauma of losing a child. We met once a week and discussed our own experiences, as well as our plans for the future. In my group, there were two women who hadn't known they were pregnant and a married woman whose husband would take her back only if she relinquished the child who was conceived during an affair she had during a trial separation. One of the women was a university student who came from a religious family in Alberta. She delivered at six months, and no one in her family knew about the child, including her fiancé. They thought she had appendicitis. We also talked a lot about the act of placing a child for adoption and how so many things had been difficult or nonsensical about the experience. Among us were women who wanted the option of open adoption, which was not available to us at the time, and there were those who wanted only to forget.

Coincidentally, as we hashed out our political views, new policies were under active consideration in British Columbia. At the time in BC, there were two options on the table concerning adoption: a passive and an active registry. Prior to this, I think all adoption records had been sealed forever, so either choice was considered an improvement. In the case of a passive registry, both the birth parent and her adult child would have to file a request for reunion in order for the relevant documents to be released to either party. An active registry would require only one party to desire a reunion, and once that request was filed, not only would the papers be released, but the other party, parent or child, would be actively sought. Given the nature of our group, it was not surprising that we advocated for a passive registry. I was chosen to speak for the group to a number of adoptive parents' organizations and to some policymakers in order to make our position clear. Although I didn't know it at the time, this would be my first taste of working in public affairs.

My life did not turn around immediately. After Tristan's birth, I obtained my certificate in early childhood education. Eventually, this led me to a university degree and into the field of communications, where I work today. I still bear the scars of my past, never quite believing I am entitled to anything worth having. It is hard to change your wiring, but I think it is possible.

I put myself through university with minimal help, but I also punished myself for the accident of Tristan's birth more severely than I ever thought I would. Work has been hard. I find it difficult to put my own strengths forward, difficult to ask for payment, difficult to consider that what I do has value. Never having been accustomed to being treated as though I deserved things, I still feel as though I am being greedy or demanding when I expect payment for my efforts. Considering the fact that I could not raise my own son, I have felt undeserving of any success. That feeling is hard to shake. Still, when I was able, I pressed forward. I continue to press forward and hope I always will.

One thing I know for sure: my son will never have to take the path I took. There are days when that is no comfort at all, but there are days when it is worth a lot. When I think of Tristan, I think of the face in the pictures his parents sent me. I think of the words in the letter I sent him. I remember, I told him not to look for me. Here is what I'd tell him today:

It was not your fault I gave you away. It was not for lack of love. It was not about not wanting you with me. It was about trying to find a way to breathe in a place and in a life where it felt as though everyone around me spent a good deal of their time trying to squeeze the life right out of me. I wanted a family who loved me, but I didn't want that burden to be placed on you, perfect, beautiful you.

I had hoped I would sort out all the details of my life before you were old enough to look for me, but the fact is, I wonder if anyone ever really fixes anything forever. It seems to me that people just go on varying the degree of their original dysfunction until it is small enough to be lived with or until it goes away. That's one of the miracles of life—we just keep working away at it. We keep looking up. I'm not there yet, but some day, I hope I will be. Next year in Jerusalem, as they say. I keep trying, and I hear that is the key.

I want you to know all mothers must relinquish their sons sooner or later. A good mother knows her time and acts on it. Sometimes, I still cry over you. Sometimes, it seems terribly unfair that our time to say goodbye came when you were so little and new. But I want you to know I would not change my mind. I hope, if you have children, that you are able to recognize that moment and release your love with love. I hope life is gentle with you. Really, that's all I want to say to you.

The pragmatic reasons for my son's adoption were simple and obvious. Then, like now, I never wanted charity. I did not want my son to be one of those kids waiting in the social worker's office. I didn't want us to receive a Christmas hamper or be asked if we needed winter clothes. In giving my son to his family, I felt I was bestowing a gift on him that had been denied me; I was giving him his dignity.

Now, all these years later, am I hopeful that he might come looking for me? Not at all. I found him a family who could love him and be better to him than mine was to me, and I don't want him to feel sad or burdened by the fact that my life was hard, not ever. He had no part in that. A passive registry would have allowed both of us to look for each other when we were ready. It would have meant that we might never meet, but I knew that when I placed him for adoption. If I had wanted him to know his family of origin, I would not have placed him.

Birth mothers and their children have very few rights. In the time it takes to sign a form, a woman goes from being pregnant and protected by her community to being just another single woman who, for whatever reason, has been out of the workforce for a few months and who is quite likely to be facing years of recovery from the sorrow of losing a child. There is no effort to address the emotional fallout of adoption for birth mothers and no resources available to them to rebuild their lives. The one right I could assert on behalf of my son and myself was our right to control the record of our shared past. We held that right, I thought, as individuals. If both of us decided to open that door and look back, if we decided to look for each other, I liked the idea that it would be possible to do so. However, if one of us decides we are not ready to see the other, it is not up to anyone else to say we must.

I will not register to obtain any of my son's information, because the moment I do, it will trigger an active search. He will be notified of my actions. I never want him to feel pressured to reunite, and I do not want to be pressured to reunite before I am ready. And one or both of us may never be ready. It disturbs me that the rights I thought I was protecting for both of us were ripped out from under us. I have only begun to allow myself to live again. It would be a crushing blow to my life right now if I had to contend with a son who wanted an explanation for his adoption on top of everything else.

When Jocheva sent Moses down the river in that little boat of rushes, I do not think she was hoping he would return to her. She was praying for his safety, his security, and his peace of mind, just as I prayed for my son's. She prayed that her son would be free of the bondage that defined her life, and so did I. I want my son to have access to all medical information if he wants it. I always wanted that for him, but I do not want him laid open without his consent. I might want to know who and where he is, but as long as BC has an active registry, as long as that information comes to me at the cost of disrupting his life, I will not seek it out. The fact that the threat is always there leaves a whiff of fear and shame in my life, where I had hoped to be able to live without those things.

My departure from my son's life was a gift to him. Like Jocheva before me, I put the safety of my child before my own emotional needs. I would not change my decision, but I have to say in my defence and in the defence of others like me, I should not be punished for loving my son enough to see my own situation objectively and place him in safe hands. Jocheva was a slave. Her son, Moses, was born a slave and rose to freedom because he was not brought up in bondage. She made his little boat watertight; she did not include letters or drawings or anything to lead him back to where he began. I believe one of the gifts of Jocheva was her absence. I tried to pass that gift on to my son. It was an act of love, and I do not want it taken away. ·

Stephanie Farrington is a writer and public affairs consultant living in Ottawa. She obtained her education at Carleton University and studied screenwriting at York University. She sometimes publishes as a poet and book reviewer and has written widely on housing and Aboriginal issues. Tristan is her only child.

overcoming adoption: from genesis to revelations

DALE LEE KWONG

WHEN YOU'RE SEVEN-YEARS-OLD AND hear something whispered, you know it's either delightfully good or really bad. The word? Adoption. Whispered discreetly in our kitchen, it has been both a blessing and the origin of pain in my life. Like a hearing deficit or trick knee, it's a handicap that I worked hard to overcome.

The secret was exposed when my father remarried. "Auntie Janet" wouldn't agree to be wed unless my sister and I were willing to be adopted by her. It had been more than a year since my mother had passed away—what seven-year-old wouldn't want another mother?

Dad said there would be other names on the adoption papers, but they were not to concern us. The names were there because we had both been adopted at birth, from different families. *What? My dead mother wasn't really my mother? Donna's not really my sister?* My father was wrong—I was concerned.

The year was 1968. No one talked openly about adoption. No one admitted that it had ever happened. Everyone played along, even the Alberta government. My adoptive parents are listed on my birth certificate as if I were born to them.

Later that day, Donna and I squabbled over a toy. More than five years her junior, I couldn't outmuscle her. Using the word like a weapon, I teased her for being adopted. She burst into tears. My father came to see what was wrong. Donna repeated my taunt and Dad said, "So what? Dale's adopted, too." And that was that. It was more than a decade before the word adoption was uttered in our home again.

᠗ The summer after I graduated from university, my parents called me into the kitchen. "Would you like to meet your birth family?" Dad asked. I wasn't completely shocked by the question; by then, I knew mine had been a private adoption. In Calgary's small Chinese community, it would have been easy to keep track of me. I considered the question.

I looked at my parents. Relatively strict, second-generation Chinese-Canadians, they had no idea what lay below the surface of my angst-filled teenage years. Thoughts of suicide, low self-esteem, and identity and sexuality issues haunted me. I'd survived, but I didn't want to appear ungrateful. I couldn't jeopardize my relationship with them; and there were no guarantees about the birth family. What if I was left with no family? Looking at their faces, I knew the correct answer. "No, I don't want to meet my birth family," I heard myself say. Relieved, my father said he would take care of it and these people would never bother me again. I was shocked, since every bone in my body screamed yes.

It was the first confirmation I had that these people, my birth family, my first first family, were out there. Somewhere. On one hand, I was comforted. On the other, I felt deeply uncomfortable. For years I worried that these strangers might show up unannounced at my door. Perhaps they shared the same fears.

᠗ Around the time of my twenty-third birthday, I entered counselling, which led to deeper questions. My psychologist suggested I apply to Alberta Social Services for my Non-Identifying Information document. I expected it to confirm the most common and likely adoption scenario, that of an unwed, young mother. I waited.

Time of birth: Unknown. I'd waited eight months to receive an unknown time of birth? The hospital records are sealed. What does some social worker in Edmonton think I'm going to do with this information? *Mother: Black hair, brown eyes.* Of course my birth mother had black hair and brown eyes—every Chinese woman has black hair and brown eyes. *Mother's age: Thirty-seven.* Relatively old, but not too old to raise a child. About the same age as my first adoptive mother was when I was born. *Marital status: Married.* How can this be? Not sixteen and single? Knocked up and unable to get an abortion in 1960? That's what I'd expected. *Religion: United.* That was about the only piece of information that made any sense. There were a limited number of churches in Calgary's Chinatown, and for many, the social aspect of the Chinese United Church was more of a draw than spiritual salvation. Still, I wondered: did she pray for me? Did my birth mother ask God to protect me? *Father: Unknown.* How could a married woman not know who the father was? *Other notes: Elder sibling.* They're Chinese, it must be a boy. Why did they keep him and not me?

I crumpled the single page and cursed the government worker who'd culled the scraps from my file. How would he feel if he couldn't access his time of birth? Time of birth seems like an irrelevant piece of information, but it's crucial to me. Blocked by some social worker's subjective judgment, I'll never be able to have an accurate Chinese horoscope. Don't even get me started about the lack of medical history. Black hair, brown eyes. Thanks for the update.

၄ The year my father passed away, I received a Christmas card with a handwritten greeting. I couldn't recall the sender, Allan Lee, but his last name was the same as my first adoptive mother's family name, and I thought he could perhaps be a distant relative. I sent a short note back, disguising my puzzlement as simple courtesy. In a return note as casual as his first, Allan introduced himself as my half-brother. Seventeen years older than me, he was the sibling mentioned in my Non-Identifying Information document.

We exchanged a series of letters over several months. I discovered that when I was a child, Allan saw me when he made weekly deliveries to our house. He claimed an ongoing relationship with my father, but I'd never once heard about him. I learned that my birth mother lived in Vancouver with my half-sister, Wendy. Allan, Wendy, and I had different fathers. I attempted constructing a storyline and couldn't. I wanted to know the truth, but Allan gave no hints. When he suggested we meet for lunch at the Bay cafeteria, my instincts told me to stay away. Instead, I asked for my birth mother's address. He sent it, and I never heard from him again.

Mei Li'an could neither read nor understand English, and I don't read Chinese or speak Cantonese. I decided to approach her through Wendy. How strange it must have been for Wendy to receive a letter stating I was her half-sister and asking that she translate between me and our mother. I never heard from Wendy, and I never met her. But I know she received and read my letter. I wonder if she thinks about me as often as I've thought about her.

꧁ It is tradition in Chinese culture to give gifts of food for special occasions. At Chinese New Year, one might give or receive expensive dried scallops, abalone, or high-quality Chinese mushrooms. Sweets are offered to take away any bitterness from the year before. *What symbolism do Chinese sausage and homemade peanuts represent?* That's what crossed my mind after I received a call from the mother of a high school friend I hadn't seen for years.

Mrs. Cheung had never phoned me before. But, chatting as if we were old friends, she updated me on her three children and babbled about having vacationed recently in Vancouver. She said she always visits Mei Li'an while in the city and that she'd been given a package for me. It contained a letter written in classical Chinese, accompanied by Chinese sausage and homemade Chinese-style peanuts.

I was flabbergasted. I immediately wanted to get the package.

Instead, arrangements were made to meet for pizza. The purpose was not for the Cheungs to give me the package, but to introduce me to Mrs. Woo. If I felt comfortable with Mrs. Woo, she would take the letter home to read before meeting with me for a full translation. I'd never met Mrs. Woo, but her son had dated a friend. "What a small world," said Mrs. Cheung. Not big enough, I thought. I supposed Mei Li'an didn't want Wendy to be our go-between, but I resented the involvement of these others. I was losing control of the situation.

Sentence by sentence, Mrs. Woo translated the letter from Mei Li'an:

> I born to poor family in poor village. As custom in China, I had match marriage to man in nearby also poor village. Husband left to join his parents in Canada. He supposed to make his fortune. Instead, he die. Alone in village, I raise young son. Life very hard.
>
> In-laws wanted to sponsor precious grandson to Canada. Because he minor, they had to sponsor me. Allan nearly seventeen when emigrate. In-laws make me work in Chinatown. I don't know anyone in Calgary, hard life continue.
>
> I raped and got pregnant. Pregnant widow living in new country. Entire community, including son, shun me. I walk up and down Centre Street Bridge contemplating suicide.

Upon hearing I'd been conceived in a rape, my thoughts drowned out the translation. No one really thinks about his or her parents making love, it's just something you assume—conception during a moment of passion. But what if that moment was violent? I'd always been hypersensitive to violence, now I was afraid of myself. *What traits have I inherited from my birth father? What if I can't be trusted with my anger because his blood courses through my veins? What if I lose control and nature is stronger than nurture?*

Then my anger shifted. *What did or didn't Mei Li'an do that caused a man to rape her? Was she flirtatious? Did she put up a fight, scream out loud, tear at his clothes?* I wished I was dead. I wanted to silence the painful thoughts. *Why didn't Mei Li'an get an abortion? Why didn't she jump from the bridge?* I was scared of my own suicidal desires. *Maybe it's her fault that I've struggled with suicide. Maybe it's her fault that I'm gay; she probably hated men the whole time she carried me. Why did she bring me into this world? Why didn't she keep me?*

I don't remember Mrs. Woo leaving. I know she finished translating the letter, but I had to hire a translator to translate and transcribe it for me. I wanted to be sure Mrs. Woo wasn't making it up. I wanted to know the rest of the story:

> I learn of family that adopt baby girl a few years before. Arrangements made for them to adopt mine. I fled Calgary after the birth, and I never return.
>
> I work in the fields, hardship my only friend. A man ask me marry him. Marriage of exchange, hard work or life as wife. I agree. I give him daughter. He die, too.

In the months following the rape revelation, I was traumatized into a catatonic mental state. Constantly confused, simple decisions overwhelmed me to the point of tears. I was incapable of working for three months. I felt dirty. I wanted to burn all my belongings. I wanted to start anew, but I also wanted to die. I'd worked hard in counselling to overcome distorted childhood feelings about adoption, but the shame and self-loathing came flooding back. *How could anyone be so unwanted that flesh and blood walks away?* I drew blood by digging my nails down my forearm. *I must be punished. I must be bad.* It felt so good to hurt. Saltwater tears stung my open wounds. I moaned. I wept for that ugly child. I screamed. The inhuman sounds frightened me. I was sure the neighbours would call the police. *That's it, I'm insane. Somehow, they knew I was crazy.* I curled up as if I were in the womb. *I am drowning at the moment of conception.* More moans. More screams. I slammed my head into the wall, wanting to die. All that happened was a headache. A big headache. That summer, walking down the Centre Street Bridge was a memorable accomplishment. I was afraid I might jump, but I knew that walking down the bridge was something I needed to do. *How many times did Mei Li'an pause here to think of her death? Did those thoughts give her strength while taking away mine?* I looked at the passing traffic and nonchalant fellow walkers. *Does anyone know about the woman who walked up and down this bridge in 1960?* I put one foot in front of the other and kept walking. *Can you see my shame?*

One by one, I shared the story with my closest friends. In the beginning, I couldn't get through it without breaking down in tears. I filled my time with hot baths, received rape counselling, doggie cuddles, uncensored journaling, hugs, research, mindless television, and more tears. By the end of the summer, I gathered my six closest co-workers and told them why I had been on sick leave. They cried, but I did not. By then I was incredibly detached from my own history. I was starting to heal.

Though it has taken years to fully recover, I worked through so many of my emotions that by the time I met my birth mother, it was anticlimactic.

Mei Li'an opened the door. I introduced myself. She screamed and ran away, leaving the front door open. I stepped inside, took off my shoes and looked around. Plastic covers on the couch, old Chinese calendars, an altar with photos of dead ancestors and incense offerings. I cringed. My family was very Canadian, and I was not comfortable in homes like this. *Silly superstitions. Chinese trailer trash.*

The translator friend finally arrived and explained Mei Li'an's anxiety at having to welcome me by herself. We sat down for tea and the Chinese pastries I'd brought. Mei Li'an seemed insulted when I asked questions of her family's medical history. No one had cancer. There were no known problems with heart disease, cholesterol, or early mortality. *She probably doesn't even understand why I want to know. She thinks I'm looking for reasons to be angry.* She did confess her problems with allergies, and suffering the same, I sometimes think of (or curse) her when I blow my nose. She waved off my attempts to learn more about my birth father. Literally, as if she were swatting a fly. She was no more interested in pictures of me as a child, teen, or young adult than I was of seeing photos of her dead husband and their life. I was curious to see Wendy, but since I was never to communicate or meet with her, I squirmed jealously at photos of her happy moments in Disneyland. They told me that Wendy was not as successful or confident as I. Wendy would be home shortly, so Mei Li'an rushed to conclude our visit. We quickly snapped a few photos. Mei Li'an asked what I liked to eat and offered to take me to dinner.

That night, sitting at a table for eight, it was apparent that the gaps between us were far and wide. The silences were not the kind you enjoy with a friend who knows you well. The silences were that of a well-educated, third-generation Chinese-Canadian daughter and her first-generation, plucked-from-the-village-and-transplanted-to-Canada birth mother. Fortunately, as promised, the seafood was amazing. The black bean steamed oysters were the largest I have ever seen, and tastier than any I have eaten since. Mei Li'an's parting gifts to me—a plastic poinsettia and more homemade peanuts. Even before I ate the peanuts, they left a bitter taste on my tongue.

In all honesty, I didn't like Mei Li'an. Her mannerisms were gruff and unpleasant. She seemed uneducated and ignorant. Her world was limited by her victim mentality and language barrier. I didn't see myself in her, but the photos told another story. Now that there was finally someone in the world that I looked like, I felt little consolation in having her round face and flat nose. Thank goodness I didn't have her poodle-permed hair or personality.

It's been almost fifteen years since I met Mei Li'an. Since then, I've paid closer attention to the history of the early Chinese in Canada. Their history led to mine. I cried when the Canadian government apologized for the Chinese Exclusion Act. Though repealed in 1947, the imbalances that legislation created continue to affect the Chinese community in ways we can never measure or fully appreciate.

I became a writer. I know that every good story has a beginning, middle, and end; but I've learned that some endings are just beginnings and some beginnings never end. From my experience working in television news, I know every story has at least two sides and The Truth lies somewhere in between. I accept that I'll never fully know my history, so I've used my imagination to construct a truth that satisfies myself. Intellectually, my adult brain understands the circumstances that led to my relinquishment at birth, but my inner child still reacts strongly to situations resembling rejection or abandonment.

I don't believe in keeping secrets. Often, their power lies simply in their existence. Secrets create shame. Secrets force fear of the unknown. What we imagine is usually worse than the truth. Once exposed, secrets become powerless. By telling this story, I take away its power over me. Not telling it implies I am guilty. I now understand that I did nothing wrong. I am not a victim of rape—I am a survivor.

Some may think this is a story of tragedy. They couldn't be more wrong. Every day that I walk with my head high, every year that I celebrate the day of my birth affirms my story of the triumph of good over violence. It is the story of a people that overcame prejudice and discrimination. This story is proof that how you came into the world does not set the course for your life.

I — Another Mother

The mystery of my history
began long before
the day my father revealed:
I was adopted at birth.

Long before I wondered
the connection to my worth.

He said there is no shame.
He was blessed for me to take his name.

My birth mother:

She was more than a vessel.
More than a womb
where I swam
in a sea of misconception.

She gave my heart its first beat.
Poured her blood into my body.

She is my history.
Knows the answers to my ancestry.

What time was I born? How long the labour?
Who cut the umbilical cord?
Or are we still attached?

Did she hold me to her breast after my first breath?
Or, did she hide from me — the face she gave to me?
And why, why did she give me away?

II — *Gum Sahn* Genesis

In the beginning . . . long before my birth, young men left China seeking *Gum Sahn* — Gold Mountain — somewhere in Canada. Dreams of *Gum Sahn*.

The young men became houseboys, ranch hands, gold miners. Their sweat fell in sawmills and canning factories. The railroad. Dreams of *Gum Sahn*.

The reward? Dominion Day, 1923, the Canadian government declared the Chinese "permanent aliens." Exclusion from voting and citizenship. Their families barred from immigration.

Separated, they wrote letters to their wives and children in China. The "bachelor men" of Chinatowns. Sleeping eight to a room. Working. Aging. Dreaming.
Gum Sahn dreams, gone!

III — Revelations

My birth mother told me:
"You were conceived in a rape."

My life began in a moment of violence
Inside a nest of cinnamon sticks
under a moonless midnight
or the back of a mahjong parlor.

A Dragon-Man, dark and faceless
forces himself upon my mother, birth mother.

Tears dignity from her torso.
Smothers her spirit.
Rips her heart from her soul.

Thunder and lightning camouflage her cries.
His fiery breath incinerates.
Stars shatter the sky.
Gods of heaven and earth collide.

He screams. Ejaculates. Demands.
"Comfort me, woman. Comfort!"

Gum Sahn . . . gone!

The heat burns.
I am volcano.
Lava bubbles hiss and moan.
Lava bubbles hiss and moan.

Flames red and orange and black
Ignite the cinnamon sticks.

The past consumed.
The present cremated.

And from the embers
my Phoenix rises.

Scorching the earth
at my birth.

Dale Lee Kwong is an award-winning Calgary poet, playwright, and performer. She is inspired by Sien Lok Park in Calgary's Chinatown. Note: some names and circumstances have been changed to protect the privacy of individuals involved. This does not mean that they or the Canadian government are innocent.

becoming real

JANE BYERS

WHEN I WAS GROWING up, *The Velveteen Rabbit* was one of my favourite books. I especially loved the part that said being real is not about how you are made but is what happens to you when you are loved for a long time.

"'Does it hurt?" asked the Rabbit.

"'Sometimes," said the Skin Horse, for he was always truthful. 'When you are Real you don't mind being hurt . . . you become.'"

I have learned that becoming a real family is a journey. When we adopted our twins, at fourteen months old, it took about nine months to feel real. The path to feeling like a legitimate family had some obstacles, notably, a probation period in which we were not yet a legal family, and being an adoptive, transracial family parented by two moms.

꩜ I remember sitting at dinner with my partner's parents, telling them we were starting the adoption process. There was silence at the table; I stared into my salad and examined the shredded beets. Finally, after he'd gathered his wits and remembered to be polite, my father-in-law congratulated us. Later, at home, I held my partner as she wept, knowing that when her brother announced he and his wife were expecting their first child, my mother-in-law had said it was the happiest day of her life.

During our first phone call with the Ministry of Child and Family Services to start the information gathering process, the intake social worker asked my name and then my husband's name, assuming we were a heterosexual couple. When I gave her my partner's name, the social worker quickly tried to correct her mistake, explaining that the ministry didn't discriminate based on sexual orientation. Yet, from our very first phone call, I was left feeling excluded and began to have doubts about the ministry's biases.

It didn't end there. Throughout the adoption process, we were told consistently that it would probably take longer to find a match for us because we were not the ideal family that many social workers or birth families imagine for adoptive children. This was always followed by an awkward explanation that the ministry was not homophobic but wanted what was best for the children in care.

The notion that a family is a mom a dad and children and that anything else is somehow less is still a deeply held belief, although one that is slowly starting to change. Thankfully, the social worker who picked us saw beyond our sexuality and was not biased in favour of one mom/one dad families. She saw our home study and thought we'd be a good match for some twins she was trying to place. This potential match came quickly, but then came an excruciating four months of waiting while a few other families were considered and the social worker tried to bring the twins' foster family on board.

They were a Christian fundamentalist couple who initially opposed the match, so we were subjected to additional screening, which delayed the adoption process by several months. We had to meet the foster family so that they could be reassured that we were worthy parents in an attempt to have them tolerate, if not support, the decision. This was a healthy step for developing a working relationship with the foster family, but I can't help but think it was an extra step that a heterosexual couple probably would not have had to take. I remember sitting in a boardroom meeting the foster parents, thinking, "There, see? We're normal. We don't have two heads." Instead of meeting with them, all I wanted to do was see the twins we'd heard so much about. I wanted to witness their every movement and gesture, knowing that at fourteen months, they were becoming more mobile and changing so much every day.

After that initial meeting, we had to spend every waking moment with the foster parents for two weeks of overlap to get to know the kids and have the kids get to know us. While the foster parents would probably have scrutinized anyone, we felt at times like they were particularly unrelenting with us, asking questions like "Who cooks?" and making comments such as, "Your son needs a man around." We were also subject to their religious biases, including the assumption that we had chosen to go to hell because of our "lifestyle choice." Still, over the two-week period, a shift occurred in the foster parents' world view, as they swapped their beliefs steeped in stereotypes for ones based on first-hand experience. They saw us caring for the children. They saw the children responding to us, gradually coming to us for their needs to be met, and saw us meeting those needs at every opportunity. During the last meal we ate together, they said that they believed the children were well placed with us and that they thought we'd be great parents. Their surprise sanction helped us get over feeling like imposters at finding ourselves parents of fifteen-month-old twins after so many months of waiting and hoping.

~ I have witnessed a range of reactions to our twins having two moms, from blank expressions to questions about whether they'll have any male role models. Even the social workers who were relatively accepting of us wanted assurances that our children would have positive male influences in their lives. They seemed to assume that as a lesbian couple we didn't have any deep or lasting connections with men. This prompted an ongoing joke with our male friends about their having to try out to be positive role models for our kids. Now, they come bearing masculine gifts, such as a bobblehead Thor, a football, and many toy trucks and tractors, vying for the honour.

Shortly after bringing the kids home, we were at a barbecue with friends, and an otherwise progressive, open-minded woman said, "Which one of you is their mother?" There was momentary silence as everyone stopped chewing their burgers to hear how we'd answer. "We both are," said my partner.

When I feel insecure about being a mother or need to feel legitimized, I turn to science. All the studies say that children of gay and lesbian parents do as well as children of heterosexual parents in terms of emotional, cognitive, social, and sexual functioning. In other words, it is the quality of the relationships, not the gender of the parents, that matters. The only indicator that differentiates children of same-sex parents from children of heterosexual parents is the social stigma they may face because of their parents' sexual orientation. In fact, one recent study shows they have healthy psychological development and fewer behaviour problems than their peers.

We are no strangers to discrimination, so my partner and I feel well equipped to give our children the tools they need to face discrimination with their selves in tact. I didn't realize until I had kids that the years I spent feeling painfully ashamed of my sexuality were merely a training ground for what was to come later. Of course, having two moms may not be the only discrimination our children face. Our children do not look like us. Although my partner is half West Asian, we both "look" Caucasian, while the twins are biracial South Asian and Caucasian. This leads to people asking us where the children are from or whose they are.

On a plane recently, the flight attendant started speaking Spanish to our kids, assuming they were Latino. When she asked where they were from, I answered Canada. I could tell from her bewildered look that she had the best of intentions, so I continued on and told her they had Asian heritage. "Oh, I could have sworn they were Central American," she replied. Our kids will probably question their identities at some point, or many points, along the way. We thought about this and were wary of unduly burdening them. But after copious reading about this issue, fretting over what our children would have to deal with because they don't look like us or like most other people in our small town, we ultimately came to the conclusion that loving the children, exposing them to their cultural heritages and to other transracial adoptees would be enough to usher them through to adulthood with a healthy sense of self. Thankfully, on this matter, we also had good support from our social workers, who reminded us of our strengths as a family and believed in us.

For many months after we brought them home, I referred to my children simply by their names, adroitly avoiding any familial references. The first time I uttered "my son and daughter," I took a deep breath first, unable to look the other person in the eye and ready to bolt should my declaration be challenged. It was the same feeling I had during my long process of coming out, taking those first, tentative steps to say my partner's name to a stranger. I was expert at using gender-neutral pronouns when describing my personal life and could censor myself with ease. I didn't feel like my relationship was legitimate when coming out, just as I didn't feel legitimate as a parent at first.

This experience of becoming a "real" family has taught me many things so far, perhaps most importantly that most people are open and curious. Even if a handful are being judgmental, they are open to changing their judgments, especially when faced with a two-year-old child's toothy grin. In that instant, there is an opportunity to connect and break down barriers, just as we discovered while living with our children's foster family. Heck, if a lesbian couple can spend every waking moment for two weeks with a Christian fundamentalist couple and come out at the end as friends, there is hope in the world.

These days, I am getting better at fielding questions from people we meet: Which one of you is the mother? What country are your children from? What happened to their real mother? Are you their real mother? I know that these questions come with the best of intentions, not from someone intending to challenge our parental legitimacy. That is why I patiently answer the appropriate questions and engage with people so they can learn what is appropriate to ask. As I become more comfortable as a parent, my response to the outside world becomes more comfortable, too.

Recently, we flew to Florida, one of the handful of states that bans adoption by same-sex couples, for a vacation. We had many stopovers and multiple seatmates on the trip and were asked many times where our children were from and whose children they were. In answering one of the dozens of questions, I caught myself saying "my son and daughter . . ." It just rolled off my tongue. There I was, sitting in my aisle seat, my children beside me, with a glimmer in my eye. My partner didn't even notice, because there was nothing strange in this sentence anymore. She was feeling real as well. She too, has a son and daughter.

On this trip, we saw my mother- and father-in-law, who are so taken by their new grandchildren that they send boxes of gifts every few weeks and they swell with pride when telling friends or strangers about their newest family members. Seeing two happy parents with two happy, engaged, laughing, tumbling children has melted away their concerns, and they are already making plans to take our children on a Disney cruise. It is our turn to be happily surprised by the turnaround and acceptance we now feel from them.

The other evening, as I was lying beside my daughter while she went to sleep, she started touching my arm and saying "Mom" over and over while looking into my eyes. It was like she was getting it and reflecting to me that it is indeed real. I returned her big gaze and said, "Yes, I am your mom."

Jane Byers is a writer, vocational rehabilitation consultant and full-time mom. She had a short story published in the anthology *Very Short Stories* (Off Cut Press) and has had numerous poems published in *Horsefly*, *Fireweed*, *Our Times*, and *The New Orphic Review*. She lives in Nelson, British Columbia.

how i met my mother

LAURA BARCELLA

I STARTED LOOKING FOR my birth mother one month after my then-boyfriend, Mark, and I moved in together. I was twenty-seven, living in New York City, as fearless and fragile as I'd ever be. This, my longest relationship, had lasted nearly two years and had armed me with a newfound faux maturity. We had spent five hundred dollars at Ikea. We'd bought house plants and mug hooks. We adopted a stray cat named Batman. But Mark never seemed sure—about the cat, about me, about anything. My adoption was a dark sheet between us. It ruffled sometimes; sometimes he poked at it. But he could never touch me, never see me through it.

"Of course I'll support you through this," Mark said when I told him that I wanted to start searching for the woman who had given me up when I was an infant. Then he stroked my shoulder while his eyes said something else.

As an adoptee (sounds like "amputee," "refugee"), being forsaken by my biological mom had cursed me, for as long as I could remember, with a feeling of intrinsic exclusion, the sense that something was strongly Un-Right. My decision to start looking for her wasn't reached lightly; it took years of existential freak-outs, antidepressants, therapy, and liquor.

The notion that she might not want to be found—or, worse, that she wouldn't care one way or the other—haunted me. I had dire daydreams of finding nothing but an obituary. I imagined cancers and car accidents; I imagined everything.

I was adopted in 1977 in Washington, DC. My new parents were a young married couple who wanted kids but couldn't conceive. I was a textbook adoptee: shy and troubled, with an intense fear of abandonment. Years later, I learned that many of my most private feelings—the anger, fear, and rootlessness—were common among adoptees, part of what psychologist Dr. David Kirschner dubbed the "Adopted Child Syndrome," in which a child had no social context in which to recognize her feelings of absence.

I became my loss; my loss became me. Grief for my missing mom infiltrated my every word, wrinkle, fear, feeling. Even the notes from the foster home where I stayed before my adoptive parents brought me home reveal traces of my budding displeasure: "Very serious;" "cries often."

I cried even more as a toddler, throwing dramatic tantrums when I didn't get candy or my way. Still, I passed for normal in my grade-school years. Classmates knew my history, but we didn't talk about it in any real way. Instead, they used my adoptee status as ammo for vicious verbal brawls (think Vince Vaughn in *Dodgeball*: "You're adopted! Your parents don't love you!").

My adoptive parents did love me, though; that I never doubted. They had told me I was "chosen" when I was too young to remember otherwise, but we rarely discussed the adoption at length. And, ironically, strangers often remarked on the "resemblance" (light skin and eyes) between my a-mom and me.

On the outside, my childhood was loving and stable. Materially, I wanted for nothing. But I grew sadder in high school and college, underscoring my misery with dark eyeliner as I sang along to The Smiths ("I know I'm unlovable, you don't have to tell me").

I tried all the antidepressants. I tried meditation and marijuana. I tried bed-hopping and boy-swapping and moving across the country. In college dorm rooms and dirty dive bars, I tried tequila shot after vodka tonic after rum and Coke after after after . . . The drugs didn't work (do they ever?), and I knew that the void I was trying to fill—the endless depression—was about my missing birth mom. What I needed, more than drinks or boys or bright city lights, was to know who I looked like. Where did my gray-blue eyes and downturned mouth come from? Which members of my family loved rock music, sweets, and animals; which ones loathed sports and spiders and stood slightly bowlegged, like me?

Lacking in hard facts about their past, adoptees may fill the void the void they feel with fantasies. For most of my life, I had imagined my birth mother like a cool older sister. Maybe she was a well-travelled artist or musician, a glamorous groupie or a vet? My fantasy mom was a creative bohemian beauty with long blond hair and vintage hippie dresses she would give me. We would drink wine together at her kitchen table. Her house would smell of old velvet, amber incense, warmth.

꧁ Soon after moving in with Mark in Brooklyn, I hired a search agent, Lana, from the agency where I was adopted. She served as a go-between for adoptees and birth parents, facilitating the discreet exchange of first names and photos. Mine was a closed proceeding, so my adoptive parents never knew my birth mom. The documents were sealed. Lana encouraged me to write a letter to my mystery mom. "I'll pass it along," she said brightly before warning that "reunification" could take months, with no guarantee of a happy ending.

When Lana called a few weeks later, at the end of December 2004, I was out for dinner with a friend. "I have an update on your situation," she said. "I've made contact with your birth mom. Her name is Shelby. She sounds really nice, but she was nervous when we talked."

Lana said Shelby had held me when I was born and that she had kept my baby picture. She also said a letter—with photos—would arrive in my mailbox soon.

And it did. Two days after my boyfriend dumped me—via a mis- ·
sive he left inside my laptop—I received a (much nicer) letter from
the mother I'd never known. She included photos: yes, she looked like
me. She had given me up when she was twenty, a petite blond college
student with a passion for music. My birth father, she wrote—her dark-
haired, working-class boyfriend—had been out of the picture since
the beginning. I don't know if she had loved him, but he wasn't in the
delivery room.

Shelby's letter prompted a shaky email correspondence. It felt like
getting to know a childhood pen pal. We asked each other the most basic
of questions: What do you do on weekends? Do you like to travel? Seen
any good movies lately? They felt awkward and unnatural, my banal
exchanges with this woman I'd felt a part of, and painfully apart from,
for as long as I could remember. The unconscious amount of power I
had given to this stranger to save me from myself—it felt foolish.

I finally met Shelby at Christmastime, a few weeks before my
thirtieth birthday. I drove to her modest ranch house in a tiny blue-
collar town in Pennsylvania. We hadn't even talked on the phone yet. I
parked in her driveway and rang the doorbell, my heart clattering.

"I am so freakin' nervous, it's unbelievable!" Shelby exclaimed when
she saw me, before enfolding me in a long hug, then looking at me, hard.
"You're so beautiful!" she beamed, blue eyes shiny with tears.

I couldn't cry; I felt strangely removed, like I was watching a movie
of myself. Maybe I was just scared shitless. She was not the striking
bohemian I'd envisioned. She seemed bright-eyed and healthy and
stable; she was married, with no other kids.

She heated up some crab chowder for lunch. We looked at photo
albums, and she told me about her family: who had died of what; who
had married whom. Ron, her gruff husband, mainly kept to the basement and fiddled with his guitar. Shelby showed me her doll collection,
which filled an entire room, and she gave me one of her favourite dolls
to take home. I didn't tell her I thought doll-collecting was creepy.

We drove to a park near her house and walked around the lake. It was too cold to stay outside for long. By 5:00 PM, I was more than ready to get home. My parents were waiting to have dinner with me, excited to hear about the "other mother." Shelby and I promised to keep in touch. "Maybe we can go on vacation one day!" she suggested shrilly before handing me a palmful of chocolates for the road. (We both love sweets.)

It's been five years since we met in person. We don't talk much—we email occasionally. I suppose getting to know each other is a lifelong process. In some ways, finding Shelby was an exercise in disappointment. She's not the mom I thought I wanted. She is not a bohemian world traveller, or a veterinarian, or an artist. She's a thoroughly average, married, middle-class American woman. She uses fuchsia fonts in her email messages and writes with lots of exclamation points, and lives in the middle of nowhere with a room full of dolls. We don't have many things in common, but the things we do have—eyes, hair, body type— are important. I'd never seen myself physically reflected in a person before. It's something I always longed for.

My life has changed in some ways since I met her. After spending most of my twenties jumping from job to job, I've managed to hold down the same position, as an editor at an Internet company, for the last two years. That's nothing, though, compared to my b-mom's record—she's worked at the same book-packaging factory for twenty-plus years!

The me of today is many things: a homeowner, an editor, a writer, a reader, a sour-candy lover, a dog owner, a one-day wannabe parent. I see a therapist who specializes in adoption issues, and I read every adoption-related book I can hunt down on Amazon. I wish I could say that reconnecting with my birth mother significantly changed my connections with other people, that it magically led me to become the happy, self-assured woman I've always wanted to be. But life isn't magic; I still struggle with self-esteem and fears of abandonment. I still turn to relationships as an easy escape from my jumbled brain.

Finding my birth mother left me with fewer questions about where I came from, yes. But I'm still on antidepressants, and I might always be, and that's okay. Now thirty-three, I've learned that my life's central challenge is accepting myself the way I am in any moment — even when it's not pretty, even when I'm sad, morose, lonely, or introspective. There was nothing wrong with me when my birth mother put me up for adoption, and there's nothing wrong with me now, no matter how wrong I may feel sometimes. I'm learning to accept that the saddest part of me — the child who felt so separate, so different from "normal" people — may be with me to stay. But if she's never leaving, I might as well learn to love her.

Laura Barcella is a writer and editor currently living in San Francisco. Her writing has appeared in more than forty magazines, newspapers, and websites, including *Salon*, *The Village Voice*, *NYLON*, *ELLEGirl*, *Time Out New York*, *CNN*, and the *Chicago Sun-Times*. She is currently editing an anthology of essays about pop icon Madonna, to be published in March 2012. Visit her personal site at laurabarcella.com and her book's website at madonnaandmebook.com.

finding sheila

LIZ M. FORBES

YEARS AGO, WITH CAUTIONARY warnings, my mother often drove me by a particular street in Victoria near the Royal Jubilee Hospital that once was the site of a home for "wayward girls" who were pregnant "out of wedlock." I always craned my neck, hoping to see what "girls like that" looked like. When, at age seventeen, I became one of those girls, I expected I would end up there. Instead, my mother sent me to live with my father in the BC interior where I endured small-town isolation and my stepmother's hostility.

I dealt with my situation by avoiding any thought or talk about my pregnancy. I had my baby with my eyes shut and never saw her. A social worker gave me papers and birth registration, and I had to give her a name. Writing the name Sheila, which I had long ago chosen for my first-born daughter, made the baby's existence real. I cried. I cried all that week in the maternity ward, hearing other babies cry, my baby cry, milk pouring from my breasts, and still I refused to speak of the birth. Once back in Victoria, the baby's father, Richard, and I resumed our relationship, but there were too many unspoken feelings to make it work. I assured myself we had made the right choice, but Richard and I did not talk about it.

Richard is black; his was one of the few black families in Victoria in 1956. And yes, racism existed. I had just graduated from high school and was living at home when I met him at a house party. I had never spoken to a black person before. He was fun, kind and gentle. Soon I was in love, but my parents, whom I had thought liberal, refused to let me date him. Between working at a bookstore and lying on my bed listening to records of Harry Belafonte and Louis Armstrong, I still found ways to see Richard nearly every day for months until morning sickness gave me away.

Richard and I were both popular top students at our respective schools, and we thought our child would easily find a good home. I had naively stipulated my ideal adoptive family on the papers I had signed. I gave birth to Sheila on August 19, 1957. Two weeks later, I began my nursing training at Royal Jubilee Hospital, living in residence. I buried all my feelings and carried on, barely.

Eleven months later, I received a call from a social worker. The residence phone was in the hall with our dorms open on both sides. "Sheila has not been adopted." I heard these words through the chatter and laughter of my fellow nurses as they passed obliviously by me.

"Children like these are hard to adopt," the social worker explained. Children like what? I thought. Was something wrong with her?

"No one wants a mixed-race child," she went on, but then added that luckily someone looking for a "hard-to-adopt child" wanted Sheila. Would I come in to sign more papers?

Distraught, I phoned Richard. I wanted to go and get her. I needed to talk, but he had a cold and couldn't—or wouldn't—drive to pick me up. Something died in me that day. I didn't care much about anything, and definitely did not care about Richard any longer. I began to drink wildly on my days off. My behaviour spun out of control. I ignored my breakdowns until the outburst of rage when I trashed a whole table of dishes and drink glasses in a late-night Chinese restaurant. My date, whom I hardly knew, tried to console me, but I ran crying and sobbing out into the night and collapsed on the street. All I could think about was my unwanted baby girl.

I left nursing in my second year, married, and had a son. The next year I turned twenty-one, a coming-of-age milestone in 1960. My father sent me a dozen red roses; my mother gave me a cultured pearl necklace. I felt it was all a mockery. My husband and I were struggling financially; I was pregnant again and depressed. I maintained a good front but I was choked with guilt over giving up Sheila. Grief bubbled up and caught me unawares. At times I wanted to die. The next child was a daughter, to whom I clung obsessively, not even allowing my husband to hold her. A son followed the next year and the depression grew deeper. Suicide haunted me, and I twice made plans. One day, I just walked into the bath-room, ran the bath, stepped in, and put a razor blade to my wrist—I felt nothing. To this day, I don't know what stopped me from killing myself.

The next day, I wrote a letter to Sheila. I told her that her dad and I had loved each other, that she came from caring people who'd made a huge mistake and regretted not keeping her. I took this letter to Family and Children's Services and requested that they give it to my daughter when she was of age. I asked if Sheila were healthy and happy, but the social worker I spoke to said they couldn't tell me. Yet I knew I needed to know something if I were to survive this trauma.

A couple of weeks later, I received a phone call to see the children's services supervisor. And I met an amazing woman named Bernice Levitz Packford. I swear her eyes bored into my heart, and she knew every-thing about me. When I talked, she listened with compassion and finally said she could give me information about my daughter. Ms. Packford indicated a manila folder on her desk. It was a report from a social worker who had visited the family about another adoption and was so impressed she had written a glowing account of Sheila's progress. Ms. Packford told me Sheila's adoptive parents were professionals, lived in a small town, and had older biological children. Sheila had dark curly hair, a great smile, loved to dance, and had won a baby contest for the best personality. She was healthy, loved, and a great joy to her family. Finally, I was able to shed some of my guilt and focus on my children at home. Getting myself back was a long process involving therapy and pills. But I was still determined to find Sheila one day.

As the years passed, I contacted Parent Finders and put ads in the papers searching for information. I followed dark-skinned girls in the streets, searching their faces for a family likeness. I even stalked a young teen in my car—right age, right skin colour—and asked her if her name were Sheila. One thing I shied away from was questioning my parents—I suspected they knew but I didn't want to hear them lie to me.

Not until my father was dying in the late 1980s did I dare to ask him. He told me Harry, his old life insurance friend, knew Sheila's adoptive family. I phoned Harry, but he was flustered and denied any knowledge. A couple of days later he called back; he swore me to secrecy: a Dr. Watkins in Kimberly had adopted Sheila, then later moved to Winnipeg. I phoned every Watkins in Winnipeg with no luck.

I kept Richard and his mother Ethel informed of my search. (Richard is an only child and Sheila is his only child.) Richard confessed he also stared at dark-skinned girls, wondering if one could be his daughter. When BC opened the adoption registry, first the passive registry and later the active one, I registered and paid my money. In 1992, I received a phone call telling me registry workers had found my birth daughter, Sheila.

For thirty-five years I had longed for this moment, but my first response was panic. Could I meet my adult daughter, not the baby I mourned for, not the child I wanted to nurture, but an adult who might hate me or be indifferent? I was terrified.

Sheila had agreed to talk to me, the social worker said. We arranged for me to phone the next night.

That evening was a blur of conflicting feelings as my buried emotions welled to the surface: Would I like Sheila? How would her presence affect our lives? Who was she? I poured a numbing glass of scotch. I had a new career, financial independence, a new relationship and lifestyle. My two sons were living their lives well, and my daughter,

Maureen, had recently given me a grandson. I was finally in a friendly relationship with Mike, the father of my three children, following our dreadful divorce.

What if I had no room for anyone else? Most of the family were aware I had had a child before I married. Mike knew I had dated Richard; they worked together. Since Mike was jealous, I had always refused to tell him who Sheila's father was. Now he would meet her and instantly figure it out. I poured another glass of scotch—my family coping technique—and fell into maudlin memories, long processed and boxed away.

Sheila lived in Ontario, and her husband, Dan, picked up the phone the next night. He said Sheila had gone out for the evening. Had she forgotten? Dan hinted at some troubles and assured me that finding her birth parents would help.

The following night, I answered the phone to hear a throaty, sexy voice. "Mum? This is Sheila." For some reason I'd thought she would sound like me, with the slightly British voice my family and I have after growing up in Victoria. But she sounded like a stranger who was calling me Mum.

Feeling stunned and disconnected, I needed a drink. When I heard clinking of ice cubes down the phone line, I understood. She explained she had panicked last night and gone out. Oh Gawd, I understood: we are alike. We talked that night and every night, sometimes late, sometimes crying, and sometimes laughing. I still stumbled over her voice until I remembered her birth father's deep, throaty voice. Of course.

Apart from threatening to run away and find her "real" mother when she was sixteen, Sheila hadn't wanted to find me until her two children were born. She had loved her adoptive parents, who had given her the life I had imagined. The fact that the Watkins were both dead now made this reunion easier. They already had four children when they decided adopt her. Sheila told me when Dr. Watkins first went to see her, the foster caregiver said, "You do not want to adopt this child, all she does is cry."

He walked into her darkened room, smelled the rank air, and examined the eleven-month-old girl. He held Sheila in his arms. "This child has ear infections and needs care. I am taking her."

Sheila and I did not physically meet for at least nine months, a symbolic birthing time. Perhaps because we were both scared, neither of us could find time for a visit. By my standards, she was wealthy and glamorous: she drove a BMW, entertained lavishly, and stabled her purebred in nearby Aurora. She had been a professional dancer, had won the world competition more than once in Latin American dancing. She was a beautiful combination of Caucasian and black. I was granola: short and overweight with greying hair; I wore Birkenstocks and no makeup, lived in a cottage in the country and managed a group home. My other three kids followed their own nonconformist paths, which didn't produce much money.

When we met at last, I'm sad to say my big concern was my clothes, my frumpiness. Ideally, I'd wanted us to meet one-on-one, in a quiet coffee house where we could strip down to our core. But Sheila didn't have enough time, and Richard's mother, Ethel, wanted to come with me to meet her. So I travelled to Vancouver with elegant, black Ethel, hat-and-glove wearing Ethel. Sheila's "new" grandmother and I rode the elevator to Sheila and Dan's room at the Hotel Vancouver. A beautiful, agitated, fashion-model woman in yellow silk answered the door: my daughter. Two adorable children peeked around her long nylon-encased legs. Sheila was in high heels; I was wearing Doc Martens, slacks, and a leather jacket. I wanted to hug her but was unable to bridge the space that hung between us.

Confused, I couldn't read her needs, and I felt intimidated. I had no map for meeting my daughter for the first time. She was annoyed with Dan, her husband, who now couldn't take the children while she visited. Sheila closed the door sharply, leaving us to wait outside. In a few minutes, she and the children emerged, all in coats. Ethel and I followed as she stalked down the hall to the elevator.

We walked to a park; gradually Sheila and I relaxed our guard. Ethel was, as always, composed. She had prayed for this day, and nothing could shake her joy.

That evening we had drinks and dinner with Sheila's father, his wife, and one of my sons. The next day, January 9, 1993, Richard, Sheila, and I attended a post-adoption reunion forum put on by Family Services of Greater Vancouver. We had special permission to attend with our daughter even though the sessions are usually only for one of the adoption mix. Sheila sat across the room from Richard and me, so she could watch us.

At lunch, the three of us talked, sharing feelings and old misconceptions. We laid many demons to rest and began the bonding process. At last I saw Sheila as a daughter I could embrace and build a relationship with—a person with whom I could be myself.

Sheila and I continued to phone, write letters, and email. She managed a few short visits to the west coast, often with the children. But even though Sheila was generous with lavish gifts and embraced the reunion wholeheartedly, there was still something missing between us. She found her relationship with her grandmother, father, and half siblings easier than the one with me. In one of her many letters she voiced her worry that she wasn't as intellectual as my other three children, and that she would have been a better person if I had raised her.

I had my own worries—that I was a disappointment to her and she would never be able to forgive me for abandoning her to adoption.

We needed the "remember when" stories as family bonds, so I told her about Harry, my Dad's friend, selling life insurance to Dr. Watkins. I told her about my Mum's friend Margaret who must have known Sheila because she was the public health nurse in Kimberly. I found photographs of me pregnant with Sheila at the same lake that Sheila frequented with her adopted family. Sheila found pictures of me in her Grandmother Ethel's albums, including a couple of me at Christmas dinner. She was delighted to figure out I was already pregnant with her in the photos.

The final barriers fell when Sheila brought her Grandmother Ethel up-island to visit me and my other daughter, Maureen. When we met for lunch, Maureen, a storyteller, began with family tales, some about me, some about herself and her brothers. As three generations of women related by blood, we sat for hours, shared stories and bonded. Sheila belonged.

Two years later, when Sheila flew in from Toronto for Ethel's ninetieth birthday, we showed her all the places in Victoria that Ethel and I loved. She saw the schools I attended and the high school where both her dad and grandmother went. We went up Mount Douglas, a childhood haunt of mine, ate lunch in Cadboro Bay, drove through the tony parts of town and along to Willows Beach where her dad and I had hung out. We visited all the memory-building places important to Ethel and me. I even cheekily showed her the lane in Oak Bay near my house where she was conceived in the front seat of her dad's car. Ethel sniffed in displeasure as we laughed.

Sheila's mission that day was to order ninety helium balloons for Ethel's birthday celebration. We found the balloon shop at 1461 Hampshire Road—exactly where I had lived when I dated Sheila's dad. The house had been demolished a few years before, but we stood in the shop where the entry hall had been, where Sheila had been present in utero, and had a staff member take our picture.

While Sheila and I went shopping, we left Ethel sitting in the sun at an outside tea table where my front gate once was. Giddy, high on life, arms around each other, we returned to see Ethel being chatted up by an attractive man. She looked beautiful. We felt beautiful. If Ethel at ninety could still draw admirers, anything was possible.

"Mum, someone should write about us," Sheila said.

In 1976, Liz Maxwell Forbes left her birth city of Victoria, British Columbia, for her adopted community of Cowichan Valley. An unexpected bonus of finding Sheila is the bond she found with her "new" granddaughter, who asks for advice on decision making and love. Liz does not have the answers.

sisters at last

NICOLE M. CALLAHAN

I WAS STANDING ON the porch when they pulled up in their rental car, practically bouncing on my heels because it seemed altogether too cool and dignified and not at all *right* to be sitting calmly in the house, waiting for my sister—my *sister*—to walk up and ring the doorbell. All I could think was, *Cindy is here. She flew all the way across the country to meet me. I cannot just sit in my living room waiting for her to knock on the door.*

I managed to wait until she got partway up the driveway, and then I bounded down from the porch and met her, breathless and nervous and a little choked up. She said hello and hugged me tightly. I thanked her for coming all this way, and we walked into the house arm in arm.

All through that first day together, our husbands stared from me to Cindy and back again. It was obvious they were eager to determine what we had in common, just as Cindy and I were. At the same time, we joked about the inevitable and compulsive search for similarities; when her husband said, "You both just tucked your hair behind your ear at the same time, the exact same way," Cindy asked, "How many different ways are there to do that?" while I told him, "You would too, if you had long hair."

꧁ My sister Cindy was born in Korea six years before me and spent her early years with her grandmother in Seoul. Her parents, my birth parents, had moved to Seattle with our half-sister Mia to establish the family business, and they sent for Cindy when she was four or five. Cindy had no memory of the mother she hadn't seen since she was a baby, and she didn't know what to expect. Right away, even at her young age, she felt frightened and disappointed by the deeply unhappy woman she met. From the day she reappeared in her parents' lives, her mother abused her.

When Cindy was six years old, her mother got pregnant again. She wasn't happy about it, particularly after learning that the baby was "another girl." When I was born in May 1981, dangerously premature, my birthparents placed me for adoption, and my adoptive parents brought me to the small town in southern Oregon where I spent my childhood. When Cindy and Mia asked about me, my birth parents told them that I had died at birth. Because Cindy had made my birth mother angry on the day I was born, her mother told her that it was her fault she had "miscarried," her fault her little sister was dead.

The abuse got worse as the years went on, especially for Cindy, the youngest. She spent much of her childhood attempting to run away from home. She would disappear for days, sleeping in the woods, or in a church bathroom, or somewhere along her route to school. Sometimes she was found and brought home; other times she returned because she was hungry and had to eat. One time Child Protective Services took her away, but her father talked them into letting her return home, promising that the beatings would stop. Within a month, her mother was abusing her again.

When Cindy was twelve, her parents finally ended their unhappy marriage. After a few terrifying months alone with her mother, Cindy went to live with her father. His new wife was kind to her and helped give her the first safe, real home she had ever known. Within a few years, their family relocated to Guam, where Cindy graduated from high school. Later she moved to Portland—where her mother and half-sister had since moved—and started college.

Cindy worked part-time at her mother's grocery store while she took college classes. Mia had told Cindy that their mother had changed, so

Cindy decided to give her one more chance in Portland. But although her mother could no longer physically harm her, the verbal and emotional abuse seemed even worse than she remembered. One night, while Cindy was working alone in the store, a couple of teenagers stole a six-pack of beer. She chased them for a few blocks before realizing that she had no idea how to deal with them even if she caught them, so she returned to the store to call the police. When her mother found out about the robbery, she screamed at Cindy in front of the police, and told her to get out. Cindy left, and she never went back.

That was the end of her relationship with her mother. Soon after, Mia moved to Los Angeles with their mother while Cindy stayed in Portland. She finished school, found a job, and got married. She stayed in contact with Mia, and with her father and stepmother. As far as she knew, they were her only family.

A few days into 2008, Cindy received a call from Mia, who told her that they had another sister. A sister who had been placed for adoption. The sister they thought was dead.

In late 2007, I had decided to write a letter to my birth mother through a confidential intermediary, requesting updated health information. I had reached an age at which it seemed important to know as much as possible about my family medical history, in part because I was expecting my first child. I was willing to pay the intermediary's fee of five hundred dollars. She called herself a "search angel" and urged me to pursue an in-person reunion with my birth parents. I emphasized that while I was open to some contact, I did not want my birth parents pressured in any way.

When my birth mother received my letter, she was unable to make sense of it, so she asked Mia to translate it. And that was how Mia learned the truth about my existence. She immediately called Cindy to tell her that their little sister was alive.

To say that Cindy has low expectations of her family is an understatement. But, as she told me later, she also never imagined that her parents could have hidden an entire *person* from her. She wasn't brought up to question her parents, and when they told her that her sister, who was born ten weeks early, had died at birth, she had believed them.

After she learned the truth from Mia, Cindy asked her father about me. She asked him to explain what happened, why they had lied. Instead he said, "Who told you there was an adoption? How could you think that was true? Your sister died; there was nothing we could do."

Eventually, with her stepmother's help, she pried the truth out of him. But she had been disappointed, yet again, by her family. Of course, her father and mother have starkly different versions of events at the time of my birth and adoption; each blames the other for what happened. Whether one parent is right, or both, or neither, it's impossible to know. After so many years, they may not even remember everything that transpired.

Cindy was angry when she found out that they had hidden the adoption from her. But she was also relieved that I had escaped her fate. "I would have fought to protect you," she told me, "but I don't know what I could have done if that woman really wanted to hurt you."

Both my birth parents did elect to share medical history with me and claimed they were eager to meet me one day, although initially they found it difficult to speak to me about my adoption. Mia was very gracious and welcoming, but I think that she, too, was afraid I would think ill of their family if I knew too many details about how dysfunctional it had been. Cindy was the only one willing to tell me what she thought might have happened, based on what she could remember and what she managed to glean from her father's terse answers. She said that I "deserved to know everything," and while I was glad for her candour, what made me feel the most gratitude was simply knowing that she cared about me already and wanted to know me.

❦ I know that Cindy is strong because she always had to be. But what strikes me most about her is her openness and honesty, her great capacity for hope and love, when her own mother—one of the people who should have loved her most—failed her so deeply. Cindy has endured things that would make some people turn their backs on the very idea of "family." Given her past, I would have understood if she said thanks, but no thanks, when she learned about me. Yet in her first letter she told me how much she wanted to know me, and she eagerly exchanged long emails with me—sometimes daily—along with regular phone calls. She asked me to let her know when she could come for a visit.

In early 2008, when we first connected, I was living with my husband and daughter in North Carolina, and Cindy and her husband were in Oregon. I felt a little surprised by how much Cindy wanted to meet me. Even though I had wondered about and wanted to know my sisters all my life, I never really imagined they would feel the same way once they knew about me. But as soon as I felt ready, Cindy and her husband took time off and booked flights to come visit us.

At first, it was far easier for us to notice the differences between us. We had, of course, exchanged many photographs prior to our meeting, but I thought this new sister looked quite different in person. I noted her cute freckles, which I have never had. Cindy commented on the fact that the shape of our eyes, nose, and mouth are similar, but far from identical. As my husband put it, "it's certainly believable that you're sisters, it's just not obvious."

She was quiet, a little shy, and I could tell that despite her happiness she was also overwhelmed. But as the hours passed, we both relaxed and began sharing more, and we began to see similarities, too. Cindy purses her lips exactly the way I do when she's thinking hard or looking at someone appraisingly to try to determine if they're telling the truth. We have some of the same nervous habits, and we're both clumsy—we actually get clumsier when we are excited, which is why, the first night of her visit, I managed to walk straight into a door frame and bruise the bridge of my nose. Like me, Cindy can really rant when she wants to—it's a glorious spectacle, accompanied by dramatic expressions, wild gestures, sometimes even fist shaking—a trait I have never liked in myself, but one that I love in her.

Over dinner, she saw me absently writing on my placemat with my fingertip—sometimes, when I am thinking or talking, I will take invisible notes without fully realizing what I'm doing, writing with my finger on whatever surface is handy—and she exclaimed, "Our dad does that all the time! I do it, too."

At first, I could only stare at her. "I've never met anyone else who does that!"

"Neither have I," she said, "except you and Dad. I always thought I just picked it up from watching him all my life."

"Well," my husband said, nodding at me, "maybe not."

As we talked late into the night, I had to keep reminding myself that this was not simply a nice new friend sitting next to me—this was my sister. My long-lost sister. It was so strange, and thrilling, and at times too much to believe. Growing up adopted, I had to learn how to make distinctions that most kids never even had to think about. I bristled when others referred to my biological parents as my "real parents"; I drew a clear line between love and blood, and put the emphasis on the former. But that was before I met my only full sister and my closest biological relative. While looking at her was not exactly like looking in a mirror, I could not deny how much it meant to finally meet someone who was a blood connection.

Suddenly I remembered being in Grade 4, the only Korean girl in my small parochial school, and telling my mother that I just wanted to look into a face that looked like mine. Sometimes I pretended that I had a sister or best friend who looked like me. In Cindy, I found that, and also much *more*—the big sister I'd always wanted and never imagined I would find, who not only knew about me and tried to answer the questions I'd had for a lifetime, but also wanted to be a meaningful part of my life.

When I used to imagine getting in touch with my birth family, I never really thought our relationship would evolve much past the occasional phone call or letter, cards exchanged at Christmas. I certainly did not picture one of them flying over three thousand miles just to meet and hug me; I just didn't think they would take such an interest in me, let alone want to be a *real* family member to me.

One evening a few days into Cindy's visit, she and I went for a stroll through the darkened, rain-drenched streets of my neighbourhood. As we walked, we talked about how our relationship might develop now that we had finally met. "I don't really know how to be a sister, because I've never been one before," I confessed to her. "I just know that I want us to be friends as well as family, and feel comfortable sharing things and asking things of one another. I want us to trust each other and be a source of support when things are tough. I know you're used to having low expectations of family, but I don't want you to have low expectations of me — I want you to believe that you can depend on me."

I hesitated, suddenly feeling a bit self-conscious, wondering if I was asking too much from a person who had only met me a few days ago. "I know it may take some time for us to get there," I said quickly. "And that's okay. That is just the sort of relationship I want to have, eventually, and it's worth as much time as it takes."

There was a little pause, and then Cindy answered, "You're already there with me, Nikki."

❧ I'm nearing thirty, and I have a child of my own, yet I can still remember how it felt to be a little adopted girl growing up in a white family in a white town. I would avoid looking in the mirror because what I saw there made me feel so alone; I longed for someone, anyone, who could understand how I felt. So it still seems too incredible that after a lifetime of wondering about my birth family, wondering especially about my sisters, I was given the chance to meet Cindy, who is beautiful and brilliant, loyal and strong — and a part of me in a way that no one else has ever been before. Having her in my life now seems like more than I deserve, the sort of happy ending I never would have dared to dream of, an imaginary friend become real.

   While our blossoming sisterly relationship has filled both of us with a sense of wonder and new hope, we do live many states apart, and we don't see each other as frequently as we would like. It's still so new and strange for me to say the words *I miss my sister.* My family and friends hear it and do a double take; they are used to thinking of me as an only child, and I am, too. I'm so glad that I now know my sister *well* enough to miss her.

   I will always remember that rainy March afternoon when Cindy and I finally met, how tightly we hugged each other, how we were both trying not to cry. We were so eager, in those first hours together, to seek out any and all similarities—we made that too significant, perhaps because we both half-worried that we wouldn't feel like "real" sisters if we didn't share certain traits or features. But I never needed to fret that Cindy wouldn't seem like my sister just because we look different, have different personalities, and grew up never knowing each other. Our relationship is not *supposed* to be one thing or another; we get to create it now, together, and choose what it will be.

   Cindy says that it is a miracle to her just to know that I am alive after all. "I feel as though I can never know or assume anything—in a *good* way," she wrote to me in a letter, not long after we found each other. "Now that I have a sister I never knew existed, I have to believe that anything is possible. I'm not sure if I could have really missed someone I didn't even know, but having the chance to know you now has enriched my life."

   We are not like sisters who grew up together; without that common family history, we know that we will never be. But we are still sisters, as grateful for one another as if we had always known each other, and I feel sure that we will always be close.

A graduate of Johns Hopkins University, Nicole Callahan has worked in the non-profit sector for nearly a decade as a writer and advocate. She lives with her family in Durham, North Carolina.

the adoption: helen's story

BARBARA-HELEN HILL

I'VE HAD THREE BABIES in my life, and the first one I was forced to give up for adoption by my parents and grandmother. Maybe in their wise ways they knew I was too young to be a mom and take good care of him. Maybe because I was living at home, my father worried he would end up supporting the baby when he already had nine to feed. I don't know the reason, but it was a painful time, and it was a good excuse for me to get drunk.

I spent the duration of my pregnancy in the Salvation Army Home for Unwed Mothers in Hamilton, Ontario, which is about fifty kilometres from Six Nations of the Grand River, where I was born and raised. I went to the home when I was about five months pregnant I think. It was shameful to be pregnant and not married in the 1960s.

I don't remember having any choice in the matter, even though I was twenty years old. I remember feeling like I was a bad girl for having brought this on my family. I remember having dreams of making something better of my life, and I even dreamed that my dad would change his mind and let me keep my child, figuring that once he saw the baby, he would have no choice but to let me keep him or her.

I felt very shy at the home at first. I was very naive in many ways and thought that everyone was there because their parents made them go there and they had to give up their babies. That was not the case: one or two girls who seemed to be older had chosen to go there, have their babies, and then give them away, like a baby was going to cramp their style.

The home was a large, old house, three storeys at least. The place was warm and friendly, and our rooms were comfortable. There was a classroom of sorts for those who were still in school. During my time there, I took a correspondence course and would go to the classroom every morning, trying to be studious and better myself. We had a common dining room, and the meals were quite good, although I didn't like the steak and kidney pie and remember trying to give it away to someone else. We were close to the Hamilton Mountain, and we walked all over. The street the home was on also had a little store and a coffee shop and a few businesses; we were only about six blocks from downtown Hamilton, so the girls and I would walk there as well. As we window-shopped, we dreamed of how it would be when we were back home with our families.

I don't recall going to the doctor for prenatal checkups, but I must have because I remember thinking that the home took very good care of me — by that, I mean I was fed well, had a nice, comfortable bed, and was warm and dry. I think we did chores, because I recall helping with the laundry, but the matrons and the Salvation Army women seemed very kind and caring to me. I don't remember how the others felt, but I know I felt good there. I know I blocked a lot out of my memories so I don't really remember a physical examination, but there might have been a doctor who came to the home to make sure that we were all right.

I do recall a visit from one of the council members from my territory who came when I was in the middle of my eighth month. I know I felt really nervous talking to him, because I thought no one knew that I was pregnant, let alone in this home in Hamilton. I was truly surprised when the matron said I had a visitor. He took me to a little coffee shop a block or two from the home and asked me to agree to give my child to a couple he knew who would be good parents and who desperately wanted a child.

I don't remember giving him that permission. I do remember saying I didn't think I could give a child to a family from my community, because I would want to see him or her all the time and that wouldn't be allowed. I didn't want to give my child away in the first place. I wanted to keep my baby, and I knew it would be too painful to know that he was that close and that I wouldn't have care of him. So I believe I said no, and he told me that the baby would then go to the Children's Aid Society (CAS).

I remember going to the hospital and having the baby. I remember them bringing him to me every day to feed and then taking him back to the nursery. I remember crying all the time. I remember crying as I fed him and held him and loved him, and then I remember walking away from the hospital about a week later to go back to the home, where my parents were to pick me up.

I wasn't able to talk about the baby for the next month. I was scared. I think I felt like I did when I was sexually abused—if I didn't talk about it, it would go away. If I didn't talk about the baby (I'd called him Michael Wade), the memory and pain would go away. I remember being told to show up at the CAS in Brantford, the nearest office to my home, to sign papers to give him up for adoption. I remember my mom and two brothers getting into a car with my aunt and going away for a "vacation," leaving my dad and me to watch the younger children. To me, it felt like my mom didn't want to help me, like she ran away. I remember canning tomatoes with my dad on the night before the CAS meeting, neither of us saying anything about my baby or where we were to go the next day.

At the CAS office, I got to hold my baby again as the social worker took my dad into her office, leaving us in the waiting room. I cried and said I wanted to keep him. I remember the lady coming out with dad and her shaking her head and me having to go in and sign the papers to let him go. I had asked CAS to put him with an Indian family if they could, and she told me she would see what they could do, because there were a lot of couples wanting children. Then I walked out of the office with my dad and went to the Kirby Hotel to drink beer. I think both of us that day knew that we did something horribly wrong, but to me, there seemed to be no other choice.

For the next twenty-five years or so, I did my best to wipe out those memories. But not a day went by that I didn't think of my baby, Mike. Not a day went by that I didn't wonder where he was, how he was, what he was doing. I didn't tell anyone I'd had a baby, so I thought it was my secret. But when I went out drinking one night, I was asked by some girls from my community why I didn't keep him. I had to tell them that my parents wouldn't let me, and I had to tell them his father wasn't there to support me either—that his father wasn't from our reserve like they thought. Everyone knew that I had had a baby; I had been secretive about the home for nothing. I started to get angry, but I kept that inside. I covered the feelings of shame and guilt with drinking.

Four years later, I had another son and refused to give him away. I thought I was being a good mom and being responsible. When my son was almost two years old, I married, and a year and a half later I had a daughter. Unfortunately, my husband abused me and my children. I dared not mention the child I had given up for adoption, because I was afraid of how my husband would react. We left him after nine years, and he died three months later from a heart attack related to alcoholism. We moved back to Canada, where I went to work in a drug and alcohol prevention office in my home community. While travelling to different communities in southern Ontario, I would look around to see if I could spot my first son, whom I thought at the time of his birth had looked like my brother. Even though I didn't know where my son was, I kept looking to see if I could find him.

I was in school in Buffalo, New York, finishing my BA, in 1996, when I had my first book published. The book was a mixture of poetry and short stories and was titled *Shaking the Rattle: Healing the Trauma of Colonization.*

It was partly the stories of different clients that I'd worked with and partly my feelings and what I'd learned; it contained narrative essays on healing and recovery from abuse and addictions. The dedication read:

> I dedicate this book to my children: Monica Lynn, for her beauty, and the courage that she has in carrying on the duties of women in our traditions and the human way. Timothy Lorne for his words, his encouragement, and his ability to grow with me. For both of them for their support and their determination to not let me lag behind in the growing up stages. For Michael wherever you are. I wish you every happiness in the world. May the Creator bless you as he has blessed me, with love and children that give happiness in endless ways. Finally for the children and grandchildren to come in the next seven generations.

I thought nothing better could happen. But while I was home for the Christmas break, I got a call from CAS saying that they had a young man looking for his mom. I stuttered and stammered and asked if it was my son. The woman calling told me yes and that we might reunite within a month. I almost fainted and called all eight of my siblings and my mom. The next day, I got another call from the CAS: my son had done the paperwork and was ready to meet me—would it be okay if she gave him my phone number? I told her of course. I waited and waited for his phone call, and about two hours later, CAS called again to say that they were having phone troubles and he'd get to me as soon as he could.

Mike was working at a library in a community next to mine and finally went to the office across the way to phone me. "Mom," he said. "Is it okay if I call you mom?" I said yes, of course, by all means. He told me where he was and how to get there. I called my sister and asked her to come with me and to bring me her copy of my book so I could give it to him.

We went to the library, and when I walked in he looked totally different than I had imagined—he didn't look like my brother, he looked like my dad and me. We introduced our support teams: he had his best buddy John with him, who was also adopted, and I had my sister. I gave him the copy of my book, and, at my prompting, he read the dedication and he cried.

We talked and caught up with each other for about an hour, and then we arranged to meet another sister for lunch and then to go on to introduce him to my mom, his gramma. It turns out that my mom and dad were friends with Mike's adopted uncle and aunt and visited them quite often. Mom said she remembered bouncing this little boy and girl on her foot, playing pony with them.

After reuniting with Michael, I went through a period of anger that I didn't understand. I loved him, I wanted him back in my life, I wanted him to be happy and not reject me as I had rejected him or what must have seemed as rejection, even though it was out of my hands. I had a hard time speaking to him. I avoided him for a few months except to keep in touch by phone. After a lot of journalling and a lot of crying, I realized that I was enraged at the fact that I had left a young baby at CAS, and that thirty-six years later, I had this young man calling me Mom. I wasn't angry at him, but I so wanted to strangle my dad and my gramma, both of whom were deceased by that point.

I always write to help me work through things, and sometimes there is something salvageable in it. I wrote the following poem for Mike, but I guess it is really about me and my terrifically strong mind that has helped me through the trauma of having to follow orders and give him up.

You're Too Little (1997)

you're too little

how can you be here?
when you're too little
you were just a baby

when I gave you away
you're too little

how can you drive a car?
when you're too little
you were just a baby
when they took you

how can you talk to me?
when you're too little
you were just a baby
when you left

how can you have a job?
when you're too little

how can you be a dad?
when you're too little

how can you be so responsible?
for all the things you say
when you're too little
you're just a babe

you left when you were one week old
you left because of orders
not mine but theirs
now you're grown
and you are here
but to me you're still

too little

Things got better. I did the grieving and got over being angry with my parents and grandmother, and we have all learned about each other. I am so blessed to have my son back, and when he and his wife got married, he asked me to stand up for him. My granddaughter presented us all with a wonderful little boy almost three years ago now, and my son and his wife adopted a little boy who was only ten days older than that great-grandson of mine.

Today, I marvel at the strength of mothers. Many will die before they let anything happen to their children. Many will abdicate that responsibility for whatever reason and turn to drugs and alcohol or other addictions. Many will get sick and not be able to take care of children, but nevertheless, they are still mothers. I believe deep down that when all is said and done, they would give up their lives for their children to protect them and keep them from harm—and maybe that is what I did.

I've learned, as a grown and somewhat mature grandmother and great-grandmother, that each of us must choose our own path. Each of us makes our own mistakes and suffers the consequences or reaps the rewards. I did suffer giving my son up for adoption, but I also reaped the rewards in the end by meeting him and building a relationship with him.

If I had a prayer for each of you reading this book, it would be that you find the peace in your heart to trust in your higher power to look after those babies. Make the most loving choices you can for your babies, and then help them make healthy choices for themselves.

Barbara-Helen Hill is an artist and writer from Six Nations of the Grand River Territory in southern Ontario. She is the author of *Shaking the Rattle: Healing the Trauma of Colonization*, and *collective consciousness*, a book of poetry. She is the mother of three children and the gramma/nana of three granddaughters, one grandson, and one great-grandson.

meetings

CHRISTINA BROBBY

I WAS TOO EARLY. I had arrived at least half an hour before Glenda would stand outside the entrance to Sloane Square underground station in the cool November afternoon sun, looking for a middle-aged light-brown-skinned bi-racial woman matching the description I had given to her earlier when we talked on the phone and arranged the meeting place. She would be looking for her new half-sister.

Having met my older adoptive sister for lunch the previous day, I was already re-acquainted with the area after many years' absence. Moving to Toronto, Canada, in 1979, raising my son, divorcing his father, returning to school to become a lawyer, moving to Whitehorse, Yukon,—plus the break-up of a long-term relationship—had kept me occupied in the intervening years. The narrow, crowded thoroughfare of Kings Road in the Royal Borough of Kensington and Chelsea was lined with ubiquitous black taxi cabs and red double-decker buses, both now upgraded and modernized. The street, still lined with small, independent shops, as well as the chain stores that became household names in England while I was establishing a life in Canada, was jammed now with people starting their Christmas shopping or browsing. I'm usually an avid shopper, but my attention faltered today. Standing in one of the chic upscale women's clothing boutiques, I fingered the fabric of some item of clothing, hardly aware of what I was looking at or its texture as my mind returned yet again to the events of the past few weeks that had brought me here from my home near the sixtieth parallel.

I had grown up with two adoptive sisters in my adoptive family: Leeann, older than me by nine years, who was my adoptive parents' biological child; and Shannon, two years younger than me, who was adopted from the same orphanage a year after I arrived. Though we were not related by blood, Shannon and I were easily distinguished from the rest of the family by the colour of our skins.

In January 2006, Barnardo's adoption agency in England sent me its summary of what was known of the first three years of my life before I went to live with my adoptive family. The summary was accompanied by a number of letters from each of my birth parents to Barnardo's.

The summary provided my father's name: Michael Andrew Wireko-Brobby. How many children have two fathers named Michael, I wondered, and was he, like my adoptive dad, also known as Mike?

In the summer of that year, Deirdre, a woman from Barnardo's, contacted me again. During a routine preliminary search for potential relatives, she had located someone named Glenda Wireko-Brobby living in England. Was I interested in the agency contacting Glenda to find out whether she was related to me? I needed no time to contemplate that question. Yes. Please. The next email from Deirdre demanded a lot more consideration. Were there things I wanted to know from this person if she was related but wanted no contact with me? I felt paralyzed, unable to take on the task. Why could I think of nothing? I had no idea, had never prepared for this day, the opportunity to know more about me. Years earlier, when I was pregnant at seventeen with my son, the doctor wanted to know my family medical background. Was there a history of twins? Any history of diabetes? Heart disease or high blood pressure? I had no history. I was a blank slate, like a classroom blackboard at the beginning of a new school year. This could be an opportunity to ask any questions I wished. Surely there should be a flood of them.

Finally, after much angst and many hours of soul-searching, I completed the list. I tackled those inquiries I considered within the realms of normalcy first: a physical description of my father, his profession, his date and place of birth. Next came the pressing questions, which surprised me, both for the fact that they were so important to me and for their content. I prefaced the questions with: "This last part sounds silly, but these are some traits/characteristics that I have and I wonder which side of my family they come from: large feet and hands; long fingers; muscular build; short in height; short-sighted; love reading, learning, travelling, outdoor activities." I sent the list to Deirdre at Barnardo's, the yearning to know overcoming my embarrassment. What did it matter if the relative thought I was mad, since she would see the list only if she did not want to meet me? I felt somewhat reassured by this.

Weeks passed without a response from Glenda Wireko-Brobby. I felt disconnected, powerless, not knowing when Deirdre wrote the inquiry letter, what she wrote, or the ultimate question—whether Glenda Wireko-Brobby was related to me.

While waiting for news from Deirdre, I spent hours every day surfing the Web for Wireko-Brobbys. One site led me to a photo of attendees at a conference in Japan. The representative from Ghana caught my attention. One of the few black faces in the photo, his face, the colour of mine, reminded me of someone—me. For the first time in my life, I looked like another person and saw before me another person who resembled me. I became obsessed with that photo and sent it to my son, asking: "Hey, do you think we're related?" My daughter-in-law responded, "How can you not be related?" My son thought this man might be my brother. He had my ears, my cheekbones, the same shape of eyes, a similar nose.

A site called Ghanaweb was a major source of information on life in Ghana—current news, politics, religion, social events. The classifieds section fascinated and amused me. Men Seeking Ladies, most of whom must be God-fearing; Ladies Seeking Men; people looking for friendship, rentals and sales of real estate, cars and other sundry items. And a section called "Looking for Lost People." It seemed that a lot of Ghanaians had misplaced people—old schoolmates, teachers, friends, family members.

My ad in Ghanaweb appeared on September 11, 2006:

> I am looking for information on my birth father. His name was Michael Andrew Wireko-Brobby and he attended the University of London and lived in London in the late 1950s and early 1960s. He had a sister who lived in London. I believe he may have later returned to Ghana. I would really appreciate learning anything about him or other potential family members.

I don't remember what I was doing when man first walked on the moon or other momentous world happenings. But the events of Thursday, September 14, 2006, are engraved in my brain as if on a tombstone. I had arrived atypically early at the office I shared with another lawyer in downtown Whitehorse. By 7:00 AM, I had turned on my computer. I sipped my coffee as I waited for the start-up procedures to complete and for the icons to appear on the screen. I clicked on my Hotmail account. Three new messages. "More junk mail," I muttered irritably. My surmise was only partly correct. Three words, in bold letters, held me transfixed. I sat for what seemed a lifetime staring at the name: "Glenda Wireko-Brobby." I waited for my grey matter to absorb the import of those words and to make sense of them, to free my hand and allow it to left-click on the mouse and complete delivery of Glenda's message. The office felt hot and stuffy, the screen danced before my eyes, bright, then far away. Finally, click.

> . . . I have in the last few days been in contact with Barnardos regarding your request for information regarding our father. He had asked me to find you but you found us first. He is very

excited about this development and is quite keen to hear from you via any contact medium. I would be happy to speak to you if that's ok with you. Hope to hear from you soon.

Our father. Two simple words. So much information. And our father, the blood connection between us, was still alive. Why had it never occurred to me that he might be? Why was I so unprepared for this discovery, in spite of the months of knowing the true circumstances of my adoption? This would not be the fictitious tale I was raised on, like an Aesop's fable that you believe without question until something triggers the truth. My fable shattered that spring as I worked through the summary and my parents' letters. The true story was more sordid, more heart wrenching, but a story that has been played out, in some version or another, since time immemorial: older man with family back in his motherland meets beautiful, innocent young blonde girl, seduces her with his charm and promises he cannot possibly keep, words of love and endearment until she finally is won over. When the inevitable consequence of unprotected sex results, he questions her faithfulness to him, whether the child can be his. Then he leaves her to bear the shame and consequences of being the unmarried mother of a mixed-race child. My mother is taken in by the only maternal relative who ever knew I existed, her older sister Joyce, whose name was part of mine until adoption erased it together with other parts of my identity.

In the silence of my office, it was still too early for the phone to start commanding my attention. I let the new history sink into my pores, becoming part of what felt like a new self, one with a birth father living in Ghana and a sister who already knew I existed and had been burdened with the responsibility of trying to find me, with few or perhaps no clues. A sister who conveyed warmth, inclusion, welcome, and compassion in one brief email.

I could not focus on my work. I wanted to run outside and yell to the whole town at the top of my lungs: "I have a new sister and a father.

I am a Wireko-Brobby. I am found. There is more of me than there was yesterday!"

The day was a blur of emails, MSN conversations, telephone calls, lunch, and coffee dates. As I shared the news with each new person, I felt more detached and remote, as if observing a play with me sitting in the audience watching myself enact the lead role on stage.

Over the next two months, as the blank canvas that had always been my companion filled with characters that became brighter in colour, the picture included seven half-siblings living in Ghana, England, and the United States, some whose voices I now knew. I had my first telephone conversation in the early hours of one morning with my sister Carmen in Ghana who, after a brief chat, handed the phone to my father. "Hellooo Teenaa," he said, elongating the words in a low, clear voice. The same tone as mine. Lots of laughing and crying, all of us admitting that we couldn't stop grinning, hardly believing this conversation was finally happening. More telephone conversations and emails, each adding to the canvas. I have two older brothers living in Ghana, one whom I had found during one of my earlier web surfing forays but had discounted as a relative because I thought his facial features were not a sufficiently close match. Later, when I met him, other features not seen in a poor photo on the Web, including the large feet and hands, made it clear we are related. I also learned that the man attending the forestry conference in Japan, who looked so much like me, was my youngest uncle, living in Kumasi, our family's home town in Ghana.

Conversations with my father were simultaneously pleasurable and frustrating. I could listen to his melodic voice for hours. Now I understood why my mother yielded to his charm and gave herself to him. Listening to his slow, measured voice, I could almost see him considering each word before it slipped from his lips. When he laughed or chuckled, I felt lighter. Frustration, in the early days, was mostly the result of poor telephone lines, stealing words from our conversations, lost before delivery from its journey between Accra and Whitehorse. I struggled with the touchy subject of how to address this new parent in my life, wishing there was an etiquette book to provide guidance. We both rejected "Michael" outright as too formal and not fitting his personality. "Mike" felt awkward as I associated it with Dad, my adoptive father, yet it was also how some family members and friends addressed this new father. "Father" eventually became my warning to him that he had done something to upset me and I was sulking. This caused more laughter, making it hard to remain annoyed for more than a few minutes. Finally, after much persuasion, I relented and joined most of the family, including cousins, who referred to him as "Daddy."

As we became more familiar with each other, we also had difficult conversations. When Daddy discouraged me from rushing off to Ghana immediately to meet him and Carmen, trying to persuade me to wait until the following year, my meltdown was pretty dramatic. He could not know how terrified I was that death would rob me of the chance of ever meeting him or touching his skin. Sobbing, accusing him of not wanting to meet me, never wanting to lay eyes on his long-lost daughter, I hung up the phone, unable to speak as I slipped into the black hole of abandonment and loss. It was a first. I had never hung up on either of my adoptive parents, never in my life ranted or made such a scene to either of them. I was the good girl. Now, in the space of a few weeks, I rebelled, feeling I had lost my family anyway. What did it matter if I screamed, yelled, falsely accused, or hung up on a stranger who sounded like me? The black hole embraced me for hours, the pain almost physical; primitive thought processes prevented my rationality from stepping in and easing the grief. Eventually the intensity of my emotions subsided, though I felt I could be pulled back into the turmoil at any time.

We re-established our lines of communication and had more difficult conversations, more firsts. A new previously unknown assertive part of me emerged: I insisted that he listen to me after he had chastised me for ten or fifteen minutes on my impetuosity and lack of consideration for others. We muddled our way through the minefields of emotions, learning how to deal with each other as we scolded, cajoled, listened, laughed, and cried. Carmen also filled in some of the blanks, explaining that our father hates surprises and does not respond well to them.

℘ Now, on this cool November day, I meandered through human and vehicular traffic on King's Road, back to the underground station, to search for the short woman who described herself as black like plain chocolate, and spoke in the same soft, slow voice as me. Tomorrow evening, with my father's blessing, I would be in Ghana meeting him and more of the Wireko-Brobby clan, including Carmen.

Waiting for the traffic light's permission to cross the street and deliver me to the station, my eyes scanned the people around the entrance, searching for the dark-chocolate-skinned woman wrapped in a red jacket. Earlier that day we attempted to describe ourselves, both struggling, giggling at our descriptions. My self-sketch in response to Glenda's description: "light brown skin, like a coffee with cream." We both described what we would wear. I had packed in the early hours of the morning days before, rejecting this and that piece of clothing until finally I felt satisfied that I was equipped with clothing suitable for a first meeting with new family. The outfit I selected to wear to meet Glenda was a mixture of old and new: a deep brown wool sweater I'd brought with me from Yukon, new beige corduroy pants purchased the day before in one of the shops on Kings Road, and my favourite brown, wool jacket.

Crossing the road with the throng of others making their way to the station and going about their daily business, I saw her. Everyone else passed through my radar, rejected. Only she remained: Red coat. Check. White T-shirt. Check. Jeans. Check. Perhaps the way she stood or carried her body left no doubt in my mind that I was looking at my sister for the first time. She saw me almost immediately and came toward me as I reached the safety of the sidewalk. We stood there, our mouths mirroring smiles, her eyes dancing.

"I knew it was you without the description," said Glenda with a laugh. "You look so much like Daddy. Oh my goodness, wait until you go to Ghana. You are going to hear that constantly." We stood taking each other in. Her laugh, like Daddy's, was infectious, though my smile seemed frozen. "I can't believe we're finally getting to meet, to put a face to a voice" she continued.

"I know. It's hard to believe," I agreed. I noticed that she too wore glasses, simple black frames well suited to her tiny face, sitting on a broad, flared nose that spread outwards as it travelled downwards.

"You're lucky, you don't have the Wireko-Brobby nose. Most of us are blessed or cursed with it," Glenda observed, as if following my thoughts.

I don't know how long we stood at the curb, interrupting the flow of human traffic as we continued the external checklist of each other's similar or different features — hair very different, mine belying my mixed heritage, with looser curls and dark brown in contrast to hers, black and thick-textured woven into extensions that flowed down her back and around her face. We shared the shape of our mouth and the lines around it; our cheekbones too were identical. At least I thought so. I wished we were standing in front of a mirror for accurate comparisons.

Finally, we moved, back across the crosswalk, retracing the steps I had taken alone earlier, heading toward the café I recommended, farther up Kings Road.

"I hope you don't mind a bit of a walk. It's about ten or fifteen minutes," I told Glenda, worried because I had no idea whether that was far or was nothing to her.

"I love walking. So does Daddy," she responded.

"Me too."

"I expect we get that from Daddy. He used to walk miles every day, as well as tending his large plot at the house on the university grounds. He will probably tell you all about it, or you will hear more from our cousins. He used to feed the family from that plot," Glenda explained.

We both laughed in embarrassment as we caught each of us checking the other out, hoping our sideways glances would be concealed by our eyeglasses as we walked. I could barely take my eyes off her.

When we stood in line at the coffee shop to place our orders, the almost overwhelming urge again struck me to tell everyone around me that this was my sister. That single piece of information would do nothing to explain the significance of the statement, but still I wanted to share it with the whole world.

Sitting opposite each other, the table wedged close to others around it, all occupied, we continued exploring our past, Daddy's life, my other siblings' lives, and where they grew up, my life growing up in my adoptive family, how I came to be living in Canada. The pace of our exchange slowed now that we were within touching distance. I noticed how small her hands were, yet the fingers, like mine, disproportionately long, pale pink finger tips and palms bright against the blackness of her smooth skin. One hand rested lightly on the table, close to her glass. No longer able to resist, not caring what people thought of two women touching each other in public, I reached my hand to hers, watching those slim fingers curl around my larger, longer ones. She had soft, delicate fingers, but her grip was firm and sure, like a baby's hand curling around an adult's. Now we both reached out several times as we sat, sometimes in conversation, other times just looking at each other, smiling, or still stealing glances at the other as we pretended to watch patrons drink their coffee immersed in their own conversations.

"I wondered if you would like to come over to meet Ato and the kids. I would love it if you did, but if you're not ready yet that's fine. This must still be so overwhelming for you. Ato and I talked about it earlier and whether to invite you instead of meeting in a public place, but we were worried it would be too much too quickly for you, and that you might not like us," Glenda said, as she laughed at her last concern.

"I would love to, Glenda. If you're sure it is not too much. I know what it is like when you have just moved. If it's better to wait until I return from Ghana, I don't mind." The last part was not strictly true. I did not want to leave Glenda. I wanted to be with her for as long as possible, to know every aspect of her life. I longed to meet her husband, Ato, as well as my niece and my nephew. But I did not want to appear pushy or overbearing.

"No, no, if you don't mind the fact that you may have to sit on a box and be surrounded by them. Chances are the boxes will still be there when you get back from Ghana and see me again anyway." Again I was treated to her eyes reflecting her laughter.

Leaving the warmth of the coffee shop, we retraced our steps. Back to the same underground station that was by now so familiar. This time we entered it together, to make our way to a south London suburb, home for Glenda and her family for the past month, an important detour before I continued on my journey to Ghana to meet more of my clan.

Christina Brobby has lived in Whitehorse, Yukon, for fourteen years. She is working on a memoir about finding both of her birth parents and families.

a mother out of time

M. JANE JOHNSTON

IT'S NOVEMBER, 1992, AND I am in the Edmonton airport, having just arrived from Vancouver with my husband, Rob. Clutching my bag in one hand and Rob in the other, I stand on my tiptoes and anxiously survey the crowd. A couple of times I think I see someone who resembles the woman in the photograph, but they look away, unseeing. My heart races. As travellers make their way out into the blue-skied world beyond the grey door, the room grows quiet. The empty luggage conveyer comes to a stop. "Where are they?" Rob asks, looking at his watch.

Today is a momentous day, never to be repeated or forgotten. I was a young teenager when I gave birth to my son, Michael, in the spring of 1971, during a time when keeping your child was never discussed as an option, social supports were not yet available, adoption records were sealed and the children given new families, new names. After decades of searching and waiting to find my son, who I now know is called Andrew, we are about to meet Ann, my son's adoptive mother. For me, time stands still.

Ann and I have spoken on the phone, and I have a good feeling about her, despite my worries.

I breathe slowly and deeply to calm myself. After twenty-two years of silence, here I stand, waiting. Waiting to finally meet the people who were given my son. As I wait, I wonder about this family that received my beautiful boy—what were they like? Did they love him as much as the children born to them? Were they able to see and celebrate his unique gifts? Were they frustrated by traits they didn't understand? Did they wonder or care about what had happened to me?

I talked with Andrew's entire adoptive family the night he and I first spoke. His family of six sat in a circle on their living room floor and passed around the phone, their excitement and curiosity so disarming, so welcoming. Ann said she had always wanted to thank me. She felt certain that she would know Andrew better only by knowing me. How was it that he was so musically gifted? Was his extraordinary language acquisition genetic? Who else had his receding hairline? Ann sounded wonderful, laughing and crying all at the same time, thrilled to be able to connect. This was beyond my hopes, and the calming effect of their family support was profound and immediate. I was well aware that many adoptive mothers felt threatened and discouraged now-adult children from meeting their birth mothers. I had also met adoptees who felt so guilty about needing to know who they were and were waiting for their adoptive parents to die before searching for their roots. After hearing Ann's voice, I knew that in the deepest expression of her character and caring, Andrew was completely free to discover himself anew. Years of oppressive anxiety began to lift for me that day.

The waiting years were difficult in the extreme, but being lucky enough to have a beautiful daughter was a healing balm to my soul. Jessica came into this world as a bright, happy, and funny girl, and I could not love her more. Like other mothers with children lost to adoption, I was fearful she might somehow be taken from me, too. I constantly had to work with intrusive thoughts that something bad might happen to her. My nightmares were incapacitating. The post-traumatic stress resulting from being a mother separated from my child wouldn't go away—the trauma was ever unfolding and only worsened with the passage of time. As my daughter matured, I more fully realized all that I had missed.

As Jessica recalls, she grew up with a brother she couldn't see. Anyone who knew me well knew I was looking for my son. Overall, I managed to keep faith that I would find him, as was my promise to him when he was but five days old. Having no acceptable place for my grief to exist or my voice to be heard, I suffered the long years of separation, often in silence. What could be done? The messages from society's dominant culture had been consistent: put the adoption behind you, get on with your life. But as mothers separated from their children well know, putting the past behind you is not possible when you live with it every day. I was a mother without her firstborn, but his mother nonetheless, with all of the same concerns I had for my daughter.

🖉 The airport baggage room is dingy, and I find myself redecorating it in my mind. I notice Rob becoming a little more agitated, and I, too, have moved from being scared about meeting my son's other mother to being worried about a possible accident. We have now been alone in the baggage area for twenty-five minutes. Suddenly, at the far end of the large room, a crack of light shines through an opening door and a figure hurries through. A woman. As she nears, I see she is olive complected, with stylish short chestnut hair. She is the picture of casual elegance dressed in a crème coloured silk blouse under a shell-pink light wool jacket with matching skirt, finished with a single strand of pearls, designer purse, and low heels. "Ann?" I call out with a wave. A big smile breaks across her face. I place my luggage at my foot and step forward. She walks quickly now, and as we meet, she wraps me in her arms, crying. A long moment goes by before her raspy voice finally chokes out her first words: "I love you." Her words surprise me and create an instant field of peace. I take her arm as we leave the airport, two mothers together. The alarms in my head wind down. I am going to be okay. We are going to be okay.

🖉 Finding Andrew was a one in five billion chance. Over the silent, dark stretch of the years, desperate, I wrote to and met with Social

Services in Edmonton, attended Parent Finders, searched databases in the library using non-identifying information, marched on the legislature to put pressure on lawmakers to open sealed records, advertised in papers across Alberta on Mother's Days and birthdays, talked to anyone who might listen or help, went to psychics, had Andrew's astrological chart done, entered therapy and analyzed my dreams for any possibility of connection. In the end, it was intuition and engaging the services of a detective that brought us together again. Our records are still sealed, eighteen years after our reunion.

The day of our meeting is emblazoned on my heart. The memory goes like this: I am at home, in Vancouver, jumping up and down on one foot, exclaiming, "I may throw up! I'm going to throw up!" My husband, Rob, while holding me from behind, calmly says, "Well, if there was ever a time in your life when you should throw up, it would be now, Jane." Ah, reunion—a high-wire act, without nets. But I wouldn't want to be anywhere else. I am finally going to have my daughter, Jessica, my stepson, Nathan, and my son, Andrew, in the same room; the corners of my world are about to touch.

"He's here!" Nathan shouts, and Rob accompanies me outside. Nathan darts out ahead and is already at the curbside. A young version of my father steps out of the cab. Andrew glances up at me and nervously asks the cabbie if we look alike. The driver cocks his head in confusion, smiles broadly, and says something in his native tongue. We all nod in agreement as if we know what he has said.

I feel myself to be underwater as I move toward Andrew and encircle him in my arms. He nervously claps me on the back, laughing. We all wave the driver off, and Rob helps carry Andrew's luggage into the house while engaging in small talk about the flight. Once inside, we find it difficult to know what to do. There is no comfort in these early moments. I busy myself making coffee while Andrew and I discreetly take turns staring at each other.

I feel myself beginning to calm down. I haven't died, I haven't gone insane, I haven't even thrown up. My early vow to find him no matter what is realized. I have somehow survived the unimaginably long and painful years of separation. We are together in the same room; it's real and it's happening.

Drinking in Andrew, I marvel out loud at our striking resemblance. I recognize his features, the way his body moves, the way he thinks. I know him deeply, and not at all. He sits at the piano and begins to play. I am stunned by his gift, inherited from my mother. I'm so moved, I quietly slip away, locking myself in the bathroom to cry for all I have missed.

Back in the kitchen, Andrew leans on the island. I stretch out my hand and place it on his. I see my father, my mother, myself. "It is perfect who you are," I tell him. He is startled and lapses into momentary silence. "No one has ever said that to me before," he replies, letting out a long, slow sigh. We look at each other in silence, experiencing the deep healing embedded in this knowledge.

It is evening now, and we stroll along Robson Street, enjoying the balmy June weather. The night is festive and alive with musicians and magicians and shoppers. Suddenly, Andrew turns to us and shouts, "I'm free!" Rob and I exchange a glance, and I ask him what he means. "For years I have had this behaviour of turning my head from side to side in crowds, wherever I go. I never fully realized until this moment that I was always scanning and looking for people who looked like me. I was always wondering who my mother was, who my family were. I can stop searching crowds now. I know who you are and where you are, and I am free to simply enjoy the night like everyone else." His words stop me in my tracks.

"Wow," says Rob. "I know what you mean, because when we're on ferries, I looked for you too. I would say to Jane, 'Look, there's a man about your son's age, and he looks sort of like Jessica." Well, Andrew, I guess we're all free now.

The long ride from the Edmonton airport gives us time to chat and ready ourselves for what is coming. I study Ann as she drives and find that I am intrigued and comforted by her way of being. Her Anglo-Argentinian accent charms me. She is beautiful—warm and positive with open, laughing eyes. Clearly, she is excited to have us stay and speaks of her many plans involving us meeting a host of people who have been important in Andrew's development over these twenty-two years.

I haven't been so sure about staying with Andrew's family, worried about the possibility of becoming engulfed in pain with nowhere to hide. The notion of entering my son's family home is difficult—I am the mother-ghost with my face pressed against the window looking in at the happy family scene. How will I cope when seeing the photographs of Andrew as infant, toddler, child, young adult, man? Will the artifacts of his baby-book firsts, report cards, and childhood stories undo me completely? What if I have a breakdown and can't put myself back together again?

We are met by three little barking poodles accompanied by Andrew's Nana. I love her instantly and see where Ann gets her warmth. Ann and Geoffrey have four children: the first two, Andrew and Heather, are adopted, and the second two, Jonathan and Sarah, are by "home production," as Ann likes to say. I survey the large, comfortable, suburban family home and know there would have been no going without for Andrew. Tea is served, and photograph albums come out of cupboards. I can feel Rob's hand on my back and my love for him has never been more real. He is my rock as I open the pages and begin the process of incorporating images of my growing son in my heart and mind, replacing vivid fantasy with reality.

"Look! Look at this! He looks just like Dad as a boy," I exclaim. It is Ann's face that crumples in tears. "It's not fair—I got to raise your son and you didn't," she says. Her tears flow freely throughout my absorption in the albums. I am aware of the unexpected reversal, and it is surprising to me. I am elated and peaceful as I see my boy on Santa's knee, on horseback at camp, clutching his little books. His happiness is my happiness; I can share in it and do.

I already know that not everyone in the family feels the same way as Ann. Andrew's adoptive father, Geoffrey, who is two years younger than my own father, has some concerns. He is British and graduated from Cambridge as a physician. He has not considered contact before and wonders what I could want all these years later. Wasn't a contract signed? He believes healthy young girls put these sorts of events behind them and get on with their lives, that nurture is more important than nature. That I provided the genetic material, but all that Andrew is today is the result of their having shaped him with experience, opportunities, and schooling.

꠵ It isn't until Geoffrey and Ann fly to Ottawa the following Thanksgiving to meet our family that Geoffrey finds his worldview shifting. He tells me that he is transfixed by my father—the way he looks, eats, and walks; the similarities to Andrew are uncanny. Geoffrey lets me know with a smile that he is revising his long-held beliefs about nature and nurture. We Johnstons all love to talk and eat and sing, and Andrew couldn't be more at home. Andrew says he has Gramma's personality in Grampa's body. Watching Andrew and my mother playing the piano for each other is among the most cherished recollections in my life. Our two families merge and celebrate not only the reunion, but our families coming together as one. It is profoundly healing for my parents, who have silently carried their own guilt and worry all these years. They did not dare to hope that I would find Andrew but now think of the Dawrants as clan. We have frequent contact, sharing holidays and exchanging regular phone calls. There have been weddings and deaths, traumas and festivities; Ann and I are now grandmothers to Andrew's two daughters, Alexandra Elvie, named after my father and Ann's mother, and Ariel Johnston Dawrant, unifying our family in name. We are a well-knit clan and can't imagine it any other way.

Ann and I recognize that our reunion is outside the normal experience—our story is unusually positive and continues to deepen, enriching our shared lives. When I reflect on the various elements of how it came to be, I realize Ann is key. I don't know if it's because she was raised outside of North America (I suspect this plays a role) or if it's just part of who she is (she is wonderful), but she has never considered her four children as objects of possession. She longed to know me and also knew that meeting me would allow her to understand Andrew better. She is thrilled to have family in Canada, and we have become sisters in a sense, frequently talking on the phone until bedtime. I love her now-adult children and have special bonds with each one. We all visit back and forth in various combinations and genuinely love and like each other. This is what is possible between people who genuinely care about the experiences of others and actively choose a preferred outcome.

I am one of the lucky ones, and I know it. In reflection, as integrated as I now feel, I also experience deep waves of sadness and even distress when I realize there are mothers still suffering the agony of separation from their children. Only four provinces and one territory in Canada have opened closed adoption files. Records have long been open in other places, including New Zealand and Australia. New South Wales, after a careful study on the treatment of unmarried mothers and the traumatic long-term effects of adoption, not only opened sealed records and changed adoption laws, but also made an official public apology for harm done. The legislative council clearly stated that although the inquiry was about past practices, the actions of the past would continue to affect future generations and as such mistakes must not be repeated.

I so wish that I could lay my hand on the shoulders of legislators here in Canada and impart the inside experience of the horror and damage inflicted on birth mothers by adoption separation. If I could do so, I know the laws would change today, allowing women to begin to repair their lives. No amount of therapy can heal a woman separated from a living child, nor is dissociation a healthy state. Being reunited is the only event that can begin to heal families who have a core need to find each other. Sealed-record adoptions are tortuous, and the trauma is now known to last a lifetime. I continue to experience post-traumatic nightmares, the protracted loss was that formative.

I have also moved away from considering the loss of my son as my story to realize that Andrew's adoption is actually everyone's story. Members of our blended family have experienced the deep healing available in the knowledge that there is no finite number of people to love and be enriched by. Our family circle has expanded to incorporate everyone, with room for more. The old fracture has largely healed and is observable by all. I will never have memories of my son's childhood, and I still grieve that loss and always will. I do have many wonderful shared memories with Andrew now, with many more to come, life willing.

Recently, after a wonderful visit with Geoffrey and Ann in Victoria, while boarding the plane for home Geoffrey remarked with wonder, "Just think: if we hadn't have gotten Andrew, we never would have met Jane and Rob." I believe that says it all. As for my first meeting with Ann in the Edmonton airport, when she whispered in my ear, I experienced just how quickly a life can transform within the spirit of compassion and openness, while embodying the wisdom that children don't belong to us, we all belong to them, and always have.

Jane Johnston lives in her beloved forest by the sea in Victoria, British Columbia. She shares her life with her best friend and husband, Rob Evans. Jane is a retired RN who specialized in maternity. She has a masters in clinical counselling with an emphasis in the study of dreams and the unconscious. She has a passion for writing, photography and videography and is currently exploring adoption issues through the lens of neurobiology and attachment in her art based research.

voices from
a family

BARBARA MACANDREW

SHAUN MACANDREW

JACK MACANDREW

RANDY MACANDREW

BARBARA MACANDREW

Our biological-born son, Shaun, arrived three weeks before our first wedding anniversary in 1958. Jack and I thought he would be the first of many children to cheer our house. That was not to be. After I had two traumatic miscarriages, our doctor told me my baby-bearing days had ended with Shaun.

In 1961, just before Christmas, Shaun wrote a scrawly letter to Santa. "All I want for Christmas is a bruber [brother]," he wrote. As if by magic, the very next day salvation appeared in the advertisements section of the *Halifax Herald*:

Unadoptable Mixed Race, and Physically or Mentally Retarded Children Looking for Homes

I read down the list and came to, "*Attractive two-year-old boy, mixed race (mother, negro; father, Caucasian), high average intelligence, excellent health . . .*" I showed Jack the advertisement. He was thrilled. We wanted this child!

Jack phoned Nova Scotia Social Services the next day and was told Randy would soon be going to the Nova Scotia Home for Colored Children, where he would stay until he was sixteen. We made an appointment to meet Randy the next Saturday.

Background: William Randall, twenty-two months. (Birth mother, sixteen-year-old black Nova Scotian; father, visiting United States navy officer trainee). First mixed-race adoptee in Atlantic Canada. (Three other black/white children were also adopted at that time in Montreal through the Open Door Society.)

I remember that Shaun was wild with excitement to meet "his new bruber." He insisted we buy a big red lollipop en route to social services. We three sat and waited for the case worker to bring William Randall in to meet us. When they finally arrived, Randy shyly hid behind the worker's skirt, eyes downturned. The case worker tried and tried to get him to respond to us, but nothing worked.

Then small blond Shaun took the red lollipop out of his mouth and marched over to Randy and handed it to him. In an instant, the lollipop was in Rand's mouth. Reticence disappeared; he sidled over to stand beside Shaun, staring up at him with huge dark eyes. Then Shaun brought him closer, so he could stare at Jack and me. After a few moments, the little boy took the sucker out of his now-bright-red mouth and offered us a lick.

Shaun, Jack, and I fell in love at first sight with this adorable child with the soft brown skin, big eyes, crisp black curly hair. Jack and I begged the case worker to let us take him home for the weekend. After some bureaucratic double-checks, we were handed a brown paper bag with all of Randy's worldly possessions inside: a snowsuit, two pairs of pants, three T-shirts, four diapers, and a toothbrush.

That night, two little boys got into their PJs; Shaun, the newly dubbed "big boy" climbed to the top bunk while Randy was assigned the bottom bunk. Jack and I went to get a book to read to them; in that minute Randy, already the athlete, leapt to the top of the bunk and snuggled up to his new "bruber." The rest of that weekend at our Purcell's Cove home was wild fun.

On Monday, the case worker came to take Randy back to the orphanage. She told us she had never seen a more shy child than Randy and didn't know if he could "adjust" to us.

When he came into the room, roaring and laughing, he jumped onto her knee, grabbed her necklace, and broke it into a shower of pearls.

She was stunned. "Well, he's not shy anymore!"

She departed, looking relieved. "I'll be back with adoption papers," she promised. And she left us Randy, our forever child, with whom we would log forty-seven years of Randy MacAndrew history. Jack and I look back on our imperfect but sincere attempts to nurture, understand, and cope with what many people in the 1960s thought was wrong: a mixed-race adoption. That "wrong" was a right choice, a decision that continues to enrich our lives. Today, it is strange to revisit people's reactions.

My mother, Ruth, adored Randy at once; Jack's family sent love and all best wishes. My brothers and sister loved him unconditionally. But my war-wounded retired cleric father was frightened for me and cold to the idea. He told me we'd end up in "a destitute coloured ghetto." Initially, he ignored Randy. But when Rand was twelve, my dad had a stroke that left him blind. Officially colour-blind, Dad finally accepted his second grandson, and they grew close at last.

Nevertheless, I discovered there were people who could never accept our new son because of his brown skin. I learned the sting of "The Hate Look" and the violence it brought. I'll never forget the morning I wheeled Rand and my groceries around the local Dominion store while a man in a pinstriped suit yelled, "Black man's whore," at me, again and again. Another shopper stopped and stared at me and my baby son, then aimed his grocery cart at us. Suddenly, something went wrong with its wheels. His cart zoomed straight toward a one-storey high display of large cans of tomato juice. Down crashed a hundred or so heavy cans, all over him.

Little Randy and I got out of there pronto. As we left, a beautiful blonde woman ran after us, laughing. "God crashed that jerk into the display," she said.

That was the way things were in the 1960s in Halifax: mixed reaction to mixed-raced people. When we moved to Prince Edward Island, Rand was a celebrity and a curiosity because there were only two other black people on the island back then. His teachers spoiled him, and he became an ace hockey star. Later, when we moved to Toronto, we had the support and love of his aunts, uncles and cousins.

But, in October 1975, *not* of the Toronto Metro Police. When Jack was in Switzerland producing a CBC-TV show, I waited up one evening until midnight for Rand, then fourteen, to come home from the Fall Frolic at Northern Secondary School; the event had ended at 10:00 PM. When the phone rang, I heard an angry voice.

"This is Constable H. at police headquarters. Do you have a son Randy?"

"Yes, I am Randy's mother."

"Well, mother," he replied, "We have your nigger son here and we are going to charge him with possession of a dangerous weapon. Get down here, girl, as quick as your ass can carry you."

Shaking and scared, I ran to Shaun, who was sleeping soundly in his room. I shook him awake and told him we had to drive to police headquarters in downtown Toronto. At the front desk, I asked for Constable H. When he came out of a nearby room, he did a double-take as he saw me—not the black woman he'd expected at all.

Instantly polite, he escorted me into the next room. There I found a terrified Randy, his lower lip wobbling as he forced back tears when he saw his bro and me. The weapon? Police had found his small Swiss jackknife in his pocket. We had a good laugh the next day when we saw the special gifts Jack had brought the boys from Switzerland: two new Swiss Army knives!

Like any flustered mother, I sometimes call Shaun "Randy," and Randy "Shaun." The boys laugh: "Hey, Mum, can't you tell us apart? I'm the white one." And, "I'm the black one."

We recall the time when Randy noticed that friends' next-door neighbours had a statue of a white boy peeing in their yard, instead of the stereotype black boy. "Hey look, Dad, black people must live there. They have a white-boy statue on their lawn."

Now it's 2010: Michaëlle Jean is Canada's Governor General;

Barack Obama is US president. Mixed-race adoptions are accepted and celebrated.

And we, the MacAndrews of PEI, married fifty-two years, are getting old. Our sons are fine middle-aged men who have fathered five children, who have given us five grandchildren. If possible, we love and care for each other more than ever.

Over the years, many people praised us. "What a wonderful thing you did adopting that black child. What a lucky boy he is." But Jack and I agree that the luck is ours. Especially we recall that day in 1997 when we first saw Rand holding his sweet baby daughter, Miranda Jo. "Luck" had just doubled itself.

SHAUN MACANDREW

When I was very little, in my early Halifax years, I was often quite lonely. I wished for a close playmate, but really, I wanted a brother. And once Randy came to live with us, I had someone to star in the plays I wrote. Okay, maybe "star" is the wrong word when I recall the morbid demise I inflicted on Randy in the second act in one of my creations. But let's face it, I gave him his start in theatre. After all these years, I can report happily that having a brother like Randy has added richness and good times to our lives. We MacAndrews share many family memories and funny stories that will carry through to generations to come. My wife, Lois, and I—and our two sons, Stewart, nineteen, and Layton, fifteen—are celebrating our twenty-fifth wedding anniversary soon, and we hope the whole clan will be there.

Time passes and we all change: I have even forgiven Randy for getting taller than me—his *big* brother—when he was fourteen and I was sixteen! That height difference doesn't matter so much now that he's forty-nine to my fifty-one.

JACK MACANDREW

When it became apparent that Barbara and I were determined to adopt Randy, Barbara's father feared the worst for his daughter and predicted dire results should we bring a mixed-race son into the family. Accordingly, the retired Anglican cleric dispatched me for a talk with the reigning Anglican bishop of the Diocese of Nova Scotia. His job was to try to talk me out of our foolhardy adventure.

The bishop and I skirmished over several issues, not making any headway, until finally he pulled out his last gambit. "You realize," said he in the most solicitous of tones, "this youngster will never be able to regard you as his true father."

"Whether he regards me as his father, a kindly uncle, or a just a good friend is entirely up to him," I replied. "Whichever, it will be better than being brought up in a segregated orphanage."

And with that, I bid the good bishop good day, and Barbara and I went about the legalities of adoption.

When we moved to Prince Edward Island, it was the time of the raising of black consciousness in the United States, with the civil rights movement on television news every night. Critics said that raising a black child in a white family would deprive him of his own racial culture. That bothered me, so, in an effort to introduce black context into the MacAndrew household, I purchased a subscription to *Ebony* magazine. I'm sure we were the only readers the magazine ever had on PEI. I learned quite a bit, but I don't think Randy ever opened an issue.

I always wondered what I would do when a direct slur at was hurled at Randy and us. When it happened, it was as unexpected and hurtful as a swift, hard blow to the stomach.

The occasion was the wedding of and sit-down dinner for the only daughter of two dear long-time friends, whom we had known since childhood. We were seated more or less directly across the table from them. It was a happy time for our friends and the fifty or so other family friends in attendance, as a wedding of an only daughter is supposed to be.

We heard the usual banging of silver on glass to prompt kisses from the newly married couple—always a sure-fire laugh-getter at a wedding in rural PEI. And then a professor at Prince of Wales College in Charlottetown got up to deliver the toast to the bride. I could see immediately that he'd drunk more than his share. I don't remember anything about his toast as he droned on, but I can still recall my growing horror at the direction it was taking: the professor was telling an explicitly racist joke.

I looked over at Randy. Fortunately, he was too young to understand what was happening . I glanced at Barbara; she was distraught. I looked over to our hosts, who wore expressions of dismay as they glanced covertly in our direction, then averted their eyes.

My mind raced: What should I do? Should I assemble my family and bolt from the place? Should I interrupt the toast-maker and upbraid him publicly? Both those actions would cast a pall and forever spoil this celebration for our friends and their daughter. I couldn't bring myself to do that. So I did nothing and said nothing. We all just sat there and endured. As soon as the dinner was over, we left, amid apologies from our friends and feelings of even stronger love for Randy. That was a long time ago, but I am haunted to this day—and will be to the day I die—over my decision to do and say nothing.

Randy developed into a gifted athlete, which registered positively with other kids of his age. Hockey was his favourite sport. On one road trip, there was an evening in the motel when the boys were asked about their ancestry. When the coach asked how many were Irish, hands went up. When he asked which boys were Scottish, Randy's hand shot up with the others of that persuasion.

But we knew that sooner or later Randy would directly encounter the "N" word. On PEI, it had not been much of a problem, but when we moved to Toronto, suddenly it was. Nevertheless, Randy continued playing hockey. One night, following a scramble around the goal, Randy and an opposing player exchanged words after the whistle—unfriendly words— and Randy wasn't backing off. Intuitively, I knew what it was about.

On the drive home, I asked him what was said. He wouldn't tell me. I pressed him, and finally he confessed: "He called me a nigger."

Barbara and I had always counselled him to walk away when that happened, but clearly there had to be a limit to non-engagement. So I gave him this advice: "Hockey fights are usually won on the first punch. So if you are going to do anything, do it first and do it hard."

The following week, I couldn't drive Randy to his game, but I asked how he'd made out when he got home. Randy had a slight smile on his face as he replied: "One goal, one assist. One fight, one punch."

RANDY MACANDREW

I began to realize my family situation was different from my friends' lives, just from the reaction of people when my parents introduced me— the confused look on their faces, the speculation of "I didn't know Jack was married before." I often had a feeling of not belonging. I don't mean to the family, but I often felt as if there was a big void, like there was a part of me missing that I couldn't identify. That confused me, made me into an astute observer of things around me. Consequently, I began to develop people-watching skills.

One time I was in a park in Toronto when I saw my friends in a heated argument with a black guy. I approached them and asked them what it was about; the Jamaican guy started calling me brother. When he was done, I told him, "I'm not your brother." I meant that I wasn't going to take his side just because we were both black. Then I turned to my buddies, who were saying "We don't see you as black." And I had a problem with that as well. I told my buddies, "Yes, I am black and proud of it." Both sides left very confused.

My brother, Shaun, taught me all about music, especially the blues. He was into people like Sonny Terry and Brownie McGee. The first concert we went to in Toronto was given by David Bowie, and Shaun turned me on to his music.

There weren't many black kids playing hockey in the seventies, especially on Prince Edward Island. One time when I was being called names, I went up to the referee and told him people were calling me derogatory names, and if he didn't deal with it, I would—and he wouldn't like what I would do. The ref went over to the bench and had a chat with the other coach. The name-calling stopped.

For many years, I didn't really understand the enormity of what my parents had done when they adopted me because I didn't understand what had been going on during the sixties. The civil rights movement in the United States was happening, with the history of slavery mixed in there, too. Halifax is a port town, and you can almost taste the intangible feelings, even today, on both sides of the race issue. But understanding all that, my parents still chose me.

The most important thing I learned from them over the years was a sense of integrity—not expressed in words but in choices they made and actions they took to practise those choices. They taught me by example that it was okay to take the path less travelled.

As I grew up, I discovered that comedy was a great way to make friends and get people to loosen up. I had to deal with the reality that some people were going to judge me by my "blackness," but eventually I developed the confidence that I could win them over by being myself. And, if I couldn't, that was their problem, not mine.

Barbara MacAndrew has worked as a journalist and freelancer for dozens of media outlets since the late 1950s. For the past twenty-two years, she has run a business, recommended in Fodor's travel guides, renting beach houses to tourists.

Shaun MacAndrew studied the technical side of theatre arts and has worked extensively as a television video editor. He now is a contractor on Prince Edward Island.

Jack MacAndrew is a journalist and television producer-writer-director who has also worked in theatre as producer of the Charlottetown Festival.

Randy MacAndrew is now lead cameraman for the CBC in Charlottetown, where he lives with his thirteen-year-old daughter.

more people to love

RAQUEL SCHNEIDMILLER

WHEN I WAS FOURTEEN, I thought I knew everything and didn't like anyone telling me what to do. At the time, I lived with my mom in a small town called Langdon, in Alberta, where I felt treated like a little girl, with a time limit on how long I could use the phone and watch TV. "The only reason your mom has rules is because she doesn't trust you," my dad told me. My parents had separated when I was six, and my farther had only become interested in my life again once I turned thirteen. "But if you came to live with me, there would be no rules because I trust you." I thought having no rules would mean I'd finally be treated like an adult. Looking back, I think that living in a house with no rules contributed to my becoming pregnant, because I was given freedom and I took advantage.

I had been living with my dad for only three months when I started to think I might be pregnant. I called my friend Cori to go to the doctor with me; I was so scared but relieved to have her with me for support. When the doctor confirmed my fears, I felt my heart stop. All I could think of was how my parents would be so disappointed in me — I could never let them find out.

The next morning, I had plans with my mom. As we were driving along, she asked me if I was pregnant. No, I said. She asked me again, and again I said no. She pulled the car over and told me that she knew for sure that I was. It never crossed my mind that Cori would tell her mom and that her mom would tell my mom. My mom was so calm; she wasn't screaming or mad at me. Then, she calmly asked once more, and this time I said yes. I was scared but relieved at the same time. I could finally talk to my mom, the one person who had always been there and supported me.

She asked me what I was planning to do with the baby. I told her I didn't know; I was only fourteen and had no idea what my options were, so she told me. I knew that I did not want to have an abortion: I didn't think I could go through that, and having watched people in my life try so hard to have children, how could I have an abortion? We then talked about giving the baby up for adoption, which ended up being our ultimate decision. Then, my mom asked me what I thought my dad would do if he found out. We both knew that he would force me to have an abortion, so I had to move out of my dad's house that day.

When I was about two weeks pregnant, I started meeting with Linda from Adoption Options, a local non-profit agency, to talk about open adoption. In an open adoption, you get to look at profiles of prospective adoptive parents that include photos of them and letters from them. You choose a few that you feel a connection with, and then you set up a meeting with them. When you find the couple that resembles what you are looking for, you start discussing the parameters of the adoption: how often you can visit, what the baby's name will be, etc. Linda never pushed adoption on me—she was presenting one option of what I could choose to do with my baby, and she wanted to make sure I was making the right decision for me. When I was four and a half months pregnant, we met with one couple that fit what we were looking for. My mom, stepdad, and I had nice long lunch together with this couple. Connie and Scott were very down to earth, easy to get along with and easy to talk to, and they lived only an hour and a half way.

Throughout my pregnancy, I remained active. I was on a school field trip swimming in the morning and then went back to school for classes in the afternoons. After swimming that day, I wasn't feeling that great, but I stuck it out as I had some major subjects that afternoon. By the time I got home, I was in a lot of pain, so my mom and Brad took me to the hospital, where the doctor told me I was three centimetres dilated. How could I be in labour, I wondered. I was only six months pregnant. I had only just started wearing maternity clothes, and the only place I had gained any weight was in my lower back; I had no baby bump.

I was transferred to a different hospital where they would be able to care for the baby, should I give birth that day. The doctors gave me a shot to stop the labour and two shots of steroids to help develop the baby's lungs. By the next morning, the labour had stopped, although I remained in the hospital for four more days so the doctors could keep an eye on me and monitor the baby.

After I got home, I took it easy all weekend, as I was still having back pain and I had trouble sleeping. When I woke up Tuesday morning, the day I was supposed to be going back to school, I discovered that I was spotting. My mom and I headed back to the hospital where they hooked me up to a fetal heart rate monitor. A little while later, a nurse came to check on me, while doing her routine check, and then turned and ran out of the room. The next thing I knew, the doctor was in my room saying he might have to do an emergency Caesarean section if the baby's heart rate dropped again. He showed us what to look for on the fetal heart rate monitor: my mom and I were to watch that the line on the monitor didn't dip down. If it dropped again, we were to tell the nurse. I felt scared, but I was determined to stay strong and do what was best for the baby.

We kept a close eye on the monitor, and everything seemed to be normal. The doctor came back into my room to check on me and the baby a few hours later. Just as he walked in, the baby's heart rate dropped again. The doctor moved me from side to side, and the heart rate didn't return to normal. After that, everything happened very fast.

"OR now," I remember the doctor shouting. I was going for an emergency Caesarean. My mind raced: would my baby be all right? Would I ever be able to have another baby?

There were so many doctors and nurses in the operating room, along with an anesthesiologist. My mom was signing the consent forms for the operation and suiting up to come in the room with me. By the time she entered the room, they were already starting to open me up. My mom was on one side of me and one of the nurses on the other side, both holding my hands. I remember the nurse looking over top of the sheet telling me it looked like a girl. I thought she should look again, as I was sure it was a boy. Even the other nurses had agreed—they'd said, "You must be having a boy—only a boy could give you this much trouble."

But it was a girl, and before the group from the Neonatal Intensive Care Unit (NICU) took her out of the operating room, they held her up so I could see her. They took her little hand and waved it at me, and then they rushed out of the room. We waited four hours before we found out how she was doing. After that, it was another three hours until I was able to see her, and that's when I found out that she weighed only seven hundred and fifty grams, a little less than a carton of milk, and was thirteen inches long. I was overwhelmed at seeing her in a warming bed with four IVs and a ventilator. She was so small and seemed so helpless, and I couldn't help but feel helpless as well.

My baby was a day old when a nurse had told me that I needed to give her a name. Having planned for an adoption, I'd never thought about names before now. I thought about it for a bit and remembered that in one of my favourite movies, *Cocktail*, I liked the girl's name Jordan, and from that moment forward, she was known as Jordan.

Jordan was in the Level 1 NICU for seven weeks, and then she graduated and was in the Level 2 one for eight weeks. During her fifteen weeks in the hospital, she had two blood transfusions and many instances when her heart stopped beating. We knew she was a feisty little girl when she was only a few days old and pulled out her ventilator tube.

I started back at school two weeks after giving birth to Jordan. The school was really good; teachers would let me out of class fifteen minutes early before lunch so I could pump milk for Jordan when the other kids wouldn't be in the office. They also allowed me to use the school phone so I could call the hospital to check up on Jordan.

After spending seven weeks concentrating on her, I had to start thinking once again about my choice for adoption. I had found out that the couple I had picked to be Jordan's parents had been chosen by another birth mother, which meant I had to start my search again. My mom and I talked about what Jordan needed from her new family. We changed a few of our original requirements: for example, we needed a stay-at-home mom for Jordan, because if she had to be in a daycare, she had a good chance of ending up sick, which could land her back in the hospital. After all that Jordan had been through in the first few weeks of her precious life, we did not want her to have to spend any more time in the hospital.

Once again, my parents and I started to look at the many files for prospective families for Jordan. We found a few that we liked, but they turned us down because they were scared Jordan might have future health problems. Then, the social worker at Adoption Options suggested that we look at one particular family in Edmonton. Our only hesitation concerning this family was that they lived three hours away. With everything we had gone through and spending so much time with Jordan, we had all become so attached to and were forming a special bond with her. We could not bear to be that far away from her.

The social worker phoned the family, Anne and Tim, to see if they would be willing to take on the responsibility of a premature baby. They said, "She belongs in our family." My mom, Brad, and I met with them and had a really nice visit. We found out that the little boy they had already adopted had celebrated his third birthday on the same day I first went into labour and that both of the kids' names started with *J*—for me, it was like a sign that this connection was meant to be.

The next day, Anne and Tim came up to see Jordan. I asked Anne if they were planning on changing Jordan's name. "No, her name is Jordan," she replied. That meant so much to me, since she was Jordan to us. My parents and I told Anne and Tim that they were the couple that we would like to have adopt Jordan.

My mom and I chose to do a giving-in-love ceremony, with all of our friends and family present. We played a few songs and said a few prayers that my mom and I had chosen, and then I handed Jordan over to her new family. Once again, I had so many emotions running through me. I was sad, but at the same time I was happy, as I knew I was doing the right thing for Jordan. I was only a fourteen-year-old girl in Grade 8. I didn't have a proper education, and without one, I couldn't get a decent job to support both myself and Jordan. Jordan's dad was not in the picture. He was not there to support us emotionally or financially. Jordan deserved to have a family with both a mom and a dad to raise, teach, guide, educate, and support her. As I handed Jordan over to Anne, I looked in her new parents' eyes and knew her presence in their family would bring them joy.

After the ceremony, Anne asked when we would like to come and see Jordan next. We asked if we could come in two weeks, and they had no problem with that. Those two weeks felt like a lifetime, since my mom and I were used to seeing her every day. Since then, my family and I have always felt very welcomed in Anne and Tim's house. I remember when Jordan was almost a year old, Anne would leave the room so we could have more one-on-one time with Jordan. When Jordan was four, we started staying overnight at a hotel in Edmonton close to their house on her birthday weekend. Anne and Tim asked us if we would like Jordan to stay with us overnight, which meant so much to me.

When we drive up to Anne and Tim's house, Jordan and her older brother, Jonathan, are always sitting at the window waiting for us, when they see us pull up outside they start yelling, "They're here!" We have always tried to ensure that Jonathan doesn't feel left out. We take birthday and Christmas presents for him as well as Jordan. Whenever we spend time with Jordan, we make sure that we spend some time with Jonathan as well.

Anne, Tim, and the kids came out to my parents' cabin and spent a week with us a few summers ago. They also came to my sister's bridal shower and her wedding two summers ago. We normally see each other five or six times a year. My sister and I have also watched the kids a few times when Tim has had conferences in Calgary.

To this day, I have never regretted my decision. The relationship that we have developed with this family has turned them into our extended family. When we go and visit them in Edmonton, it's to visit the whole family, not just Jordan. I know Jordan is also very happy, because she always tells me, "I am so happy I am adopted." When I ask her why, she says, "Because I have more people who love me and I have more people to love."

Raquel Schneidmiller lives in Calgary, Alberta, but grew up in Langdon, a small town outside of the city. She started working in oil and gas in 2003 and received her Applications to Engineering certificate in 2005. When not working, she enjoys playing baseball and travelling.

instead

BONNIE EVANS

FALSE MEMORY. I AM what, perhaps five or six? The house is old, Victorian, high and dark, surrounded by a small overgrown yard and a black iron fence. I am with my mother, and we are at the orphanage that was my home for the first four months of my life. We are bringing my outgrown clothes and castoff toys to the children who live there. Through the front door into an entry hall, dark faded wallpaper and steep narrow stairs lead up to the bedrooms and nursery. A woman stands at the top of the stairs looking down at us, backlit by an upstairs window, her red hair a nimbus of fire around her head. I believe this to be my birth mother. I know that I'm adopted and that I came from this house, but I'm not yet old enough to understand what this means. I think that, like the old woman who lived in a shoe, she had too many children so she gave some of us away. The proof is her red hair. My mother wants a girl with red hair; she's always inspecting my white-blonde locks for hints of strawberry. The woman speaks, but what she says I no longer remember. We follow her up the stairs to the nursery. A long row of iron cots along one wall, high, narrow windows at the end of the room. This was your bed, my mother tells me. Which mother? I can't remember.

I was born in 1942 at the Florence Crittenton Home for Unwed Mothers in Fargo, North Dakota, then transferred to an orphanage run

by the Children's Home Society. At the time of my birth, the law stipulated that no child be given for adoption before the age of three months
so that he or she could be assessed for physical or mental defects. Thus
children like me — and in 1942 there were an estimated eighty thousand
of us in the United States — spent our early days in institutional rows of
iron cots, like cabbages lined up in a supermarket's produce department.
Prospective parents like mine came to such institutions to pick out a new
son or daughter. How, I wondered, did they decide which one to take?

We turn myth into truth over time. Someone has written a history of
the Children's Home Society. I haven't read it, but on the website selling
it, the book cover shows a large white framed building set on spacious
grounds. So vivid, so absolute is my memory of that dark Victorian
house that, despite the evidence, I cannot believe this is the same place.
I test my memory. Where was my father, my brother? Did I see other
children there? Were the iron cots occupied? I remember nothing else.
I've stripped the story to its essential elements: the mothers, the stairs,
the red hair, the iron cots.

Even in 1942, adoption had come a long way from the notorious
baby farms of Victorian England. Only a generation before I was born,
the Home Children, orphans or children of poor or single mothers,
were shipped out from Britain to the colonies as free labour. They
were chosen on the basis of usefulness — a strong boy to help with farm
work, or a capable girl to work in the kitchen. There were no social
workers inspecting their living conditions and often no formal adoption
process. The emphasis was on their labour; the children themselves,
once described in the *Globe and Mail* as "guttersnipes," were sometimes
viewed with hostility and suspicion. For proof, you need look no further than the Canadian classic, *Anne of Green Gables*. When Marilla tells
Rachel Lynde that she and Matthew are adopting, Rachel is horrified
and full of tales of ungrateful orphans who poisoned the families who
took them in or burned down the house. Marilla has her own doubts:
"At first Matthew suggested getting a Home boy. But I said 'no' flat to

that . . . no London street Arabs for me. Give me a native born at least. There'll be a risk, no matter who we get. But I'll feel easier in my mind and sleep sounder at nights if we get a born Canadian."

By the time I was born, much had changed. Formal adoption laws had been put in place to protect the interests of the child. Adoption records were "sealed" in order, according to lawmakers of the day, to protect adopted children from the "stain of illegitimacy." Gradually, adoption agencies were formed, and social workers were brought in to inspect and approve potential homes and to give guidance to the new parents. Parents were told to present their children with an "adoption story" that would parallel the birth stories of their friends, and to tell it from the beginning, so the child would always know and never be shocked by the realization that she was adopted.

Innocence. There are dozens of photographs of me as a toddler, as a preschooler. I look radiantly happy in those pictures, posing and smiling, my whole face lit up. Then the pictures stop. I don't know if it is coincidence that they stop at the point when I start school. But it feels symbolic.

I am eight or nine. I know, now, that the woman at the top of the stairs is not my mother. That no one knows who my mother is. Other children know that they are Swedish or German, Catholic or Lutheran. I know that I am Adopted. In my school, every child is white. Every child is Christian. The despised minorities aren't black or brown; they are the poor kids with their hand-me-down clothes and dirty necks, the boy with the polio-withered arm, and me, the girl who was adopted. Other kids avoid us as if we were contagious, or taunt us into tears and rage. I am no longer innocent. I know what a bastard is.

I have absorbed the lessons implicit in my adoption story, that my mother wanted a baby girl with red hair, that the only redhead available had a birthmark, a red stain across her cheek to match her hair. That they got me instead.

Nightmare. In my dream, I walk along the beach at our summer cottage. Above the beach, in the trees, there appears to be a barn. I walk up through the dry sand and go inside. The barn is lined with stalls, and in one of them is a small red plane, not much taller than I am. As I stand in front of it, the propeller on its nose begins to turn and the plane moves toward me. I want to run but I cannot move. Just as the propeller is about to hit my face, I wake up screaming, only to sleep again and dream the same dream again and again.

Thus, being unblemished is added to the other elements required for safety, for belonging. I had to be pretty; I had to be nice; I had to be smart. I had to prove to the world that my parents hadn't made a mistake, and I had to be grateful, very grateful. "We didn't have to take you, you know," my mother would say when she was angry with me. "Who asked you to," I would reply. And the battle lines were drawn.

While I had figured out by the time I was in high school why I had such an antipathy for girls with red hair, I was well into my thirties before I understood the genesis of my nightmare. Red plane, damaged face.

The best of times, the worst of times. I am in the Grade 5 section of Mr. Shearer's Grade 5/6 class. I sit toward the back of the second row, farthest from the door. The Grade 6 kids are in three rows on the other side. From there, my nemesis, Marilyn Anderson, rules both grades with a sharp eye and a nasty tongue. No one escapes, but I am her favourite victim. I am too smart, always with my hand waving frantically in the air. I know, I know! Call on me. I am taller by a foot than any of my classmates and unfashionably dressed. I leave a trail of litter wherever I go—pencils, mittens, erasers, and boots. I am a foreigner, a clumsy and awkward Gulliver among my tidy Lilliputian classmates.

We are studying Asia in geography class—and here you have to remember this was sixty years ago. India is particularly fascinating. In India, we learn, they worship cows. I am enchanted. I know cows; I like cows. I fancy a dim, placid, bovine god.

A few days or maybe weeks later, for who knows what reason, Mr. Shearer is explaining to the class the difference between obscenity and profanity. Obscenity, he tells us, relates to bodily functions — the words we think of as "dirty." Profanity, on the other hand, is the use of religious words that express a lack of regard or contempt for God. My hand shoots into the air; I bounce up and down with excitement. "So then," I say, "in India, if I said, 'Holy Cow,' that would be profanity because they think cows are gods." Mr. Shearer looks startled, my classmates snicker. But I am exalted. I have had a thought entirely my own. That comic book cliché, the light bulb turning on above the head, is exactly how I feel. The taunts, the bullying fade in importance. I've turned a corner, and a new country of the mind has opened before me.

If this were one of those children's series of biographies I read by the dozen as a child (*Clara Barton, Red Cross Nurse*), I would have gone on from that moment to discover radium, or the cure for cancer. But I was still me. My delight in ideas could only give me respite from the chaos of my days. School remained a mixed blessing, but home was increasingly a battlefield.

Uncivil war. I am standing at the top of the stairs in the grip of a white hot rage. Maybe I am seven or eight. I don't remember the quarrel that sent me to my room, my mother threatening at the bottom of the stairs. I turn and blurt the unforgiveable: "I hate you. You aren't my real mother. My real mother would never . . ." Would never what? Again, I don't remember. But I do remember the sudden silence, my mother going quite still, then turning on her heel and walking away. Twenty minutes later, I approach. She stands at the stove, her back to me. I weep with remorse: "I'm sorry, I'm sorry. I love you. I'm sorry." She doesn't turn, won't speak, won't forgive. That I am inconsolable doesn't matter. There is nobody here who will console me.

My mother was and remains a mystery to me. She would never, even when I was an adult and we had achieved a tentative peace, talk about herself or her past. She was born in 1901, the year of Queen Victoria's death, eight years before the publication of *Anne of Green Gables*. The daughter of Danish immigrants, she had a hard, impoverished childhood. Her father, I was told by an older cousin, was a drunk, and her mother ran a country store, working from sunup to sundown, while her three children, my mother the middle child, ran wild. She met my tall, handsome, hard-working father when he was demobbed after the First World War. Together they built a life, a successful business, social prominence, a beautiful home. For nearly twenty-five years they worked and played together. Parties, nightclubs, concerts, movies. My mother's diary, Valentine's Day, 1940: "Violets from Tommy." The only thing missing in this perfect life was children.

I was to have the childhood my mother never had. She gave up her parties, her concerts, the nightclubs, and the movies. She had waited a long time to be a mother. She was going to be a perfect mother, and her perfect children would be the proof.

I am in Grade 3, and Miss Fleming, the music teacher at my school, is getting married. My mother is having a shower for her, and all the teachers are coming. I am beside myself with excitement and importance. My teacher, Miss Oleson, a small, spare woman, whom I adore, arrives early. Under the guise of showing her the house, my mother takes her upstairs to my bedroom, shows her my messy room, opens the closet door so she can see the pile of dirty underwear lying in a heap on the floor. Miss Oleson shakes her head in sympathy, tells my mother how I throw my coat on the cloakroom floor instead of hanging it up neatly. "See," my mother says to me. "Nobody likes a messy girl." I am stunned. Humiliated. Betrayed.

Humiliation was only one of the weapons in my mother's struggle to turn me into the daughter she wanted. Spankings, criticism, and hostile silences all played a role. I, for my part, grew more and more withdrawn, escaping into books, daydreams, and lies. I lied to my mother because I was afraid of her, afraid of the punishments that came like lightning strikes from a sunny sky, reprisals for things I didn't even know were crimes. I lied to my friends in order to be somebody. The violence escalated as I grew older. The wooden yardstick broke across my backside and was replaced with the wire handle of the fly-swatter. Always the arguments seemed to circle back to the facts of my origins. I wasn't grateful. She wasn't really my mother. The funny thing is that she had one weapon in her arsenal that she never used, probably never knew she had. I wanted her to love me.

Memory moves forward. I am in my forties and sitting in the office of yet another in a series of therapists who try to help me unravel my discontent, my depression. She has given me a homework assignment: write down ten occasions in my early life when I was happy. She reads the list, then comments. "Do you notice anything about this list?" I don't. "There are no people here. You are always alone." She was mistaken; there was one person, there was Miss Murray.

Because I was a child in the era of polio epidemics, my parents bought a summer cottage on an isolated lake in Minnesota where there were no other children. It was my parents' greatest gift to me. I had a small wooden boat, a 5 HP Johnson motor, a peanut butter sandwich, and a fishing rod. For whole days I would lose myself in any one of a thousand places on the lake, at the beach, in the woods, and nobody worried, restricted me, or set rules about where I could or couldn't go. It was the closest I ever expect to be to heaven. And I had Miss Murray, an elderly spinster who had a cabin a quarter mile down the road from us. I spent hours with her every day. She loved me absolutely, listened to all my childish grievances, and kept my secrets, always took my side against my brother and mother. We played Chinese checkers on rainy days; on sunny days, we walked through the woods or went swimming, she wearing her funny 1920s era woollen bathing suit. She told me stories of plants and wolves and deer; she listened to me sing "The Tennessee Waltz" at the top of my lungs over and over and over. I never had to pretend with Miss Murray. I don't think I ever lied to her.

I believe with all my heart that without those summers of freedom and Miss Murray's love, I would never have made it to adulthood.

Fast forward now, through the agony of adolescence, the first failed marriage, the melodramatic lens through which I viewed my life. I am in my early thirties, a wife and mother myself. My father has summoned me home; my mother is dying after a long and painful illness. The hospital room is crowded with my father, my brother, and my cousin Vivian. My mother is semi-comatose.

"Frances," my father says in a loud voice to rouse her. "Bonnie is here." My mother opens her eyes for a moment. "Poor Bonnie. You must be so tired, dear. Why don't you go lie down on the sofa?" And then she's gone again.

I've never before heard such affection in her voice. She is no longer the powerful force I have struggled against all my life. She is weak and vulnerable. And it occurs to me that she must, after all, have loved me. I sit vigil by her bedside. I listen as she mumbles in the dreamscape she now inhabits. Each day she moves back and back in memory. And on the last day, she is a child again and cries out, "Mommy, mommy, help me, help me." I cannot stop crying.

We are at the bank, my brother, my father, and I. A lawyer is removing the contents of my mother's safe deposit box, each item named and placed on the table. The Last Will and Testament of Frances Thoms; Certificate of Adoption for Cheryl Ann Goodman. So there it is. At the one moment in my life when I least care about any other mother than the one who raised me, I discover her. I had a name in those months before real life began. I wasn't just a cabbage, waiting for someone to take me home and turn me into something else. For a few years after that, I imagined the life that girl might have had, saw her hovering at the edges of my peripheral vision.

ॐ Birth mother. I don't like that phrase. There's too much mother in it. And yet . . . and yet. I was closer to fifty than forty when my brother, who had been searching for his birth mother, called to say that in his search for his mother, he had found mine, and did I want the information. I wasn't sure. On the one hand, there was medical information I wanted—a bout of breast cancer and two daughters made that seem more important than it once had been. On the other hand, I was the mother of grown children—I hadn't thought about adoption or my birth mother for years. I was, or so I felt, all mother, no daughter. Oh grow up, I'd think when friends still dealing with living mothers would complain about their relationships. I could no longer relate to the daughter's plight. I was a mother, full stop. And I had no desire to be a daughter ever again.

But curiosity, and the desire for a medical history, won out. There was an approach, initial reluctance on her part, then correspondence and an agreement to meet.

Nervous. I can see no family resemblance at all. She is tiny—too small to be mother to someone as tall as me. We sit in her tidy living room. She offers tea. She talks about her teaching life in the schools of California, her years in Japan, her divorce, and her husband's subsequent suicide. Her daughter and her grandchildren. Finally she looks at me and says, "What do you want to know?"

"My father?" I ask.

She tells me then. About the hired man on her parents' Depression-era farm, how he began to sexually assault her when she was eight years old. How in her senior year of high school she realized she was pregnant. How she finished school, then left for Fargo, telling her parents she had a job as a maid. How she wrote to them all through her time at the Home for Unwed Mothers, letters full of news about her job and the family she worked for. How she went on to university, married, taught, and never looked back, never told a living soul that she'd had a baby. "You may not have had an easy life," she said to me, "but don't kid yourself that it would have been any better with me."

I cannot say that I am who I am because of my adoption. I cannot separate adoption from the facts of a difficult childhood. I do know that meeting my birth mother made a difference, filled some of the void. I admire her tremendously, am awestruck by her sheer grit and determination. And I think I recognize in her a love of knowledge, an intellectual curiosity that mirrors my own. There are now solid bits of fact and history where before there was nothing or at best fantasy. But it's too late. The void, the sense of otherness, of non-belonging is so much a part of me with all its ramifications—good and bad—that our visit really didn't change me. Perhaps if I had met her when I was in my twenties, perhaps if, like so many adopted children today, she had been known to me all my life, it would have made a difference.

I look, sometimes, when I'm in the supermarket, at parents who are walking with children clearly adopted, Chinese perhaps or African, and I think to myself, my God, how will they cope when these children are twelve or thirteen or fifteen and ask questions that can't be answered? Maybe it will be different for them. There is so much more information now, parents can prepare better. But I think the void will be there for those children as it was for me.

I wonder at the vividness of those childhood memories and their ability to sting after all these years. I no longer blame my mother for the mistakes I've made along the way. It would be outrageous after sixty years to claim that I am who I am because of my adoption or my mother. As in every life, there have been good choices and bad.

I would like to be able to say that my childhood doesn't matter anymore. I would like to be one of those smug people who say, "My parents spanked me and it didn't hurt me any." The truth, however much I'd like to deny it, is that it did hurt—does hurt. Real pain causes real scars. They don't go away.

This morning, standing at my window, looking out over the long sidewalk that leads to my house, I watched a mother and her toddler—a little girl in a fluffy white dress. Mom stopped to chat with a neighbour. The little girl, unnoticed, wandered down the sidewalk toward the intersection. I watched the mother, suddenly aware, run after the child, yank her arm, and drag her back, her angry walk too fast for the child, half stumbling, half running. I know, because I am an adult, that mom is angry because she has been frightened. But it's hard not to interfere. Transference, the therapist would call it. But I know that yank that feels as if it will pull your arm from its socket. I know the bewilderment at a parent's sudden and inexplicable rage. I resist the impulse to call out—oh don't, don't, please don't.

Bonnie Evans spent most of her adult life in British Columbia working as a teacher, a writer, an editor, and an administrator. For the past five years, she has lived in Calgary, Alberta, where she plays with her grandchildren when she isn't working.

a grandfather's perspective

JIM TAYLOR

FIVE YEARS AGO, I went to Ethiopia to become a grandparent. My wife, Joan, and I accompanied our daughter, Sharon, who was adopting a ten-month-old Ethiopian orphan.

Never having found a mate who measured up to her standards, Sharon found herself in her late thirties facing a childless future. She tried artificial insemination. She tried—and almost succeeded—with in-vitro fertilization. Finally, she turned to international adoption.

The year before, we had taken Sharon with us on a trip to Africa. The continent enchanted her. The children we visited in an orphanage in Tanzania captivated her. So when the adoption agency she was working through offered her an Ethiopian child, she leaped at the chance.

I was in Toronto on a business trip when my wife telephoned me. "Hi, Grandpa," she said. Both of us started crying—we had almost resigned ourselves to never being grandparents.

We knew that Sharon, as a single mom, would need additional help during those first critical days of adoption. So, in mid-March 2005, we accompanied her to Ethiopia. Because we wanted to know something about our new granddaughter's heritage, we went a week early to travel around some of the historic parts of the country—particularly Gondar, city of kings, and Lalibela, where a twelfth-century emperor carved thirteen churches out of solid rock.

In the country's capital, Addis Ababa, we finally got to see our new granddaughter. She lay on a carpet in a foster home, with eight other children also awaiting adoption.

"If you can pick out your child from the others," an attendant teased us, "you can keep her."

We had seen only one picture of the baby girl who had been named Rediet (pronounced "ready-yet")—"blessing" in Amharic, the national language. We knew nothing of her history, except that she had been abandoned as a newborn. She still had a withered umbilical cord attached when someone—we will never know who—left her at the gate to a rural school for the blind, run by missionaries.

Sharon picked her infant daughter up. Then, the three of us hugged a bewildered, unresponsive infant, ours eyes so overflowing with tears that our glasses fogged up, our throats choked up so much we could not speak.

The next day, we brought Rediet home to our guest house. Sharon spent three days trooping from one government agency to another, completing the paperwork that would allow her to take her new daughter out of Ethiopia and into Canada.

A chance conversation made me aware why poor nations often resent richer nations. During our week of travels before the actual adoption, we shared a sightseeing minibus with a young Ethiopian couple. He had spent seven years attending school in the United States; she had never been outside of Addis Ababa.

He favoured international adoptions. "It gives children a chance that they would not have otherwise," he said. "As orphans, they will always be at the bottom of the ladder here. They will be denied opportunities that others have."

She disagreed. "But they will lose their language and their culture," she protested. "Even if you teach them about it, it is still not their culture, and they will be strangers in their own country."

"But . . ." he began.

She cut him off. "You're taking our babies," she snapped at us.

I could sympathize with her sense of loss, although it was also our gain.

In recent centuries, the imperial nations thought they brought the benefits of modern medicine, literacy, education, technology, and trade to their colonies. The colonies saw mainly a steady erosion of their natural resources, customs, and language—as well as their people. Some were taken forcibly as slaves. Others, the best and the brightest, left voluntarily to seek fame and fortune in London or Paris or New York.

The British Museum in London has preserved probably the world's greatest collection of artifacts from around the world—manuscripts, statues, crowns, jars, and vases. From a colony's perspective, however, most of those artifacts were looted. They were taken, without payment or permission, by Europeans who assumed the right to help themselves to whatever they found, since the local owners were obviously too primitive to understand their value or to preserve them.

Now, those local people see the pattern repeating. Parents from rich nations adopt children from poor nations; the flow never goes the other way. And good intentions are muddied by unscrupulous predators who adopt children for use in the sex trade or even as unwilling donors for organ transplants. Little wonder poor nations get cautious; little wonder the approval process can take a year or more.

The Alberta and federal governments wanted to ensure that Sharon would be a competent mother, that the baby would not be a burden on taxpayers. Ethiopia wanted to protect its children from exploitation. There were police checks, financial checks, and health checks. If Sharon had gotten pregnant the conventional way, no one would have questioned her. But for an international adoption . . .

One woman asked Sharon, after she returned to Canada: "How much did you pay for your baby?" As if one could buy a daughter in a discount store. The short answer is: nothing. Sharon did not buy Rediet from anyone. A longer answer is that the adoption process cost roughly twenty thousand dollars—all paid as fees to organizations, government agencies, hotels, and airlines for specific services.

The Dalai Lama established a chain of schools in the Himalayas for children smuggled out of Chinese-occupied Tibet. Children as young as five had to walk out over nineteen-thousand-foot mountain passes in deep snow. Some lost fingers and toes to frostbite. But they are not available for adoption because the Dalai Lama realizes that no matter how well intentioned the adoptive parents, the children will grow up Canadian or British or German, but not Tibetan.

Nevertheless, whatever Ethiopians think about international adoptions in general, they showed us no hostility.

Six families, including ours, travelled together to Ethiopia under the auspices of Canadian Advocates for the Adoption of Children (CAFAC). Three families adopted their first child. The others already had children, some by previous international adoptions. But they wanted to give a few more children a better life.

To our granddaughter's Ethiopian name of Rediet, Sharon added the Canadian name Katherine. I can't claim that Katherine Rediet Taylor's life will be happier in Canada than it would have been in Ethiopia. But I can state that without people like us, she might not have had a life at all. She was abandoned at a rural school. It's a recurring litany at orphanages: Abandoned by his mother at the hospital. Left at the police station. Found at the door of the church. At least those mothers hoped that someone would look after their infants. Other children had less chance: Mother dead of AIDS. Parents killed in car accident. One newborn dumped just hours after birth in a pile of old car tires, his umbilical cord still attached. Another boy's distraught mother tried to suffocate him with a plastic bag; he suffered permanent brain damage.

These children are alive today only because of altruism—what the Dalai Lama sometimes refers to as the finest virtue. Without it, there would have been no school for the blind at which to leave Katherine, no orphanage to take her to. And no CAFAC to match adoptable children with potential parents.

Katherine was not an easy adoption. When we got her, she had an ear infection that kept her awake at night, screaming. In a crowded orphanage, with two or more children stacked in each crib, and then in the foster home awaiting our arrival, she had had little personal attention and no encouragement. At ten months old, she couldn't roll over yet, let alone crawl. She showed no interest in toys. When we touched her hands, she withdrew them.

I remember holding her in my arms on one of my night shifts, synchronizing my breathing with hers to soothe her. She was, for a few moments, silent. Ethiopians have very dark irises. I remember looking into those almost black eyes and knowing that I could not, ever, betray her wordless trust.

Fortunately, once she came to Canada, she progressed rapidly. She learned to crawl, to play, to talk. Sharon's friends had somewhat unorthodox teaching methods—they taught Katherine to cough and burp. Among her first words were, "'Scuse me, I burp."

After two years, Sharon and Katherine were both passing social workers' reviews with flying colours, and Sharon felt capable of adopting a second child. Joan and I were nervous—we knew from experience that two children are not just twice as much work, more like four times as much. But if Sharon wanted to give us a second grandchild, we would support her. She asked for a boy this time. She told us she would name him Stephen, after her older brother, who died of cystic fibrosis shortly before his twenty-second birthday.

In October 2008, she got word that a boy had been found for her. His Ethiopian name was Tekalegn (pronounced "teck-uh-lin"). Sharon asked an Ethiopian woman in her Edmonton congregation what Tekalegn meant. The woman paused, and then said, "It's hard to translate. It means something like 'replacing something precious that was lost.'" The coincidence took our breath away. It still does.

Joan and Sharon happily prepared for Stephen's arrival in the six months before he was to come home. They repainted "Stephen's room." Joan knitted sweaters for him. Katherine, now three, set aside toys for her little brother. She imagined him as a ready-made playmate. She couldn't imagine what having a baby would be like.

As it turned out, he wasn't a baby anymore. His birth certificate claimed he was not quite a year old when Sharon brought him back to Canada. But he already had six teeth. He ran. He pushed kitchen chairs around and had sufficient manual dexterity to put caps on pens.

From the bits of information we have been able to piece together, we learned his mother died. He lived for eight months with his father and two older children in a mud hut. They signed him over to a local orphanage, who sent him to CAFAC's foster home in Addis Ababa. From there, he came to frosty Edmonton. In an estimated eighteen months, he lived in four places, hearing at least three languages. The experiences set him back emotionally; he's still recovering.

But I delight in watching his progress. From being withdrawn, he has become cuddly. From sullen silence, talkative. From angry, co-operative — at least, on his better days.

As I've watched those two grandchildren develop, I've given considerable thought to the conversation we had with the husband and wife on the bus in Ethiopia. And while I have sympathy with the woman's view, I find myself increasingly supporting her husband's.

Because an infant does not have a culture. Not yet. Culture is not bred into DNA. It is learned, absorbed, by living within that culture, by being immersed in it. Ethiopia is a spectacular country, with its own unique language, a rich artistic tradition, and an illustrious religious heritage. Former emperor Haile Selassie claimed direct descent from biblical King Solomon. The Church of St. Mary, in Axum, in the far north of the country, may preserve the original Ark of the Covenant that Moses built to house the Ten Commandments. But a one-year-old child knows nothing of that.

Katherine and Stephen will grow up as Canadian as any child born in Canada. They have known no other culture — although they will, over time, be introduced to as much information as possible about the land of their birth. Is that a loss to them? I think it is more a loss to Ethiopia than to the children. The child is not robbed of her culture; the culture is robbed of the child. That's essentially what happened in Canada's Indian Residential Schools. A dominant European culture robbed Native communities of all their children, attempting to raise them in a different culture. The results, as we now know, were catastrophic. What we don't know, what we can never know, is what might have resulted from leaving those children in their home environment.

Ethiopia's rate of infant mortality, for example, is twenty times higher than Canada's, its per capita income forty times lower. By international reckoning, Canada has near-universal literacy (although Canadian agencies estimate that 40 per cent of Canadians are functionally illiterate); only one-third of Ethiopians qualify as literate. Canadians, on average, live thirty years longer than Ethiopians. Under those circumstances, does remaining in one's home culture outweigh the risks?

Obviously, exporting children to Canada is no solution. A long-term solution requires improving Ethiopia's situation — economically, socially, environmentally — so that all children can benefit, rather than a select few.

I love my adopted grandchildren dearly. They run to me with arms extended. "Gran'pa!" they call. I sweep them up and they wrap their arms around my neck. But they're starting to notice that their arms are not the same colour as mine. We are not genetically related. There is no way the two of them will ever resemble a blue-eyed, blonde-haired Scots-Irish descendant. Their mother is even more fair-skinned than I am. The difference doesn't bother them, yet.

But someday, I'm sure, Katherine and Stephen will wonder why they're different. Why they were taken away from their home country. What their biological mothers were like. Even if these questions don't

occur to them, their schoolmates will almost certainly draw the differences to their attention.

Sharon has never hidden her children's origins. They enjoy Ethiopian
food. Pictures of Ethiopia flicker on Sharon's computer screen. Their
bedrooms are painted with African scenes.

I hope, I trust, I believe that Katherine and Stephen will survive the
adjustments that confront all adopted children. So much will depend on
the friends they choose, as they grow toward adulthood.

That's where I discover a streak of prejudice within myself that I
hadn't known I had. Because I picture my grandchildren in a cluster
of kids. Mostly black kids, like them. In that context, I'm an outsider.
And despite years of battling prejudice, a shadowy recess of my mind
still seems to harbour unflattering stereotypes of black youths. I don't
want my grandkids to hang out with dropouts, gang members, Rastas. I
want them to associate with—well, with educated, intelligent, purpose-
ful kids. Like me.

I hope—dear God, how I hope!—that I never yield to the tempta-
tion to blame their genetic ancestry as Katherine and Stephen grow, as
they test their limits, as they test *our* limits. If they carried my own DNA,
I couldn't. But they don't. Somehow, I have to wipe that awareness out
of my mind, to see only two delightful children whom I love with all my
heart.

Jim Taylor has been a writer and editor for more than fifty years. He is
the author of fifteen books and has ghost-written six more. He writes
two newspaper columns a week but is otherwise semi-retired, living in
British Columbia's Okanagan Valley. His daughter and grandchildren live
in Edmonton, Alberta.

when everything goes just right: a love story

LORI MCMINN

IN 1980, I WAS the new kid at a big Catholic high school in Edmonton, Alberta. That first day of Grade 11 was the scariest day of my life. I had just moved from a school of four hundred students in tiny Belleville, Ontario, where I had perfect attendance, was on the honour roll, and played on most of the sports teams. I was a geek who always dreamed of fitting in with the popular kids, but I was happy with my best friend, Paula. I worked hard in school and didn't waste much time with hair, makeup, purses, or clothes.

One of the first people among my new school's fifteen hundred students was a boy named Garrett. He was seventeen, two years older than I was. He was tall, lanky, and lean, with dark skin, hair, and eyes. He wore the uniform of the day: tight jeans, sneakers, and a New York Islanders' hockey jersey. He was cocky and impressed me with his confidence. We began a stormy relationship. He was verbally abusive, and I was totally out of his league, having never had a boyfriend before. He had me chasing after him all the time and believing him when he told me that the other girls who wanted him were more sophisticated and attractive than I was. He discarded me a few times, but I didn't see the mistreatment the way I needed to, I didn't realize it was abusive.

After one school-year of dating, Garrett's father committed suicide. Soon after, Garrett became physically abusive, and just a few months later, I became pregnant. Garrett played a smooth game at first, telling me he would take care of me. But one day, when he got angry with me, he said, "You better be nice, cupcake, because I'm all that you've got!" I promptly went downstairs and told my mom about my pregnancy. "You are *not* the only one I've got," I told myself.

After I told her, mom was quiet for a few moments. "Well, what are we going to do about this?" she said, and I knew I was not alone. I told her that Garrett and I had been contemplating abortion. She was quiet again, then said, "That baby inside of you did not ask to be conceived by you." She took Garrett and me to Planned Parenthood, and I remember being shocked that Garrett came along. But by that point, I had already decided I wasn't having an abortion. Maybe, if I'm honest, it was to spite Garrett, because I knew he wanted me to have one, or because my mom's words gave me pause.

Later that month, my mom and I discussed adoption, and a representative from the city's children's services came to talk to us. The answers to the questions we asked were very unsettling: I would not be given any information about my child's adoptive parents, ever. And they wouldn't get any information about me.

Luckily, my family had a friend in Father Conrad Verreault, the Catholic priest at the church on the military base where we lived. My mom played the organ there on Sunday mornings, and I played on Saturday nights. Father Verreault became aware of my predicament and came to visit one day to talk about it. When my mom and I told him we were considering adoption, he told us he knew a beautiful family in Quebec City. In his work as military chaplain, he had been stationed there for a few years before coming to Edmonton. He had met a man named Pierre, who was a military lawyer. Pierre's sister and brother-in-law had been trying for years to have a child with no success. Would I consider them?

After Father Verreault left, I felt here was the answer. Mom and I agreed that this beat the Edmonton agency's proposal hands down.

We both liked, respected, and trusted Father Verreault—if he said the family was beautiful, that was enough for me. A few weeks after we advised him of our decision, I received a letter from Pierre's sister, Danielle. It was all in French, but from the few words I could pick out, I was convinced I'd made the best decision.

In the meantime, I continued with high school until the fifth month of my pregnancy, when I started to show. After that, I continued my studies by correspondence. At the rate I was going, I would have enough credits to be able to graduate with my class. I might not have had the necessary prerequisites to attend college or university, as my parents had hoped I would. I didn't reject or endorse that idea. I don't think I could imagine life after this baby-and-Garrett drama. Garrett had made some suggestions that we should get married and keep the baby, and I was desperate to hear that he loved and wanted me. At one point, when my parents heard about this idea, they very quickly got me into counselling.

Usually, his romantic ideas didn't last long before he was ditching me for some other girl he imagined he could get, or playing his head games, or worse. There were many violent incidents. I decided not to tell Garrett about my decision. He was under the impression the baby would be adopted through the agency, that there would be no information for us, ever, and he seemed satisfied with that. He had bigger issues to worry about, and I knew better than to trust him. I felt a need to protect the baby from him and was beginning to feel angry toward him. Making this choice for our child without him made me feel better, like I had the upper hand, like this was one thing I got to control, so I kept it from him.

Through counselling, I met Phil, a social work student on a placement at the military base where we lived. At our first meeting, I told him I was only there because my parents had forced me to go. At the time, Garrett had been being sweet to me, so the tune I sang was that I knew Garrett and I could be happy if my parents would just leave us alone. Phil suspected, correctly, that I was being abused, and that I was afraid to consider going to college or university because I was beginning to believe what Garrett told me constantly: that I wasn't smart enough, good enough, pretty enough, popular enough. Phil took me to the University of Alberta, where we had lunch in the student cafeteria and toured the campus. I realized that, apart from my growing belly, the kids there looked just like me, sounded like me. Slowly, I started to believe that I had what it takes to go to that school.

The night my water broke, one month later, my mom and I had visited her friend Mrs. Evans down the street, who had held a military wives gathering. I excused myself early, because I wasn't feeling well, and went home to bed. The baby was moving around a lot, so sleep was impossible. Later, my mom came home after helping Mrs. Evans rearrange her living room after the party and went to bed. At 11:30 PM, the baby kicked, and my water broke. I was so excited—my ordeal would soon be over! I went to get my mom, who hadn't yet drifted off, and we clambered into the family Suburban for the trip to Charles Camsell Hospital.

At 10:15 the next morning, June 18, 1983, my baby boy was born. The nurses knew that he was to be adopted, so instead of just bringing him to me, they asked if I wanted to hold him. Instinctively, I said no; I didn't want to make it harder later on. They placed me in a room with expectant mothers, so that I wouldn't be exposed to moms bonding with their babies. I had five days in hospital with baby boy Holstein and could visit him in the nursery, bottle-feed him, and bring him back to my room whenever I wanted. I did this often and remember looking into his eyes and wondering, "Does he know what I'm about to do," which caused me to break down many times. Garrett came to the hospital twice. The first time, he offered me fifty dollars. The second time, I had just finished some adoption paperwork that I scooped up and stuffed under my food tray before he saw it.

On the fifth day, Father Verreault and Danielle came to the hospital.

She was tiny, all of four-foot-two, with blond hair, tanned skin, and green eyes (the same as me), and spoke very little English. She told me she was so happy, and we hugged. She spoke to Father Verreault in French, and he translated for us. "Danielle wants to know if you have a name for the baby." I said no, and he continued. "She has a name: Pierre Gabriel." I told her how beautiful it was, how perfect.

"Danielle wants to know, do you have some clothes for the baby?" I told them I did not. "She brought some clothes," Father Verrault said, and Danielle handed me some clothes to dress the baby in. But my hands were clumsy and inexperienced, so I handed them back to her. She had been a nurse in a Quebec hospital, and her sure, experienced hands had those clothes on in minutes. That was the clincher for me: this was the best decision for Pierre Gabriel.

I carried him to the elevator and out of the hospital, along with Father Verreault, Danielle, and my mom. I handed him to her, and the three of them drove out of sight. Mom and I got into the Suburban and drove in the opposite direction in silence until mom said, "I thought I would feel really bad right now, but I feel good." So did I.

Two months later, Garrett committed suicide, and my ordeal really was over. I went to university, graduated with a bachelor's degree in speech-language pathology, and moved across the country to take a job at a small-town health unit in southwestern Ontario. As the years passed, I hoped to hear from Danielle, but I didn't. It upset me at first, because she had promised to send some letters and pictures. But now, I think that was probably for the best.

When Pierre was fourteen, I began searching for the Quebec agency with his file. I wasn't trying to find him—because I knew his adoptive parents' names and where they lived, that would have been easy. But I had serious worries about his mental health, because of the history of suicide on his father's side, and I thought Danielle and Gilles should know. I thought they could keep an eye out for signs through those difficult teen years. When I finally tracked down the right agency, I was told they could not pursue contact with him until he was eighteen, but I sent them a letter about my concerns anyway.

When Pierre turned eighteen, I contacted the agency again, because the rule in Quebec was that if, after the adoptee turns eighteen, either party wants to initiate contact, the agency would act as the facilitator in that. So, the agency began the process of trying to contact Pierre, and I waited with my heart in my throat. I worried that he might not know he had been adopted, and that I would be causing a big shock to him and his family. It took nearly a year, since the agency would not disclose the reason for its call to either adoptive parent and needed to speak to him directly.

Finally, a worker named Ginette called to tell me she had met with my son. He was now nineteen years old and called Gabriel, not Pierre. She said he was tall and handsome and seemed well-adjusted and articulate. What's more, he had always known he was adopted, which was a relief to me. He had a girlfriend, lots of friends, a huge family, and a job and plans to travel. He wondered why I was doing this now. Unfortunately, he said he had no time to deal with this issue at the moment. I was disappointed but still grateful to have found out so much. I was surprised at the feeling of relief and completeness I had just from speaking with Ginette about him. That was enough for me.

Two years later, I got a call from Ginette at work. I knew it was her, because of her accent, so I knew that Gabriel had changed his mind. She confirmed it and encouraged me to begin with a letter. She advised me what to say and which photos to include. They should show my own physical development through childhood, my teenage years, and the present, and include photos of other family members. Eleven years after Garrett died, I had contacted his mother, Ginny, and she was aware of this new development. She sent me three pictures of Garrett, including his high school photo at age seventeen. Within days of sending my letter to the agency, I received a letter and photos from Gabriel—it was a rush! He was tall and dark like Garrett. He had my nose, chin, and smile but Garrett's eyebrows and hands. Gabriel's letter was in French, which I did my best to muddle through, and then asked a friend who spoke the language for help. Gabriel had great things to say about his adoptive parents, about how they taught him to respect me and my decision. He also expressed how difficult it was to write the letter and that it would be easier if we met.

So, on the following Sunday, after feeling nauseated all week, I called him. Gabriel was now twenty-one years old. His mom answered the phone. "Je veux parler avec Gabriel, s'il vous plaît," I sputtered with my high school French. Later, Gabriel would tell me he had been in bed with his girlfriend at the time, so he had some explaining to do, and I learned to call later than noon after that. His English was a little bit better than my French, so we managed to make a plan to meet. My husband, Mike, and I would drive up to Quebec City on Labour Day weekend. I asked if he'd like to meet at his house or some neutral place, like a coffee shop. "Or maybe some place they serve lots of wine?" I suggested. He laughed at that, our first joke together.

After we arrived at the hotel in Quebec City, I called Gabriel to make plans to meet. "I'll be there in one hour," he said. I hung up the phone and went into panic mode. One hour? I needed to shower, I needed to eat, but I felt too sick. I needed something to wear—but not those jeans, they're too tight. And not that shirt, it's too flirty! Mike laughed at me. I was really in a state. But I showered, dressed, and went down to the lobby, with Gabriel's photo in my hand and my heart in my throat. I saw him come up the escalator, with a photo in his hand. All six-foot-three of him, looking just like his photo, but with a much shorter haircut. He came up to me, glancing at the picture in his hand, and we embraced a little awkwardly. "You cut your hair," he said. "So did *you*," I replied, and we laughed together again.

Ginette had coached us each on what to bring to the first meeting: lots of photos that showed our families and our changes over the years. So, Gabriel opened up his backpack and took out his album. He had photos of his arrival at the airport in Montreal, where more than seventy relatives and friends were there to greet him and his mother. His grandmother held him in every photo. He was well-loved and much-wanted; it was my dream come true. He had been a very chubby baby and a good-looking youngster. There were photos of him and his parents, Danielle and Gilles. They had divorced when he was ten, around the time they had told him he was adopted. There were photos of his friends, some he had known since preschool. They all knew he was adopted, too, and some of them were hoping to meet me this weekend.

I showed him some more of the photos I had received from Garrett's mother, Ginny. I brought more pictures of Garrett's family, including his sister, Lorrie. Lorrie and I had been friends in high school, and she had a son who was three years younger than Gabriel. When he saw the pictures of Ginny's home in Red Water, Alberta, I blurted out: "That's Ginny's house." I had agonized over this moment for many months, and then I blurted again: "Garrett killed himself two months after you were born." Gab was quiet, then said, "That's heavy." Then we moved on to more photos.

Ginette had reassured me that most adopted children are most interested in finding their birth mother, so I hoped that I hadn't screwed this up, but I didn't have any idea what else to say. Often over the course of that weekend, I told Gabriel how amazing his resemblance to my little brother was. I apologized a few months later for failing to acknowledge his very strong resemblance to his father. It was my own bit of crazy, I thought, my leftover anger toward Garrett. But after meeting Gabriel, I could no longer be angry at Garett for what an amazing gift he had given me. I was able to say a quiet thank you and express to Gab the obvious: his eye colour, hair colour, hands, skin tone, eyebrows, and, of course, his height were all Garrett. From me, he got knobby knees, double-jointed thumbs, and chubby cheeks.

Later that weekend, I met Danielle again. Twenty-one years later, she looked exactly the same. Over the course of many visits, she and I would sit together with the French-English dictionary and a bottle of wine or two and talk about the amazing gifts we had given each other. And she said, "This is the end of a beautiful love story. How this story *should* end."

Since then, Gabriel has visited me and my family many times. My daughter Haley and my son Harrison are delighted with their big brother. I know they don't get to see him as much as they would like. In the first year after we met, we saw each other every month; I always say it was like being in love. I couldn't eat or sleep. I thought about him all the time and drove around thinking about him with this goofy smile on my face. The same thing happened to my mom and my dad after they met him. I have all these goofy-happy pictures of my mom at that Thanksgiving gathering Gabriel attended. He stayed with us for four months one summer and worked at a local factory. His English has improved greatly; my French, not so much. Thank goodness for Babelfish. He attended my Holstein Family reunion in Manitoba two years ago and bonded with my younger cousins. He whipped their butts at both tennis and cards and taught them to swear in French.

It hasn't all been rosy. He had tough questions about my decision to give him up, and my mother and I relived the events and came up with answers together—my recollection was that of a child's, and I had needed an adult to help me. I couldn't have made those important decisions myself. He wondered whether I could do it all again, would still have let him be adopted. I had to tell him about my childishness, his father's abuse, and how I wanted him to be protected and cared for. And after I found out about his parents, and they about me, I felt obligated, and fortunate to have had that option.

It also wasn't all easy for my family; Mike struggled a bit with accepting Gab, and all that went with him. I was ready to accept it all and wanted to do everything I could. After all, I had not contributed anything to his upbringing. So, when he and his cousin wanted to move into our tiny house with our two kids, I made it happen. It caused some problems when I extended that welcome without consulting with Mike, but we overcame it, and today, all is well.

Gabriel came to visit for Thanksgiving weekend in 2007 and met his paternal grandma, Ginny. Theirs was a wonderful reunion. I know it meant a lot to her after having lost her son to suicide. "The clouds have parted, the sun is shining again," she said. And Gabriel, so young, but so graceful with relatives due to all his experiences with all his French family's relatives, has been so kind and so good to all of my family and Garrett's. I am so proud to be his birth mother, and I feel at peace with myself and complete at last.

Lori McMinn works part-time as a speech-language pathologist with a pre-school speech and language program in Simcoe, Ontario. She lives with her husband, Mike, daughter, Haley, ten, and son Harrison, seven.

lost and found

JUDITH HOPE

SOMETIMES I HEAR HIM crying. Sobs drift through the heat vent below my bed. Whimpers prod the thin skin of my sleep. I groan, throw back the covers, and head downstairs to my son's bedroom. His body is curled tight, knees to chest, face buried in the pillow. I sit beside this gangly teenager, stroke his black curls, rub his back, and whisper that everything will be all right. His body is taut, muscle and bone. He pushes me away, but I stay until he yields a shiver of resignation and the sobbing winds down. Then, the head rocking begins, side to side, back and forth, repetitive self-soothing motions. This is not the first time, nor will it be the last. He's been pushing and pulling me for most of his life.

Scott and I met our son just a few days before Christmas 1994. There is scarce information in his file. His name is Ho Nam, born October 19, 1993. He is a ward of the court, abandoned by his teenaged birth mother. The biological father was a casual boyfriend, a used car salesman from Macau. There are no known physical or mental abnormalities. After giving birth, Cheung Wing Sze surrendered her baby to the Hong Kong Society for the Protection of Children, a residential crèche on Portland Street. Located in the heart of Mong Kok, the six-storey institution, grimy with diesel dust, towers over the nearby shops that sell building and plumbing supplies. The neighbourhood is bordered by street markets where tourists bargain for knockoff Gucci handbags and fake Rolex watches.

We are asked to wait in the playroom while one of the staff fetches Ho Nam. This child has held the accumulation of our hopes and prayers since we began the adoption process. The application is long. It asks whether we prefer a boy or girl. Would we accept a special needs child? If so, then to what degree? We list our education, Scott's salary, our marital status, and how long we plan to remain resident in Hong Kong. Three friends send in signed testimony attesting to our character.

Months pass. Then, one day, Miss Wind Soong, a petite woman dressed in a navy skirt, white blouse, and sensible shoes, shows up at our door. She arrives with a measuring tape, notebook, and pen. She is our assigned caseworker from the Hong Kong Department of Social Services, Adoption Unit. She measures whether we have the physical space for an additional family member. She questions our motives and my husband's job security, probes our health and finances, and queries our marital and emotional stability. She asks why we want to adopt when we already have a biological child. I am in my late thirties and have been unable to conceive since the birth of our son three years earlier. Scott has four siblings and I three; it never crossed our minds that we would have just one child. My husband is a journalist, and Hong Kong has been our home for the past three years; as foreign residents, we qualify to apply to adopt.

Miss Soong suggests that we stand a better chance if we are willing to accept an older male child. These children are more difficult to place, she explains. Contrary to the plethora of abandoned baby girls spilling out of orphanages in China, infertile Hong Kong couples prefer newborn girls. As citizens, they are given priority over foreign residents. "In the Chinese culture," Miss Soong says, "adoption still carries a certain stigma to it. Most couples prefer daughters because they will be married out and not carry the family name or receive its inheritance." Scott and I are shocked that this discrimination against women still prevails in the mid-1990s. "We counsel adopting parents to discuss the adoption openly with their child from an early age, but few actually do," she says.

Ho Nam toddles down the linoleum corridor; his tiny fingers clasp the hand of a young woman dressed in a white uniform. The boy is a mere fourteen months old, dressed in blue corduroy overalls. His hair is sparse, and his face and hands are scored with a tired rash of eczema that gives him the appearance of a wizened old man. A nametag attached to a frayed piece of string is knotted around his right ankle. His chart reported developmental delays, yet here he is walking. He looks at us: me, a tall woman by Chinese standards, and my husband, Scott, a taller still Caucasian man with brown hair and hazel eyes. We smile. Ho Nam clutches the staffer's leg and begins to cry. She picks him up and quickly ushers us into a room that contains a table and plastic chairs; scant toys line the shelves. I take a plastic toy car off the shelf and beckon him to come play with us. He buries his head in the chest of the staffer and cranks up the volume of his cries. We leave quickly, but there is no doubt in our minds that this little man belongs with us.

The next day, we return. This time, Matthew, three years older than Ho Nam, joins us, keen to meet his new brother. When we ask to see where the babies sleep, Miss Soong and the staff reluctantly show us a large room filled with a dozen stainless steel cribs. At the end of each is a Fisher Price activity centre. The room is unnaturally silent. The babies are uniformly dressed in faded pyjamas. Ho Nam sits in the middle of his crib watching Cantonese cartoons on a television mounted on the wall. Miss Soong tells us that the babies at this home are very well behaved—they never cry. I suspect the children know the futility of crying. The overworked staff has little time to attend to their longings to be held and comforted.

We take the boys to Hong Kong Park, a sanctuary of lush gardens and playgrounds in the heart of this concrete city. Miss Soong has told us that the crèche is understaffed. It provides what she calls sufficient stimulation, but playtime is sporadic, depending on whether a volunteer is available. Matthew leads Ho Nam to his favourite place in the park, a large sandpit filled with half a dozen mechanical digger toys. The playground is crowded. In an unsolicited gesture, Matthew slips his arm around Ho Nam's shoulders as the boys wait their turn. To pass the time, Scott picks Matthew up and swings him around. Never once does Ho Nam takes his eyes off the pair of them. After a few minutes, it's Ho Nam's turn. Scott lifts the little boy above his head and then hugs him close before spinning him around. Ho Nam smiles and then begins to giggle. He knows no English and our knowledge of Cantonese is meagre, but our son-in-waiting clearly communicates, "Again, do it again."

Three days before Christmas 1994, Ho Nam moves in. We name him Jonathan. Officially, he is still a ward of the court, but if the probation goes well, he will legally become our son at the end of six months. The first thing we do is snip off his nametag. A thin scar from the string brands his ankle. I rub cream into the dry skin. He squirms and pulls away but gradually yields to my touch. From the moment he arrives, he won't stop crying. Each time he cries, Scott or I pick him up, play with him, change his diaper, feed him, or rub cream into his eczema-covered skin. For three solid weeks he cries himself raw, until he discovers that he doesn't have to cry to get our attention.

Jonathan is not a helpless newborn when he arrives but a full-blown walking wonder. No longer does Matthew have the sole attention of two adoring parents. Instead, he has to compete with this toddler terrorist who destroys his meticulous Lego creations and loses his pet turtles. Now, Matthew has to wait his turn and share his toys. This is not quite the package he had hoped for when he asked for a baby brother.

"Mum, I want a baby sister," he says one night as I tuck him into bed. He doesn't realize that Jonathan can't be returned or traded in for another baby. Scott is winding up his contract with his company, and we won't be around long enough to complete another local adoption. Our sights are already set on moving back to Australia.

"Well, dear, if you really want a baby sister, we'll just have to pray for one," I say with faltering faith.

"I'll take care of that," Matthew says without missing a beat, looking up at me. Every night as I tuck him in, he put his hands together and prays: "Dear God, please send me my baby sister."

Six weeks later, Scott looks at me quizzically. "You taste different, like when you're lactating. Are you pregnant?" I shake my head, but the next day, I pick up a pregnancy test from the pharmacy. In the privacy of the bathroom, I watch a faint blue cross solidify on the white plastic disk in my hand and I smile. Our daughter, Annie, will be born three days shy of Jonathan's second birthday.

We move back to Australia, to Armidale, a small university town halfway between Sydney and Brisbane, close to Scott's parents and sister. We live in a one-hundred-year-old cottage across the street from a busy garden centre. The owners keep a small collection of birds and a jungle gym to occupy children while their parents shop. Jonathan and Matthew play in the yard. I keep an eye on them while weeding the petunias. Without warning one day, Jonathan bolts out of the gate and runs across the busy street. A car swerves and barely misses him. I run after and hold him tight. My heart pounds as he squirms. "Do you want to get killed?"

"I want to see the cockatoo," he says.

One Saturday each month, the main street transforms into a craft market. This day, Scott and I take the children and leisurely stroll the market's length. A couple of teenagers play their violins, busking for coins. A man beckons us to his stall filled with plastic stacking bins punched with tiny holes. We join the small crowd as he orates the benefits of vermiculture. Impulsively, we buy a worm farm and a pound of red wrigglers. I turn around; Jonathan is not with us. He has disappeared again. Scott and I each take one of the kids, split up and start searching. The market is crowded, and Jonathan is nowhere to be seen.

I am worried and angry at the same time. I don't like feeling this way. An hour later, Scott finds him trying to climb into the fountain, oblivious to our concerns.

I love each of my children. With Matthew and Annie, the bonding came in utero, an instant, unshakeable love. It bothers me that my love for Jonathan remains rooted in choice, a decision born from an act of my will. Of course I love my son, but why am I not *in* love with him? He is the squeaky wheel, the needy one, demanding, in my face, distracting, a study in motion and mischief, never able to sit still.

℘ Flash forward five years. We live in Calgary, Alberta, now, a career move for Scott with the benefit of being close to my mother and brother. The children settle into school; we go to church, make friends. Life is good until the headaches begin. Not minor headaches or even manageable migraines but pain so bad it sends Scott to the hospital. He has just been diagnosed with metastatic melanoma, and the prognosis is not good. The doctor says the cancer has spread beyond cure to his brain, liver, and lungs. We have to tell the kids.

The school bus drops Annie and Jonathan off at the corner. From my kitchen window, I see them laughing. Jonathan scoops up a handful of snow and tosses it at his sister. She jumps over the hedge and runs in the front door with her brother chasing after her. Matthew is already home. Scott and I gather them around the kitchen table as they snack on cookies and hot chocolate and tell us about their days.

Then, Scott says, "We saw the doctor at the cancer centre today, and I have some news." The clamour around the table stops. Annie comes over and climbs into my lap.

"You know I've been having these really nasty headaches? It seems I have a cancer called melanoma. Kids, the thing is, the tumours have spread to my brain, liver, and lungs. The doctor said it's spreading too far and too fast to cure it."

"Dad, what are you saying?" Matthew asks.

"Honey, the doctor said that there is no cure for Dad's cancer, and his body can't fight it off forever. He . . . he may not live long enough to see Christmas this year," I say holding onto Annie and fighting back tears.

Jonathan is so quiet you would think he isn't here. Usually, he would be tapping a spoon against his mug, interrupting one of his siblings or jumping up to get something. Right now, he just sits there staring at his dad. Scott beckons and lifts him onto his lap. He reaches for Matthew's hand, but he resists. "No. Mum, Dad, that can't be right," Matthew says, getting up from the table and looking out the window. "Dad can't die," he says.

"Matthew, it's going to be all right," Scott says.

"No, Dad, it's not," Matthew says. "It's not right, and it's not fair."

"You're right, Matthew, it isn't fair," I agree.

For one terrifying year, we fight the cancer, weaving and ducking with an unseen foe until Scott's body can wrestle no longer. Before he dies, we speak about Jonathan. His birth mother abandoned him. His biological father is a mystery; we don't even know his name. "I'm leaving him, too," Scott says, fearing that his death will only enhance Jonathan's sense of abandonment.

In the months following Scott's death, Jonathan withdraws. He flies below the radar, playing with his Lego for hours. At bedtime, I pray for him, kiss him goodnight, and hold him tight. His body stiffens at my touch, he turns away, and the head rocking begins, his face swish, swish, swishing into his pillow.

Jonathan won't get out of bed. His eleven-year-old body goes limp as I lift him carry him to the shower, strip off his pyjamas, and walk him in. I have to dress him, feed him. He has withdrawn, regressed, become like a needy toddler once more. I walk him to school as he drags his heels. I hold his hand and won't let it go lest he run. I force him to go to school because his pain, mixed with my own grief, is unbearable.

At home, he pushes all my buttons, knowing exactly what to do to provoke a yelling match. He smashes his bedroom window and kicks in his door. He lashes out and runs out the door too fast for me to catch him. I find him in the park atop a hill, sitting on the memorial bench I had installed to remember Scott. We walk home in the dark.

It's nearly Christmas. I thought I had a handle on this grief, but I am powerless. The thought of putting up a tree, baking, writing cards, and decorating the house, it all rings hollow. I call a travel agent and tell her to get me a beach, a buffet and a direct flight. She books us a last-minute, all-inclusive week in Cuba.

I lie on a long stretch of white beach beneath the same brilliant sun that triggered the cancer that killed my husband. The resort has every imaginable offering: catamaran rides, live entertainment, and a spa. If kids are hungry, they wander at will to the café by the pool and order what they want. The dining room is a divine feeding trough that never closes. The heat and the lull of the ocean begin to ease the tension in my neck and shoulders. The boys go exploring while Annie stays close by and makes sandcastles.

But at night, Jonathan can't sleep. His head rocks back and forth, swish, swish, swishing against the crisp pillowcase. Contained together in the small space of our hotel room, none of us can sleep because of the heat, the noise, because of Jonathan. I try to hush him, but he is riled and angry; he wants to run, but I block the door. I've had too much to drink. It's late, and what we all want and cannot find is just a little peace, a little quiet. I'm not thinking straight. I raise my hand and slap my son, a stinging backhand across his face. I am shocked. I never meant to harm him. I only wanted to get his attention. His pain rubs against my own gaping grief wounds. I want to reel back the past twenty minutes and start over. I want to reel back the past two years, but I can't. Instead, I have become the worst mother in the world. We need help and there is none, not in this place anyway. I feel so alone.

We fly home on Boxing Day. All the way home, the satellite news broadcasts reports of a terrible tsunami that is swallowing coastal villages in Indonesia, Sri Lanka, India, and Thailand. The closer we get to home, the higher the death toll. I look at Jonathan slumped into his seat, sitting as far from me as possible. He is sullen. I am sad, devastated by my own tsunami.

We meet with Claire, a child grief counsellor and mother of two young boys. She brings Jonathan and me into her cozy office at Hospice Calgary. Behind the sofa is a Heaven Wall plastered with children's drawings of their dead parents in heaven. Jonathan is reluctant to be here. He fiddles with the toys in a miniature sand box, buries a plastic dinosaur headfirst into the sand. I sit on the sofa and hold a mug of hot tea.

She unrolls a stretch of blank newsprint across the floor, hands him coloured markers, and says, "Draw what you remember." Jonathan looks at her for the first time. She takes him back: long before his daddy fell sick, long before we moved to Calgary, back to the beginning of his story. Knowing that we are Christians, she asks him where God is in his story. Jonathan shrugs. I fill in the blanks. For the first time, I feel safe to tell him all I know about his birth mother, the things that weren't recorded in his file, told to me by Miss Soong.

"When your mother found out she was pregnant, her own mother told her get an abortion or leave home, as she, too, had been an unwed mother. The thought of ending the life growing inside her was unbearable, and Wing Sze found her way to a hostel for pregnant women run by the church." He draws a stick figure of a young woman with a big belly standing at the steps of a church.

"After you were born, she took you to the children's home. Every week for the first nine months of your life, she would come back to see you, never quite able to sign off on the adoption papers." He draws a cot with a baby and his mother standing by. "Then, one day, she just stopped coming." Jonathan looks at me, throws the marker on the floor, and walks out the door. Claire says it's all right; we are not done yet.

Claire tells me that the first months of a child's life are crucial for healthy psychosocial development. Even though Jonathan has no conscious memory of his time at the children's home, his abandonment is buried in his psyche. Without that bonding, Jonathan and children like him experience great difficulty attaching to anyone. This push-me-pull-you syndrome is not unique to our experience.

We return each week until Jonathan's story measures nearly twenty feet in length. Each session, Claire unrolls his artwork and starts at the beginning. She coaxes him to use his words, speak out his story right through his father's sickness, dying, and death. "Where is your daddy now, Jonathan?" Claire asks. He draws a garden, filled with flowers. Scott sits on a bench, wearing his broad-brimmed Australian hat. He is smiling.

Something has happened over these past several months with Claire. Imperceptible at first, but there has been a gradual restoration of the old Jonathan. He understands that his birth mother loved him to the point of going against her own mother's wishes to terminate her pregnancy. He is finding safe places to store the bad memories of his dad's dying. He begins to create meaning from his losses. Even more significant is the work that has happened in me. Somehow, these sessions with Claire have changed the way I feel about my son. I look at Jonathan and can honestly say that I am in love, a deep unshakeable love with my boy — not the boy I want him to be, but the boy he is.

I walk in the door after work. I can tell that Jonathan is home; I nearly trip over his shoes, jacket, and backpack, abandoned in a heap in the front hall. The stovetop is splattered with orange macaroni and cheese. A pair of socks lies discarded on the floor by the family computer. I hear him drumming on his kit in the basement.

"Jonathan, this is a home not a pigsty," I yell above his rat-a-tat-tat-tat drum solo. He doesn't acknowledge my presence; he probably doesn't even see me, performing to an audience of thousands.

"Jonathan!" I put my face in front of his. Momentarily, he stops and looks up.

"Honey, get upstairs and clean up your mess," I say with limited restraint.

"I will."

"Do it now please, I want to start dinner."

"Just wait. I said I will," he says and lifts the sticks up to start again.

"Jonathan, get upstairs and pick up your mess," I say, feeling the irritation start to grind against me.

"You only adopted me because you wanted a personal slave," he yells, crashing down on the cymbals for effect.

"If I wanted a slave, I would have adopted a better one than you!" I yell back.

We look at each other in a moment of stunned silence. Then he smiles at me and we both shake our heads and laugh.

"Give me five minutes, okay?"

"Sure, no problem," I say.

Sometimes I hear him crying. Not so much anymore, but occasionally the grief revisits, perches at the head of his bed, and whispers that no one understands, accuses him of being worthless and unlovable. He turns up the volume on his iPod to drown out the voice. I head down to his room, stroke his hair, and rub his back. No longer does my son push me away. I want to be here, and he wants me to stay.

Judith Hope is a writer, speaker, and columnist. Born in Toronto, she has lived a far-flung life in Kenya, Belize, Hong Kong, Australia, and currently Calgary, Alberta. She is the communications coordinator for Hospice Calgary, a centre that supports bereaved families and people facing life-threatening illness.

acknowledgments

WE WOULD LIKE TO extend our heartfelt thanks to all the frank and fine contributors to *Somebody's Child* who shared their life stories with such honesty and self-understanding. We would also like to thank the University of Victoria and its Faculty of Fine Arts and Wilfrid Laurier University and its Laurier Brantford Campus for supporting us in the work of creating this anthology. And, of course, we would like to thank the terrific, hard-working people at TouchWood Editions, particularly publisher Ruth Linka and publisher emeritus Pat Touchie, for believing so strongly in *Somebody's Child* and playing such a vital role in bringing it to life.

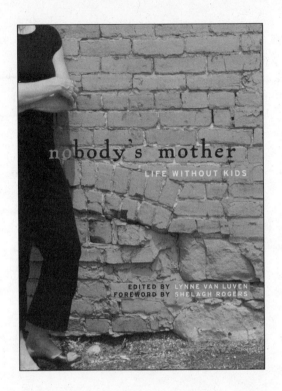

Nobody's Mother: Life Without Kids
edited by Lynne Van Luven
foreword by Shelagh Rogers

The 21 essayists in this lively anthology vary in age and background. They write frankly, provocatively and sometimes humourously about being childless, whether by intention, circumstance, or a twist of fate.

978-1-894898-40-9 • $19.95
5.5 x 7.5 • 240 pages • softcover with flaps
touchwoodeditions.com

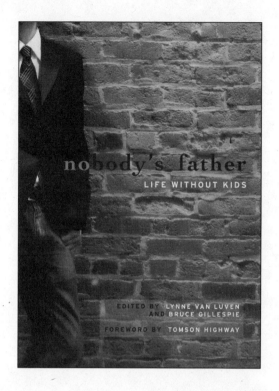

Nobody's Father: Life Without Kids
edited by Lynne Van Luven and Bruce Gillespie
foreword by Tomson Highway

The 22 essayists in this illuminating anthology come from all walks of life. They are gay and straight, young and old. They are writers and artists, teachers and priests. They are doting uncles and favorite babysitters, each one redefining the role of a father

978-1-894898-74-4 • $19.95
5.5 x 7.5 • 256 pages • softcover with flaps
touchwoodeditions.com